I dedicate this book to:

My father, who I was too young to remember, but who has inspired me to follow his dream of a prosperous Uganda.

My mother, who has always encouraged and supported me to pursue my passion of working with animals and changing the world.

My siblings, Betty Nakalema, Peter Martin, and Apollo Katerega, who greatly treasured me, but never lived to see me realize my dreams.

My brother, William Kalema, and sister, Veronica Nakibule, who have greatly supported me in my chosen career with wildlife including visiting the gorillas at Bwindi to better understand my work.

My husband, Lawrence Zikusoka, for taking on the challenge to experience a large part of this conservation journey with me.

My sons, Ndhego and Tendo, for their companionship and curiosity on this exciting journey.

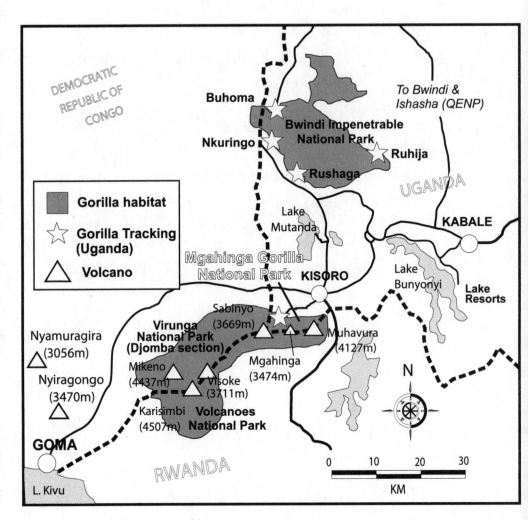

DEMOCRATIC REPUBLIC OF CONGO

Buhoma

To Bwindi & Ishasha (QENP)

Nkuringo

Bwindi Impenetrable National Park

Ruhija

Rushaga

UGANDA

Lake Mutanda

KABALE

Gorilla habitat

Gorilla Tracking (Uganda)

Volcano

Mgahinga Gorilla National Park

KISORO

Lake Bunyonyi

Lake Resorts

Sabinyo (3669m)

Nyamuragira (3056m)

Virunga National Park (Djomba section)

Mgahinga (3474m)

Muhavura (4127m)

N

Nyiragongo (3470m)

Mikeno (4437m)

Visoke (3711m)

Karisimbi (4507m)

Volcanoes National Park

GOMA

RWANDA

0   10   20   30

KM

L. Kivu

Map by Andrew Roberts andrew@eastafricamaps.com

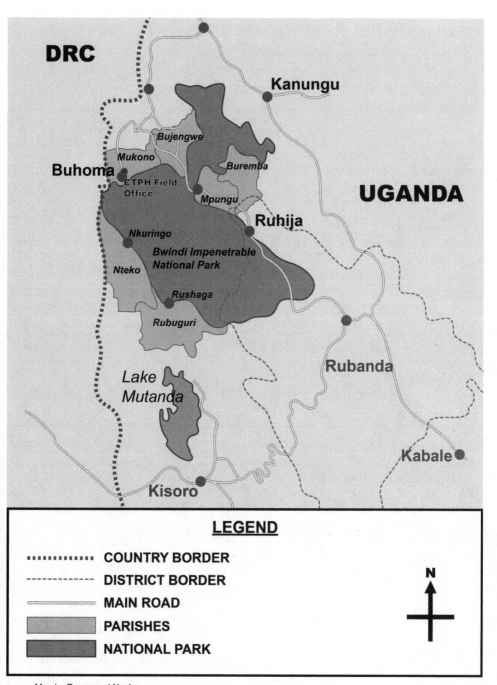

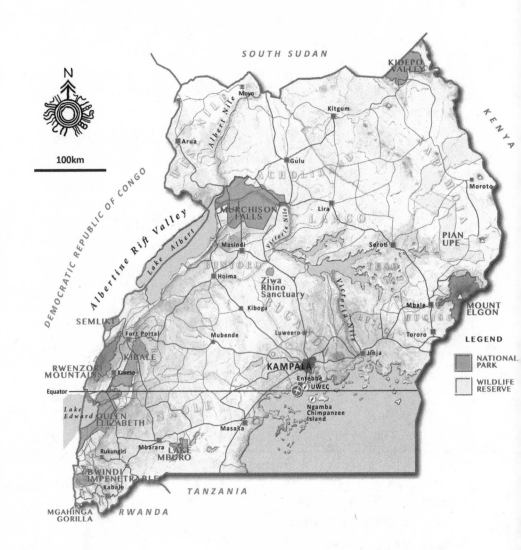

N

100km

SOUTH SUDAN

KIDEPO VALLEY

KENYA

Moyo

Kitgum

Arua

Gulu

DEMOCRATIC REPUBLIC OF CONGO

Albertine Rift Valley

Lake Albert

Albert Nile

Victoria Nile

ACHOLI

LANGO

Lira

Moroto

KARAMOJA

PIAN UPE

MURCHISON FALLS

Masindi

BUNYORO

Hoima

Soroti

TESO

Ziwa Rhino Sanctuary

BUGANDA

Kiboga

Mbale

BUGISI

MOUNT ELGON

SEMLIKI

Fort Portal

Mubende

Luweero

Victoria Nile

BUSOGA

Tororo

KIBALE

RWENZORI MOUNTAINS

Kaseso

KAMPALA

Jinja

Equator

Lake Edward

Entebbe

UWEC

Ngamba Chimpanzee Island

LEGEND

NATIONAL PARK

WILDLIFE RESERVE

QUEEN ELIZABETH

BUNYOLE

Masaka

Rukungiri

Mbarara

LAKE MBURO

BWINDI IMPENETRABLE

Kabale

TANZANIA

MGAHINGA GORILLA

RWANDA

Map by Andrew Roberts, andrew@eastafricamaps.com

Contents

Abbreviations and Acronyms

AWF	African Wildlife Foundation
APS	African Primatological Society
BMCT	Bwindi and Mgahinga Conservation Trust
CBDOTS	Community Based Direct Observation of Tuberculosis Treatments Short Course Therapy
CCAHWs	Community Conservation Animal Health Workers
CDC	Centers for Disease Control and Prevention
COVAB	College of Veterinary Medicine, Animal Resources and Bio-security
CTPH	Conservation Through Public Health
DFGFE	Dian Fossey Gorilla Fund Europe
DRC	Democratic Republic of the Congo
GCCoffee	Gorilla Conservation Coffee
HUGOs	Human and Gorilla Conflict Resolution Teams
ICCN	L'institut Congolais pour la Conservation de la Nature
IGCP	International Gorilla Conservation Programme
ITFC	Institute of Tropical Forest Conservation
IUCN	International Union for the Conservation of Nature
JGI	Jane Goodall Institute
KWS	Kenya Wildlife Service
MAAIF	Ministry of Agriculture, Animal Industry and Fisheries
MOH	Ministry of Health
MTWA	Ministry of Tourism, Wildlife and Antiquities
MUK	Makerere University
MUST	Mbarara University of Science and Technology
MGVP	Mountain Gorilla Veterinary Project
PHE	Population, Health and Environment
QENP	Queen Elizabeth National Park
RVC	Royal Veterinary College
TB	Tuberculosis

UNESCO	United Nations Educational, Scientific and Cultural Organization
UNITES	Uganda and North Carolina International Teaching for the Environment
UNITeS	United Nations Information Technology Service
UNP	Uganda National Parks
USAID	United States Agency for International Development
UWA	Uganda Wildlife Authority
UWEC	Uganda Wildlife Education Centre
VHTs	Village Health Teams
VHCTs	Village Health and Conservation Teams
VSLA	Village Savings and Loan Association
WCN	Wildlife Conservation Network
WHO	World Health Organization
WWF	World Wide Fund for Nature

No one who looks into a gorilla's eyes—intelligent, gentle, vulnerable—can remain unchanged, for the gap between ape and human vanishes; we know that the gorilla still lives within us. Do gorillas also recognize this ancient connection?

—*George B. Schaller, October 1995*
"Gentle Gorillas, Turbulent Times,"
National Geographic

Foreword

W*alking with Gorillas* is the story of a very remarkable woman. I first met Gladys when she came to one of my lectures in London in 1993, and we had the opportunity to talk—albeit briefly—afterward. It was immediately apparent that there was something special about this vibrant Ugandan woman—a sense of purpose and love for her work were strikingly apparent.

After that first meeting, we crossed paths from time to time, and I followed her career with increasing interest. In some ways her trajectory was not unlike my own, but hers was a more difficult path. She had been interested in animals from an early age, and was even teased by her schoolmates for believing that animals were sentient beings—most Ugandans were very like the professors at Cambridge University who told me, in 1962, that the chimpanzees I was studying should be numbered not named, and that only humans had personalities, minds capable of problem solving, and above all, emotions such as contentment, sadness, frustration, anger, and grief. Luckily, I knew this was not true—I'd had a wonderful teacher as a child—my dog, Rusty!

Gladys felt the same. From the start she wanted to be a wildlife veterinarian—and like me she had a supportive mother, who encouraged her to follow her dreams. And this she did, even through very difficult times in Uganda. During the reign of Idi Amin she learned about the dark side of human nature as many of her family and friends were killed, including her father, who was kidnapped and murdered, when she was just two years old. I learned about our dark side, during World War II, but I did not have to take refuge in a foreign country as she did, and I only lost one close family member, my much-loved uncle, shot down over Egypt.

Despite this, and still following her dream, Gladys succeeded in becoming an excellent veterinarian. And like me she was eventually able to work with apes: I studied chimpanzees, while she became very committed to mountain gorillas.

Early on in her gorilla work, she realized the importance of working with local communities, increasing their ability to earn a living without destroying the environment and poaching animals, including gorillas, through her initiatives such as Gorilla Conservation Coffee—just as I initiated the Jane Goodall Institute (JGI)'s method of community-based conservation around Gombe National Park. Under Gladys's guidance, poachers became Rangers, trained to protect the gorillas. And she realized the importance of improving education and health facilities for communities living near Gorilla habitat. In many ways the programs that she helped with resemble Tacare—JGI's method of community-based conservation.

A defining moment in Gladys's career came when she discovered that gorillas were suffering from some diseases that had been contracted as a result of human contact, highlighting the danger human disease posed for these close relatives of ours. So she became a strong voice in Uganda to advocate the One Health approach that is now operating in many parts of the world. There is little use protecting gorillas—or chimpanzees—if they then catch a human disease and die—therefore it is important to ensure the best possible health facilities for local communities—and their livestock—in order to do as much as possible to prevent the emergence of new zoonotic diseases, such as COVID-19. Gladys was able to create a partnership between the Uganda government's Ministry of Health and the Uganda Wildlife Authority, which helped her to develop her plan.

The outbreak of the COVID-19 pandemic posed a real problem because the great apes are very susceptible to respiratory diseases, especially influenza. To minimize the risk, all gorilla and chimpanzee tourism in Uganda was temporarily stopped. This was clearly a wise decision as gorillas in the San Diego and Prague zoos became infected with the disease. In a captive situation it is relatively easy to isolate and treat patients, but an outbreak among wild gorillas would be a different matter.

Unfortunately the lack of tourists created another problem: many of the villagers who had relied on the tourist industry for their livelihoods, either as guides or in the hospitality business, suddenly found their source of income had dried up and some of them turned to poaching in order to survive. But Gladys, who had played a key role in developing gorilla tourism after the war, was—as one might expect—able to come up with a solution. She initiated a program to encourage small-scale family farming, and to increase the potential of making money from crops such as coffee. In other words, to reduce the villagers' reliance on tourism.

It is hardly surprising that this remarkable woman has been the recipient of countless awards and prizes. Her story is amazing, and I recommend this book to everyone interested in conservation, alleviating poverty, and the role of women in society. But perhaps most important, it is a truly inspiring story of how one determined and dedicated woman overcame many setbacks and faced many dangers to follow and realize her dream. She has made a huge difference to conservation in Uganda, and she is an inspiring example to young—and not so young—people everywhere.

—Jane Goodall, PhD, DBE and
UN Messenger of Peace

Preface

I have always wanted to be around animals and growing up, I cannot remember a time when there were no pets at home. My elder brother Apollo Katerega, who was ten years older than me, also liked animals, especially dogs and was always bringing stray dogs and cats home. I was the last born of six children. My sister, Veronica Nakibule, who I followed, was five years older than me so we were just outside each other's age bracket for playing. Thus the pets at home became my main companions, and we developed a strong bond.

Along the way I eventually fulfilled my lifelong dream to not only become a veterinarian, but a wildlife veterinarian. In 1996, I began taking care of the critically endangered mountain gorillas of Uganda. Since then, they've increased in number from six hundred and fifty to 1,063 individuals in Uganda, Rwanda, and Democratic Republic of Congo (DRC). There are no mountain gorillas surviving in zoos outside their range countries, and their only hope is keeping the populations thriving where they are naturally found.

The gorillas have shaped my life's calling since I first studied them as a student at the Royal Veterinary College, University of London. I've treated them as the first full-time wildlife veterinarian in Uganda, and supported them as Founder and Chief Executive Officer of a grassroots NGO and nonprofit, Conservation Through Public Health, more commonly known as "CTPH," that promotes biodiversity conservation through not only improving the health of gorillas and other wildlife, but also the health and well-being of the people and livestock with whom they share their fragile habitats.

When CNN came to interview me for *African Voices* in 2014, I was honored and elated that wildlife conservation was becoming as important as other pressing issues in Africa, which still has the highest population growth rates and poorest people in the world with least access to health and other social services.

During the interview, one family of gorillas that I have worked with for twenty years came to the park offices for us to introduce themselves to the rest of the world through CNN. Zain Verjee, who is one of the most engaging interviewers I have ever met, was fascinated and amused by the Mubare gorilla group and was truly impressed with the dedication and efforts of the park staff who look after them and the surrounding community who have decided to coexist with the gorillas rather than hunt them. That day, Zain challenged me to start writing a book. And so I have, despite immense challenges along the way.

This memoir is about a conservation-focused journey that led me from making veterinary calls on the gorillas to building teams that make medical calls on people who share a fragile habitat with the mountain gorillas. I started out at the age of twenty-six, very eager as the first veterinarian employed by Uganda National Parks (which later became Uganda Wildlife Authority), primarily to look after the gorillas. But I couldn't ignore the poverty around me. My heart went out to the Bwindi community and their children whose smiles and waves always melted my heart as I climbed the steep hills to get to my gorilla patients. It did not take long for me to realize that it was not really possible to ensure the survival of gorillas, other wildlife, and critical ecosystems in Africa without helping their human neighbors.

During my walk with gorillas, I started improving the health of people and animals together with a "One Health"[1] approach. When COVID-19 reached my country, CTPH swung into action to protect the gorillas and people. After all, we had spent years establishing an approach to reduce the impact of contagious diseases. In the process of training other vets I got COVID-19 and developed severe symptoms. Thanks to talented Ugandan doctors working in under-resourced healthcare systems in Africa I miraculously survived. This frightening experience made me think more deeply about my legacy.

---

1   One Health is a multidisciplinary approach with the goal of improving health for all living things: animals, people, plants in our shared planet.

I invite you to enjoy reading about my incredible journey as a Ugandan woman whose mission to save gorillas has led me down many different and interesting paths, hopefully resulting in a better future for one of our closest living relatives as well as other important biodiversity, and ultimately ourselves.

PART I

Becoming a Conservationist

Chapter 1

Early Years

I was the last-born child in a family of six, entering the world on Thursday, January 8, 1970, at Mulago Hospital in Kampala; I was a bit of a surprise for my parents and siblings, but I was loved. At the time of my birth, Mulago Hospital was one of the best hospitals in Africa. But after Idi Amin came to power a year later, it became known as a place of horror where many doctors were abducted and murdered, and was made famous in the film *The Last King of Scotland*, depicting Amin's bloodthirsty dictatorship.

I came from a family of political leaders dedicated to creating a Uganda where its people could thrive and live in peace and harmony. My maternal grandfather, Martin Luther Nsibirwa, had been the prime minister of the Kingdom of Buganda between 1929 and 1941 and again in 1945. Buganda—the kingdom of the Baganda people—is a subnational kingdom within Uganda comprising of all of the country's central region, including the capital Kampala.

Uganda was a British protectorate at the time. Tragically he was assassinated on September 5, 1945; he was sixty-two years old. My mother, Rhoda Kalema, only sixteen at the time, along with the Baganda people, blamed his assassination on those who objected to my grandfather acquiring land from influential chiefs to expand Makerere College into a University—the University of East Africa. Unbeknownst to the assassins, the parliament had passed the land acquisition bill on September 4, 1945, just the day before my grandfather died.

Yet his legacy to create more opportunities for Ugandans lived on both in my mother and the man she married, William Wilberforce Kalema. In 1962, my father joined Uganda's first parliament after independence from the British, and together with my mother became part of the Uganda People's Congress. Both of them were passionate and committed to helping Uganda grow. In 1964, my father became a senior government minister in President Obote's administration. Little did I know how this would impact my own life and that the shadow of assassination would rise again soon after my birth.

The decade of my birth was a terrifying and volatile one for many Ugandans dominated by civil war and dictatorship. In January 1971, the then president Milton Obote, was overthrown in a coup d'état by General Idi Amin of the Ugandan Army while my father was with the president at a Commonwealth Heads of Government meeting in Singapore. At the time, my father was responsible for Commerce and Industry as a Senior Cabinet Minister. He was passionate about developing the local industries in Uganda and encouraged Ugandans to participate in the economic development of their country and build a brighter future. Prior to that, my father was Minister of Communications, Works and Housing, and led goodwill missions to several countries in the Far East and Eastern Europe, where he negotiated gifts and lucrative trade deals that would benefit the country and its people. This included the Mandela National Stadium, built by the Chinese government and later named after the former South African president, Nelson Mandela, someone who my father greatly admired. Though President Obote remained in exile in Tanzania, my father returned to Uganda in February 1971 to be with his family.

Soon after Amin began his reign of terror as Uganda's president, his attention turned toward my family. On January 20, 1972, nearly two weeks after my second birthday, my father left our house at 6:45 p.m. and was never seen again. He had been abducted and murdered by Amin's soldiers. He was only forty-five years old; seventeen years younger than my grandfather when he was assassinated. It seemed as if history was repeating itself with a father leaving behind a young family.

This tragic event shaped my early years, and I developed a strong bond with my mother, Rhoda, who at just forty-two became a single mother to six children living in a hostile environment. Like her, I had lost my father at a tender age, but unlike her I did not have the benefit of getting to know my father. My grandfather had taken a great interest in her education, which was unusual in Uganda in the 1930s where girls were not expected to pursue higher education. Yet for him, education was important, so important that he lost his life because of it.

With her husband's assassination echoing her own father's, my mother's hopes and dreams destroyed in the cruelest possible manner, she decided to leave politics behind, for her sake as well as her children's. I recall how my brother, Peter Martin, was traumatized by our father's loss as he blamed himself because when he'd set off from home to visit friends, he had seen two vehicles with men in dark glasses parked outside our gate. Peter hadn't realized that they had come for our father. When he returned home, it was to the news that our father had vanished.

My mother acted quickly to protect us and sent my two older siblings, Katerega and Veronica, to stay with her younger sister, Auntie Gladys Wambuzi, who I was named after. Although my aunt only lived a few miles away, my mother wished for them to have a normal school routine, and they only came home at the weekends to join family and friends in mourning. Because of my age, I remained with my mother. Thankfully, my eldest siblings, Betty and William, were already studying outside Uganda at Nairobi University in Kenya and Cambridge University in England, respectively. Peter, who followed William, was able to spirit away to Reading University in England.

The full year after my father's murder, my mother desperately waited to retrieve his body. Tragically, she was given many false promises, but my father's body was never found.

We had just moved to the suburb of Nakasero, an affluent part of Kampala, to a spacious three-bedroomed bungalow when my father was killed. Now my mother became the only breadwinner of the family and started making clothes, including school uniforms for friends' children. Instead of fleeing Uganda, she decided to stay in the country despite the hardships and threats she endured under Amin's rule. Like her father and her husband, my mother was passionate about creating a Uganda where all could prosper. Her courage and bravery are qualities I appreciate now. From her I developed a strong urge to continue my father's dream of developing Uganda. It became a driving force in my life.

Being the youngest of my siblings, who were between five to nineteen years older than me, meant that I did not often get the opportunity to be with children my own age, so when I did, I took full advantage of it. Consequently, I loved school.

When my sister Veronica was eight, she returned from my Aunty Gladys's house to live with us again and when I turned five, I joined her school. I recall one specific memory from my primary school when my sister's friends decided to play a cruel April Fool joke on her. Idi Amin's children also attended Kitante Primary School and they told Veronica that I had been fighting with one of his children. Terrified, she rushed from the senior end of the school to chastise me. I was shocked by her accusation. The mere notion of the consequences of doing such a thing horrified me. When she discovered that it wasn't true, she was so relieved that she started crying. She did not know how she would have explained this to our mother, after what had happened to our father. My cousin Nakato Kiwana recollected how prayers were held for children whose fathers had disappeared or "not returned home." When President Amin's children joined the school, the headmaster warned the students not to get into conflict with them. Those were terrifying times for us all, as Amin's reputation as the "Butcher of Uganda"[1] grew.

One way that I could escape from this cloud of terror was through our animals at home. We always had dogs and one of them, Poppy, liked sleeping under my pram, earning me the nickname "Poppy" from my godfather, Uncle Sam Wambuzi.

My older brother Katerega was also an animal lover. Once he too returned from my Aunty Gladys's, he started bringing stray animals home. The first one I remembered as a child was a stray pygmy cat called Pilli, who became my favorite. She was absolutely tiny and never grew beyond the size of a kitten. Unfortunately, the dogs often chased Pilli and one day, killed her; I was devastated by this loss.

I had grown up in a culture that believed that animals did not have souls, yet, in spite of my cultural programming, I disagreed that animals were non-sentient. Something deep inside me knew that they had as much soul as any human, and I mourned them in the same way.

I was also able to recruit others to my cause, namely the children who lived next door, Flavia Mpanga and her sister, Susie, who became lifelong friends. They often remind me how I made them participate in my pets' funerals where I would cry as I recited a prayer while we buried them in the ground with a cross.

However, the defining moment for me arrived with our new neighbors, the Cuban Ambassador to Uganda, His Excellency, Franco and his wife. They lived in the house opposite ours and became friends with my mother, often coming to visit her.

Not long after moving in, they acquired a pet vervet monkey named Poncho, who liked to sit on our gate and stare down at me. I was fascinated by his fingers and fingernails that looked exactly like mine—so human. When I wasn't looking, Poncho would jump down into our compound and start pulling the cats' and dogs' tails. Sometimes Poncho would steal bananas from the kitchen window. When you chased after him, he would jump over the gate and run back home.

One day when I was practicing the piano, I felt like I was not alone, and realized that Poncho was watching me, intently, through the window. Having begun to understand how playful and intelligent Poncho was, I decided to leave the room and left the door slightly ajar to see if he would try and imitate me. Sure enough, Poncho climbed onto the stool and played one note with one finger! I was so excited that I rushed into the room, and of course Poncho ran away, back through the window to his home across the road. He was my first venture into studying primates.

By the age of twelve I had decided to become a veterinarian. When any of our animals were sick, I would insist on missing classes to accompany my mother to the small-animal clinic, a ten-minute drive away in Wandegeya. I hated seeing animals suffering and was determined to dedicate my life to making them better.

Most people in Uganda do not consider veterinary medicine a worthwhile career because people don't place much value on pets in a developing country with so much human suffering. In spite of this, I was fortunate to have a mother who understood my passion and encouraged me to follow my dreams.

I was also very fortunate that my mother had the means to send me to schools outside of Uganda, where she could continue to keep me and my siblings safe. At the age of seven, I attended my first boarding school—Greensteds School in neighboring Kenya. Though I missed my mother terribly, I enjoyed the fun learning environment, which was like a holiday camp. It was my first time in an international school with equal representation of children originating from Africa, Europe, and Asia, and gave me the opportunity for my leadership skills to develop in a multiethnic environment. I played the queen in the school play "Sleeping Beauty" and won the form prize.

When Idi Amin was overthrown in 1979, it was safe for me to return to Uganda and at the age of ten, I joined another boarding school, Kabale Preparatory School, which was tougher, but also nurturing, and located in a region I was to return to when I started my walk with gorillas. In the same year, my mother joined a new political party—the Uganda Patriotic Movement, which later became the current ruling party, the National Resistance Movement. I treasured the few times she was able to visit and take me out of school for lunch during her political rallies in Kabale. However, I didn't realize her life was in danger until one day when my teacher, Miss Kigorogoro, gave me a big hug and told me that my mother had been released from jail. I was so shaken that I cried. I had not known that while I was away from home she had been arrested. My family had wanted to shield me. This was the second of three arrests over the years as she got more heavily engaged in politics.

My boarding school education spanned countries and continents, including the UK, where at twelve I learned to thrive in an environment as a minority and the only black person in my year. It was there while at Dollar Academy in Scotland that I first discovered racism, after a boy in my class called me "nigger." It was a rude awakening after my shielded upbringing in Uganda, and thankfully my British dorm mates who also lived outside the UK reported to the matron and he was reprimanded. Although my sister Veronica and cousins who also attended school in the UK also faced isolated incidences of discrimination, most students were very friendly. Dollar Academy made us believe that anything is possible. Veronica followed her dream and got into Princeton University to study computer science and electrical engineering.

My time in Scotland also showed me how much people valued their pets. This gave me the confidence a few years later to apply to study veterinary medicine at universities in the UK. I spent many school holidays in Aberdeen at the home of my parents' friends who they had met as students at the University of Edinburgh in Scotland, Professor Arnold Klopper, who was Afrikaans, and his wife, Mary Klopper, who was British South African. They had left South Africa because they were opposed to the apartheid regime. Their friendship began when my father, who was heading the African Students Union at Edinburgh University, reached out to Mary after Nelson Mandela was first arrested in South Africa in 1956.

After two years in Scotland, I returned home to attend King's College Budo, the third school and first coeducational school to be built in Uganda by the Church Missionary Society in 1906. My parents had met there as teenagers and all my siblings had attended. I was excited to keep up the family tradition, but I was a rebellious teenager and felt the school was too restrictive and claustrophobic. In my final year, age sixteen, my friends and I decided to leave the grounds without permission to go on a day trip to Kampala. Our grand plan went askew and we were caught in our adventure. Not only was I banned from joining a school trip to the national park, which broke my heart, I was also given an indefinite suspension. This meant that although I could take my exams as an external student, living in a teacher's home, I was also separated from my dormitory mates. Yet, being suspended proved a blessing in disguise as I'm sure I spent more time studying than I would have if I'd been distracted by my friends. When I received my exam results, I was delighted to be among the top five Budo students. This helped to pave the way for me to attend the school of my choice and follow my dream of becoming a veterinarian.

Going to as many as six schools in three countries during my primary and secondary school years opened my mind to different ways of learning and taught me to relate with people from different cultures and backgrounds, some of whom became lifelong friends.

While my decision to become a veterinarian never wavered, it was the last school that cemented my career path.

Chapter 2

The Birth of a Conservationist

The 1970s was a devastating era for Ugandan wildlife, particularly that of the African elephant and rhino, both hunted by poachers for their ivory and horn. Conservation was of little concern to Idi Amin, who himself started killing animals in the national parks where hunting was not permitted, and encouraged people to enrich themselves from the ivory trade. The once bountiful herds of the national parks dwindled to the point of extinction, and in the case of the rhino, became extinct in Uganda in 1985.

However, even during this dark period in Ugandan history, there was a source of light; hope brought about by the courage and bravery of two visionary men, Dr. Eric Edroma and Mr. Kenneth Lukyamuzi. Dr. Edroma later gave me my first job when he was the executive director of Uganda National Parks and shared the story of how they started the first local conservation NGO. Both men approached Idi Amin to set up a national wildlife club for children, knowing that one of the few things that he cared about was children and their education. They used this as a way to encourage Amin's interest in conservation. Hence in 1975, the Wildlife Clubs of Uganda was born.

My own introduction to the Wildlife Clubs of Uganda was far less dramatic and began out of boredom during the long school holidays. I was seventeen at the time and waiting to start my A levels. I remember feeling restless and eventually asked my mother to take me to visit the Wildlife Clubs of Uganda.

It was a small but vibrant office in the Ministry of Tourism, Wildlife and Antiquities in Kampala. The first person I met was the General Secretary, Mr. Charles Birigenda, who offered me an opportunity to volunteer.

One day, a park warden, Fred Katego, came to visit the offices and told us about the newly discovered mountain gorillas in the southwestern part of Uganda in a forest reserve called Bwindi Impenetrable Forest. I became intrigued with his story and asked him how I could visit the mountain gorillas. He told me that the mountain gorillas were not under the management of the national parks and were still wild, and not habituated to human presence. Yet the dream remained—I had many hurdles to jump and mountains to climb before that dream became a reality.

After the holidays, I started at my new school, Kibuli Secondary School.

The headmaster, Mr. Kawasi, was passionate about teaching and took the time to get to know each of us. He appointed me to head the Students' Council, which really helped to build my leadership skills.

My new school brought with it the opportunity to revive the school's Wildlife Club.

I felt inspired and motivated by my new project and started off by setting up a birdfeeder outside Mr. Kawasi's office. I hoped by appreciating the beauty and variety of birds we had, Mr. Kawasi would also come to appreciate the benefits of reviving the wildlife club. We held school debates covering various topics about the value of wildlife and the need to conserve it.

I took my duties as head of the school wildlife club very seriously and when I attended my cousin's wedding in Nairobi, I visited the Kenya Wildlife Club offices there to learn ways I could help develop the school's wildlife club back home. I was greatly inspired by their programs and dedication to conservation and even convinced my mother to give me a loan so that I could pay them to design and print stickers for our Kibuli Secondary School Wildlife Club before returning to Uganda. The stickers had a giraffe in a circle with the words HELP TO UPLIFT OUR ENVIRONMENTS. It was my first significant foray into conservation and raising awareness about the importance of preserving and protecting wildlife.

Once back home, I redoubled my efforts and after much persuasion, the club finally managed to convince the headmaster to organize a school trip to Queen Elizabeth National Park, which had been established in 1952 when Queen Elizabeth II and Prince Philip visited Uganda.

We traveled by Uganda Railway. To my surprise when the train arrived, people rushed to get aboard and we had to quickly appoint two of the strongest students to jump in and book seats in the economy class for all thirty students and two teachers.

When the eight-hour journey finally began, the train kept stopping whenever the driver wanted to and often where there was freshly cooked local food, which was more appetizing than the bland and boring omelets served on the train. We all ventured to sample the local food, which was delicious. Not surprisingly, the train also started without warning, but because it moved slowly there was enough time to jump on before it picked up speed—definitely something I had never experienced while traveling on British Rail!

From the windows of the moving train, I reveled in the stunning green and changing landscape of Uganda from lowland plains to rolling hills to the vast savanna. I also came face-to-face with a level of poverty I had never seen before where one woman kept hiding in the toilet with a big bunch of *matoke*, savory bananas—the staple food of Uganda, whenever the conductor came to check the tickets. Though the students made fun of her, I could not help but admire her pluck to get on a train without money and make it to the other end without getting caught.

Finally, after 340 kilometers, we arrived in Kasese at six in the evening. To my great relief, we found a truck waiting for us, kindly sent by the park's chief warden.

Tired, we all clambered into the truck and stood for an hour on the fifty-kilometer drive to Mweya, the park headquarters. Eager to spot wildlife in the dusk, we saw only a few old ambling buffalo and some antelope that we could not identify.

The following day a warden came and explained that there used to be many animals, but sadly they had declined due to the excessive poaching during Amin's regime, and now there were very few. So few in fact, that he could even arrange for us to go on a walking safari.

As we walked on our safari the next day, as promised, we did not come across any dangerous animals. Even as I felt relief not to have to fear attack from leopards or lions, I felt saddened by how greed had devastated Uganda's wildlife. But we enjoyed being in the wilderness among the acacia and euphorbia trees. We spotted a few small antelope, oribi, that jumped when you got too close and warthogs running with their tails in the air. I was particularly fascinated by the Uganda kob, a medium-sized antelope, only found in Uganda and Sudan with a unique mating ritual called a lek, where males have to fight for exclusive access to the females in a territory. They battle it out by tangling their horns and jumping toward each other, until one of them concedes by laying his head on the ground. We enjoyed the distinct song of many species of birds, which filled the air as we walked.

Nighttime was spent in front of the campfire talking about the animals we had seen—it was a magical time for me and a turning point in my life, where I decided to become not just a veterinarian, but one who works with wildlife. I had no idea that was an occupation that simply didn't exist in Uganda at the time. The three days we spent there went by in a flash and all too soon it was time to return to Kampala. We made the most of our drive back to the train station eagerly scouring the land for wildlife, particularly the big cats. Although we did not spot any leopards or lions, we did catch sight of elephants, which lifted our hearts.

The journey back became memorable when we heard a very loud rattling sound and saw a huge plume of dust coming up from the train, which suddenly stopped—the train had derailed! We were stuck in the middle of nowhere with no way of informing parents. Somehow, the problem was resolved and we resumed the journey, arriving in Kampala six hours later than planned.

We found my mother and sister, Veronica, waiting anxiously for us. But many parents had gone back home. I immediately asked my family to help drive students to the school. By the time I went home, I was exhausted, but exhilarated.

This trip had been truly exciting and rewarding in so many ways. Yet it would be some years later before I realized the full impact of that school trip and running the Wildlife Club.

As my time at Kibuli Secondary School came to an end, I found that the hardest part of starting something new was letting go. Yet, knowing that this was unavoidable, I passed the baton on to other devoted members of the wildlife club. Twenty-five years later, I became the Board Chairperson of the Wildlife Clubs of Uganda.

At nineteen, a new adventure awaited me after leaving High School, but it wasn't without its obstacles. Having studied at Dollar Academy in Scotland, I was aware of the importance animals had in British society and preferred to do my university training there. However, setting up the wildlife club was so absorbing and exciting for me that it took up most of my time and my study time suffered. Consequently, I got a B in biology, C in chemistry, and D in physics. This would have been sufficient to get me into Makerere University in Uganda, but the UK veterinary schools would accept nothing less than a B grade in all three subjects.

I received this devastating news about my grades while I was in the United States visiting my brother William and his family who lived in Wilmington, Delaware. I called my mother and sister, who refused to believe the problem was insurmountable. Their belief in me seemed boundless. I found a college in UK, where I could re-sit my exams, and my family funded the course.

Soon, I found myself traveling to Oxford and D'Overbroecks College. My time in Oxford was tough both academically and on a personal level where I had to learn to look after myself and get around on my own. Though I was wobbly on a bike, I quickly found that the most convenient means to get around the city. I bought a bicycle for forty pounds, which I sold for ten pounds to the same person when I left Oxford.

After sitting two sets of A level exams and getting five As and one B, it was more than enough to get into my first choice, the Royal Veterinary College, University of London.

It was now January 1990, and I had eight months to go before starting university. While I stayed with cousins in London in the meantime, I decided to earn a living before going back to Uganda for the summer holidays, which was an adventure in itself! First, I tried working at a fast-food restaurant, only managing one day at McDonald's—clearly not a good fit.

Next, I decided to seek work in a clothing store. I got my first lucky break working in a boutique near Bond Street on South Moulton Street that sold very trendy clothes. I even got to meet the famous singer Annie Lennox, who shopped at the store. Unfortunately, the shop closed three weeks after I started working there. It was short, but gave me the opportunity to develop my selling skills and I grew in confidence while there. Encouraged by my new skills, I landed a job at the famous and exclusive department store, Liberty, in the heart of the West End. There I learned how to engage and speak to people I did not know, and acquired marketing and sales skills that would prove invaluable later on in life. I got an opportunity to practice these skills when I returned home that summer holiday and worked in a craft shop at the Sheraton Hotel in Kampala.

I also used the time to travel for one month around Europe on a train with my good friend from Kings College Budo, Cathy Sebukima. We had a budget of twenty British pounds per country and had to spend some nights in trains from one city to another. We visited France, Italy, Portugal, Spain, Switzerland, Austria, what was then Yugoslavia, and Germany. I experienced both kindness and crime. One time, my handbag was stolen in Barcelona after someone sat next to me in the train station, which left me without money. My next stop in Venice, someone kindly let me ride in a gondola for free. Thankfully, I was able to call my guardian, Mary Klopper, who wired some money to me and enabled us to continue the trip.

As we continued to explore Europe, I was amazed at how similar some of the countries were to Uganda, such as the former Yugoslavia, where the food markets were identical. There was even a similar incident to the one I had witnessed when taking students on the wildlife club trip to Queen Elizabeth National Park. Just as the lady had hidden on the train with her bananas, a man hid in the toilet to avoid paying for his fare. More than anything, this trip taught me that there were far more similarities than differences between cultures.

Finally, it was time to come back to London, which would be my home for the next few years. I was ready for my next adventure: The Royal Veterinary College, London beckoned.

Chapter 3

The World of Veterinary Medicine

I couldn't sleep the night before my first day of university. I definitely made an impression on the receptionist when I arrived laden with three suitcases at the entrance of my new Hall of Residence, Canterbury Hall in Cartwright Gardens. He looked at me and my suitcases, stating, "The rooms aren't that big, you know!" Thankfully, my room on the second floor was large enough to accommodate me and my suitcases.

There were eighty students enrolled in my year, 60 percent of whom were women. There were very few people of color, and I was the only woman of African origin. Michael Sento was from Botswana, and Renata de Rosayro was from the Caribbean.

The course was both hard and demanding. At the time, veterinary medicine was one of the most competitive degrees to study.

Consequently, I soon discovered that everyone was among the top of their class in their schools. We frequently had exams, and those who excelled were those who worked harder than the rest.

Yet, now I had finally made it, I wanted to experience university life fully. Soon I was knee deep in a host of social activities—I tried to go to all the parties I was invited to, and to also get engaged in sports. I joined the mountaineering club and rowing club, but when winter came, I soon gave that up as I couldn't cope with the cold.

I made friends with students in the dorms who were residents at Canterbury Hall, including Sonia de Brun from South Africa who was studying at the London School of Economics. Two years earlier my brother Katerega had tragically died from epileptic fits. He had studied at the London School of Economics a decade earlier. When Sonia brought me to the events at her university, I felt connected to my older brother again. At these events I met other African students who reminded me of my parents: they were interested in politics and social justice and aspired to become political leaders in their countries.

I recall one particular day when they started singing, "Martin Luther King makes me proud to be black, Malcolm X makes me proud to be black, Nelson Mandela makes me proud to be black, Idi Amin makes me proud to be black!" Shocked, I immediately stood up and said, "Not all charismatic black leaders are good people," and related the terrible horrors Idi Amin had inflicted on my family and Uganda as a whole.

Needless to say, trying to keep up with it all eventually became too much for me, and I failed my first-year exams. It was very humbling for me and I had to spend the summer studying to retake the exams. It led to a lot of soul-searching, and I discovered the book *The Power of Positive Thinking* by Norman Vincent Peale. This helped me feel closer to God and focus on what I felt was my chosen calling. I was elated when I passed my exams.

However, I had another hurdle to overcome: how to pay for my veterinary education.

I applied to the Kulika Charitable Trust and traveled to their offices in London for an interview. When they asked how I would handle large animals, I tried my best to convince them that technique is more important than strength. A few weeks later I received a letter with good news that they would be sponsoring my whole course. I was overjoyed. When I told my mother, she got down on her knees to thank God. Her prayers had been answered, as had mine.

Relieved that my funding for university was now guaranteed, I became immersed in my studies, which mostly included studying domestic animals. This gave me a solid grounding in basic veterinary medicine and essential practical skills. However, I kept an eye out for a way to work with wild animals.

We were expected to do seventeen weeks of practical study, and I used the opportunity to work at a vet practice that attended to exotic wildlife at Twycross Zoo, specializing in primates. It was a wonderful introduction to working with wildlife, and I was eager to gain as much experience as I could.

Later on, I worked at a veterinary clinic that also looked after animals at the Longleat safari park in Wiltshire, England, where I was in my element. Dr. Gerry Benbow, who was the vet attached to Longleat, had a passion for wildlife. We went out to Longleat Safari Park one day a week, and his wife also made me delicious sandwiches for lunch. I joined him in treating giraffes, zebras, lions, and other species native to Africa as well as animals from other continents. We also got to treat an unusual patient, the Ankole cow, a traditional cattle species from Uganda. Back home, he would have been considered a food animal. Here, he was a tourist attraction worthy of specialized veterinary care. He developed a very thick coat to cope with the cold British winters and without a doubt lived much longer than he would have in Uganda.

I was also fortunate enough to work with vets at London Zoo and Whipsnade Wild Animal Park, which had archives of veterinary case studies on the Virunga mountain gorillas. I got to treat rhinos, which had become extinct in Uganda. Whipsnade also offered me an opportunity to see animals in a more open environment closer to what one would find in the national parks in Uganda.

Working with captive wild species was the highlight of my veterinary studies in the UK, and I took every opportunity to learn and discover as much as I could.

I was even more excited when I saw an announcement on the university notice board about a talk on the mountain gorillas of Rwanda, given by Dr. Barkley Hastings, the first veterinarian to work with mountain gorillas, and Dr. Ian Redmond, the first research assistant of the late Dr. Dian Fossey, who conducted the first long-term study on mountain gorillas. They also showed us a portable anesthesia machine used to sedate the great apes in the wild.

The talk fueled my growing desire to work with the mountain gorillas, and I approached Drs. Hastings and Redmond afterward to ask if I could shadow them in their practice that coming winter break. I was disappointed by their answer. They told me that unfortunately Ugandans were not allowed in Rwanda because the governments were fighting. However, they said that they would put me in contact with the resident vet, Dr. Liz Macfie.

I assured them that I understood, and that I'd already set up work experience to work with the chimpanzees at Entebbe Zoo over Christmas break, but I knew these chimpanzees were kept in cages. Dr. Redmond asked me to share photos of the primates' living conditions with him when I got back, as he was concerned about the welfare standards.

Sometime after this, I was stunned to receive a letter from Dr. Liz Macfie, who told me that Mr. Alan Rogers, who worked with the Global Environment Facility, had asked her to contact me. This felt like destiny because I couldn't recall ever meeting him. She also added that she was about to leave Rwanda to work with a different organization in Uganda and would contact me again to see if I could join her there.

All too soon, the Christmas holidays were upon us, and I found myself spending a memorable week at the zoo in Entebbe. With funding and support from the Jane Goodall Institute (JGI), the zoo had acquired many captive chimpanzees, rescued from the illegal wildlife trade, mostly from neighboring Democratic Republic of Congo (DRC). Sadly, their mothers were hunted from the forest for meat, and, because they were too small to eat, they would be sold as pets, and, consequently, many ended up in Entebbe Zoo, which later became the Uganda Wildlife Education Centre. Like Poncho, the monkey who had first introduced me to the fascinating world of primates, the chimpanzees were also playful and mischievous and when you were not looking, would escape from their flimsy cages. When I carried them back, they often wanted me to hug them, because they still missed their mothers' care. I learned that chimpanzees were fully dependent on their mothers for the first five years of their life. When I got back to London, I called Ian to see where we could meet so that I could share the photos of the captive chimpanzees at Entebbe Zoo. He suggested that we meet at London Zoo, where he was going to attend a talk on the chimpanzees of Budongo Forest in Uganda.

The presenter, Vernon Reynolds, was passionate about the chimpanzees and how much hope he had for conservation in Uganda, yet he was not Ugandan. Vernon and his wife Frankie had studied the chimpanzees in 1962. They returned after thirty years to establish the Budongo Forest Project.

Ian Redmond introduced me to Vernon Reynolds and I shared my photos of the chimpanzees with them both. Vernon invited me to visit Oxford University, where he was professor of biological anthropology.

A few days later I contacted Professor Reynolds to see if I could conduct research on the chimpanzees of Budongo Forest, as his talk had inspired me. It wasn't long before I found myself on a train to Oxford, and a meeting with Vernon, who graciously offered me an opportunity to conduct research the following summer. I was eager to study the behavior of chimpanzees, but Vernon suggested I study the parasites in their fecal samples, which had not been done before.

In the summer of 1992, I set off to Budongo Forest for my first study of primates in their natural setting. I made the four-hour journey with Vernon, Frankie, and their son Jake. When we got to Budongo, I was given my own room and a place to set up my research equipment. I carried with me the book *Diagnosing Helminthiasis through Coprological Examination* by D. Thienpont, which we still use to this day. That night, the sounds of screaming kept me awake. It turned out to be tree hyraxes, small mammals the size of rabbits that are related to elephants, specific to Budongo Forest. We got up at 6 a.m. to view the chimpanzees as they climbed out of their nests, and then followed them and waited to collect their dung when they defecated from the trees.

However, after bringing back the fecal samples from the forest and processing them onto the slide, I realized that there was not enough electricity to power the compound microscope that I had borrowed from the Royal Veterinary College (RVC) and had to find a way to improvise. Jake suggested that we turn the crate upside down and shine a flashlight underneath to provide a light source for the microscope. With this new light source, I was able to examine the parasite eggs. By the end of my time there I had not only learned to track chimpanzees and collect and analyze their samples for intestinal helminth parasites, but also to write a good scientific report about my findings, thanks to Vernon, who ruthlessly edited my first draft.

After the study, I was excited to get back to London to share my findings and research. Going through Customs with chimpanzee dung was a bit nerve-racking because I was worried that they would stop me from bringing it into the UK in spite of my supporting paperwork, but thankfully I made it through without any problems. I felt a great sense of achievement and purpose. It brought me closer to my dream of becoming a wildlife veterinarian.

My experience and study of the chimpanzees of Budongo had opened a new world for me, and I became fascinated by their behavior. I was captivated by Dr. Jane Goodall's close relationship with the chimpanzees at Gombe National Park, and how much we could learn from them. Like humans, different parenting skills resulted in different outcomes for their children's future. When Jane came to speak in London, I jumped at the opportunity to attend her lecture. Afterward, I went to speak to her and she invited me to Gombe. My sister Veronica went with me and we were the only Africans in that lecture hall. I could tell that Jane was pleased to see Africans at the event.

I was so inspired that I proceeded to attend more Jane Goodall talks, much to the disapproval of some of my classmates who expected me to spend more time working at a small-animal clinic than attending talks about wildlife. But attending these talks fed me and deeply motivated me.

As a veterinary student, I had no idea that the road I had chosen to travel would take me on such a great adventure that would impact my life and those around me. Two and a half decades later I was honored to be featured among seven alumni with unique careers on the RVC Wall of Achievement.

Chapter 4

First Contact

There is more meaning and mutual understanding in exchanging a glance with a gorilla than any other animal I know.
—Sir David Attenborough[2]

The Bwindi Impenetrable Forest is the second stronghold of the mountain gorilla. This critically endangered species was first discovered in the Virunga Volcanoes in 1902. Ninety years later, there were now only about six hundred mountain gorillas left in the world. I was in the final stages of my veterinary degree when I received word from Dr. Eric Edroma, the Director of the Uganda National Parks, that the gorillas of Bwindi had been habituated and invited me to conduct research on parasites and bacteria in their intestinal tract. I felt an excitement I couldn't comprehend or explain at the time; almost as if I was coming home. In many ways I was.

Upon arrival in Uganda, I went directly to Makerere University Faculty of Veterinary Medicine, where they kindly secured space where I could culture bacteria, specifically salmonella and campylobacter, from the gorilla fecal samples I would collect as part of my research, to determine if they affected the gastrointestinal system of the gorillas like they do in people. I also finally met with Dr. Liz Macfie in person. She had been appointed to the position of country director for the International Gorilla Conservation Programme (IGCP) in Uganda and it was great to meet her in the flesh.

I was also lucky that the timing of my trip coincided with my sister Veronica's wedding, where I was the maid of honor. Immediately after my sister's wedding, my mother drove me to Dr. Liz Macfie's home in Kampala, where we packed our luggage into her four-wheel-drive Maruti and started the long journey to Bwindi. (She reassured my mother that I wasn't going to be attacked and eaten by gorillas.) Our first stop was six hours away in Kabale, known as the Switzerland of Africa because of its hilly nature and cold climate, not typical of the rest of Uganda. After two nights in Kabale, we started the three-and-a-half-hour-long journey on a rough and winding road over steep hills to Buhoma, the main tourism site in Bwindi. I reveled in the beauty of the green terraced hills, cultivated to avoid soil erosion and separated by patches of forest; it was a scene I would become accustomed to as part of my working life.

When we finally reached Bwindi, the evening mist was rising, and I felt like I had reached the ends of the earth. Bwindi is a local name and means "place of darkness" owing to its thick and dense forest canopy. It was one of the most remote places I had ever been. It had become a national park in 1991 and declared a UNESCO World Heritage Site in 1994. My study took place not long after this, and there was a real air of hope among the communities as revenue from tourism started to trickle in to boost the local economy.

When we arrived at the camp, Liz pointed to a small hut at the top of the hill to show me where I would be staying for the next four weeks. My heart sank as I watched the local domestic staff carry my heavy luggage to a small, compact hut. I'd never lived in a mud hut in my life. The forest was between 3,904 to 8,553 feet above sea level and offered me stunning views of Bwindi Impenetrable National Park. That night I could not sleep, primarily because I felt too exposed in my new home and was scared of wild animals. I prayed to God to keep me safe and had to tell myself that I was going to be all right. Leopards had become extinct in Bwindi and logically there was nothing to fear.

I woke the next morning, sleep deprived, but eager to begin my work. My excitement faded as I felt a burning in my throat. Overnight I had developed a cough and a runny nose. My heart sank. I knew what this meant. All primates are susceptible to the same respiratory viruses. After years of wanting to study the mountain gorillas, I was not sure if I would be able to see them, let alone complete the research. I spoke to Liz about my symptoms and she confirmed my fears: I could not go to the gorillas when I was sick. However, recognizing the urgent need for my research to continue, she offered to introduce me to the park rangers who I could instruct on collecting the samples for me. At least I would still be able to analyze the samples while I waited to recover from my cold. When Liz introduced me to the park staff, chief warden Ignatius Achoka and his team, they were very welcoming and pleased to see a fellow Ugandan studying gorillas. I explained my research and what I needed them to do. It was my first-ever training session—one of many to come.

Before leaving Bwindi to attend other meetings, Liz also introduced me to the Peace Corps volunteers who were engaged in what was at the time a new brand of conservation through the International Gorilla Conservation Programme (IGCP). IGCP's mission was to help the Uganda government establish ecotourism through sharing proceeds from gorilla tourism with the local community. These American volunteers would become my friends and community during this period. The Bwindi Impenetrable National Park was unlike the older parks in that almost all the park staff were from the local communities. What also really touched me was that many of the park rangers were former hunters who had poached animals in the forest to earn a living for their families, and after having been employed by the National Park, they were now earning a larger and more regular income protecting the wildlife instead. Because they knew the forest so well, they were well positioned to catch other poachers. We started to call these rangers born-again poachers. It was an important insight as I began to understand that conservation wasn't simply about the animals, but also about communities.

By the third night, I was sleeping like a baby and started looking forward to snuggling up in my warm blankets as the cold nights drew in. I also had to get used to other inhabitants in my hut. Liz had left me with two cats from Kampala, who loved to catch rats, which as much as I love all animals I had a phobia of. The cats left me "gifts" of rat guts on my bed.

In between analyzing the samples that the rangers brought to me, I read *Gorillas in the Mist* by the late Dr. Dian Fossey and eagerly awaited the moment when I could meet the mountain gorillas in person.

During my quarantine from the gorillas, I also got to meet the locals. One day, an old man came walking slowly but steadily to my hut and introduced himself as Mzee Dominique. He knew enough of my local language in Buganda so that we could communicate. He pointed to his big hut that was four hundred meters away from mine, and told me that he was the one who sold the land to IGCP. He then proceeded to advise me not to stay in the mud hut by myself because if I got bitten by a snake the venom would kill me before I could get any help. He also added that *muzungus*, the local name for white people, were strange people who were able to live alone, but me being an African should not risk my life in this way. He advised me that I should look for a room in the trading center of Buhoma and stay next to other Ugandans. His words both scared and greatly amused me. If only he knew how accustomed I had grown used to living like a *muzungu* in London, he would have been shocked! I thanked him for his advice and politely explained that I didn't mind staying on my own, and would call on him if I needed some help. Mzee Dominique shook his head in disbelief and walked away. He became a lifelong friend, and when he died twenty-four years later, I attended his vigil to bid him farewell.

Contrary to Mzee's belief, my evenings were rarely lonely as I would have dinner together with the Peace Corps volunteers Thor Hanson and John Dubois, who had a wicked sense of humor. I enjoyed hearing from Thor, who was a conservation biologist, about how the gorillas were doing each day since I could not visit them yet and John would sometimes add to the conversation with anecdotes like, "Boy do they fart." (Gorillas need to pass gas because of their high roughage diet.) Much as I loved these anecdotes, I was impatient to experience them for myself.

Finally, the day arrived when I stopped coughing and sneezing and I was ready to trek the gorillas. I listened intently to the briefing by the rangers, concentrating on how to behave when with the gorillas. Habituation is a lengthy process to ensure the safety of gorillas and humans. A wild gorilla group is almost impossible to see because when you are within one hundred meters of them in a thick dense forest they slink back into the bushes. But just because the gorillas are habituated doesn't mean they don't need to be approached with great caution. The ranger, William Betunga, who would be taking me and a group of tourists into the forest, emphasized the need to stay still if a gorilla charged, unnerving but essential advice. He also reminded us never to track the gorillas when sick, nor get closer than five meters. Finally, he stated the importance of digging a hole thirty centimeters deep if you needed to defecate to protect the gorillas from contact with human fecal matter.

We entered their forest home of the Katendegyere group, which had eight gorillas. After walking for an hour, we came across their night nests. Gorillas build a new nest every evening to have a comfortable rest at night. We counted seven nests that were woven with folded twigs and leaves. The ranger explained that only seven gorillas in the group were old enough to build their own nest, ranging from juveniles above four years old to adults. I eagerly measured and scooped the fecal samples in separate plastic containers that I labeled according to the size of the lobe diameter before placing them in a ziplock bag. I tucked the samples into my backpack while the tourists peppered me with questions.

Two hours into the trek as we ventured deeper into the forest, up a fairly steep slope, the ranger told us that we were getting close and should get ready to leave our backpacks, which contained food, with the porters, along with our walking sticks. The origin of this rule about the walking sticks is explained in Thor Hanson's book *The Impenetrable Forest*.[3] While habituating the Katendegyere gorilla group, the country director of the Peace Corps Volunteers came to Bwindi as part of the mock tourism trek to get gorillas used to visits by white people. On one occasion the silverback gorilla grabbed a stick from one of the visitors and was about to beat him with it for daring to threaten him in his territory. My heart started beating faster as I knew we were close, and I eagerly gave my walking stick to the porters who had accompanied us.

And then I saw him. Kacupira, an adult male silverback, my first encounter with a mountain gorilla. He was on his own that day, which was unusual. He was extremely calm, chewing on a piece of bark. He had a deformity on his hand, earning his name, Kacupira meaning "Broken Hand." I was amazed at how close we were able to get to him. With a distance of five meters between us, Kacupira looked huge and unnervingly accommodating to our presence. I stared into his deep brown eyes. When he glanced back at me, I immediately felt a deep connection to one of our closest cousins with whom we share 98.4 percent genetic material. The hour went by far too quickly.

The next day I visited the Mubare gorilla group and saw all thirteen gorillas in the group, where the lead silverback, Ruhondeza, meaning "he likes sleeping so much," had six females with four babies and two juveniles. One of the juvenile gorillas was named Bob, and when I asked why he had this English name, the trackers said that he was very playful and liked cheekily peering from behind the leaves at tourists. Mubare gorilla group was the first group to be habituated for tourism in 1993, and took two years to habituate.

When the team of Ugandan trackers first began the habituation process, they would be charged within ninety-five meters and continued to get charged until the gorillas could be viewed without charging at five meters. Then when they were visited by *muzungus*, they started charging again at twenty meters until they stopped charging at five meters, signifying they were now ready to be visited by tourists, who were mainly white.

These were magical weeks where I could immerse myself in the world of gorillas. I got to name the youngest gorilla in Mubare gorilla group, calling him Kawere, which means "young and helpless," and also named his mother, Mama Kawere. Liz warned me that Kawere may not be appropriate if he grew to become a big silverback. Sadly, Kawere never got the chance to outgrow his name. He died prematurely at the age of four after being found alone in the forest when his mother abandoned him, for reasons we do not know.

There were five adult males in the Katendegyere gorilla group. The lead silverback was called Mugurusi, which means "old man." He was estimated to be over fifty years old. One of the big young males was a blackback called Katume, who was quite aggressive and liked to charge. There was only one female, Nyabitono, who was small and shy with her juvenile, Kasigazi. It was amazing to see how different the group dynamics were. The Katendegyere group was more restless, unstable and less accommodating to visitors than the Mubare gorilla group possibly because of having one female, whom only the lead silverback gorilla could "officially" mate with.

The plight of the Katendegyere group was more dire than I'd realized. There had been eleven gorillas, Thor told me, but four of them had recently crossed over into Zaire (as it was known then before becoming the Democratic Republic of Congo when President Mobutu Sese Seko was overthrown in 1997), to look for food and never returned. In an effort to find the missing gorillas and herd them back to the group, we set off very early in the morning with Charles Kyomukama, the best tracker that Thor knew of. We walked for four hours before we reached the border in the forest. Two hours after we had crossed over into Zaire, we finally came across their night nests, which from the appearance of the fecal matter, turned out to be two days old. It was now 2 p.m., and Thor started to get anxious about not being able to find them that day. He believed that it could take several hours to find their night nests from the previous day. I insisted that we should try and continue looking. After an hour, Charles indicated that we really needed to get back before dark. We could not spend the night in the forest. Reluctantly, I accepted that we had lost all hope of finding the gorillas. We could not confirm whether they were still alive or had been eaten, because unlike in Uganda, where the local Batwa hunter/gatherers avoided the gorillas because they believed it was bad luck to look in the eyes of a gorilla, people in Zaire ate gorillas because they believed that eating a gorilla would give them its strength. It was an important lesson in how different cultures could determine the fate of wildlife. Being able to easily cross between Uganda and Zaire through the unofficial border of Bwindi and Sarambwe, also made me realize how vulnerable the mountain gorillas were and how much protection they needed.

I made another trip to Zaire during my research that summer to witness how other countries handled gorilla tourism, this time with Stephanie, the Australian manager of African Pearl Safaris Lodge. Founded by a Ugandan entrepreneur, Mr. Tumusiime, it was the first company to take tourists gorilla trekking in the Bwindi Impenetrable National Park in 1993.

The official crossing over into Zaire was anything but simple. Our difficulties began as soon as we reached the border check point when Stephanie was asked to pay one hundred francs (equivalent to one hundred US dollars) to bring our vehicle into the country. As neither of us had the funds, we decided to leave the vehicle in Uganda and continue on foot. However, they still had questions for us, demanding to know what we were going to do in Zaire. They were surprised to hear that a Ugandan was going to track mountain gorillas, but that did not stop them from also asking us for a cholera vaccination certificate, claiming an outbreak. If we wished to proceed through the border, then we would need a cholera injection. I shuddered when they showed me the dirty, used needle with white solution that looked like penicillin antibiotic. When we refused to be injected, they finally stated that if we wished to proceed, we would need to pay them twenty francs each, which was definitely the lesser of two evils. Stephanie quickly paid them, and we were soon on our way again.

I was struck by the thousands of tents of the United Nations Refugee Agency (UNHCR) that lined our route to the camp where we were to track the gorillas. Yet it wasn't surprising given the recent civil war that had seen thousands displaced and genocide that had resulted in millions of Tutsi and moderate Hutus being killed through bloody ethnic cleansing.

We hired two local porters to carry our bags, and started walking to the camp next to the trekking point in Jomba. We finally arrived one hour later at 6:30 p.m., and then started to put up our tents. Two young Congolese men of not more than twenty years old offered to help us erect the tents, one of them was called Michael Jackson and the other was called Johnnie Walker, clearly not their original names, but ones they had adopted possibly to gain the trust of international travelers. Stephanie and I were thoroughly amused by their stage names, but realizing that we needed them, we accepted their help also to get us some dinner.

In the morning, we bought our gorilla permits and went tracking. Much to my surprise, we did not hike the volcanoes. Instead we found a family of about eight gorillas within an hour's hike in a bamboo forest. The guides gave us a very short briefing and did not mention anything about the risk of human disease transmission to the mountain gorillas. In fact, the ranger told people to get as close as they wanted, much closer than the five meters advised by rangers in Bwindi. I was so shocked that I had to tell him that I was working at Bwindi, and he became uneasy and then whispered to me, "You can go closer, but don't tell my bosses." However, I kept the recommended distance, deeply disturbed by what had transpired. I felt very concerned for the health of these gorillas, and when the visit finally ended, we decided to get back to Uganda that same day. It was clear to me that the political unrest in Zaire had severely disrupted conservation and sustainability. It also highlighted how difficult it was to monitor the gorilla tracking rules and ensure that they were being followed by all three countries (Uganda, Rwanda, Zaire) who were lucky enough to have a mountain gorilla population. It made me appreciate the great effort that had been made by Uganda National Parks and IGCP in Uganda.

Without a doubt, gorillas are impacted by human visitors beyond the potential for disease transmission. The study I conducted in the Bwindi gorillas compared the research group in the eastern sector of Bwindi at Ruhija with the two tourist groups in Bwindi's northern sector in Buhoma. The findings proved significant, with the two families of gorillas visited by tourists recording a greater parasitic burden compared to the one family visited by fewer researchers. Gorillas visited by large groups of people could be experiencing greater stress levels, which might lead to reduced immunity, consequently increasing their parasitic burden. It was a sobering thought and brought into question the need for a delicate balance to be struck in order to protect the gorillas while acknowledging the benefits of ecotourism in supporting the gorillas and the neighboring human communities alike.

Far too soon, my study ended, and I was sad to leave this amazing place that had opened my eyes to the world and plight of the mountain gorillas. I really felt I'd come home and didn't want to leave. People had been so friendly, welcoming, and generous. I recalled how the rangers often invited me to share in their cooked lunch during the gorilla treks because I never had time to make myself a packed lunch. Thor and I often joked about the fact that "cold beans and matooke never tasted so good" as when you were exhilarated, tired, hungry and thirsty after a steep hike to find the gorillas. Most of all, I was so grateful to Liz Macfie for giving me this opportunity and the valuable support. I realized how deeply I had fallen in love with the gorillas, the Bwindi Impenetrable Forest, and the charming Bwindi community, and I promised I would return. Something special had happened in Bwindi that solidified my intention of becoming a full-time wildlife vet protecting the precious wealth and heritage of Uganda.

I eagerly shared the findings with my supervisor Dr. Mark Fox and The Zebra Foundation who funded the research, as well as at the British Veterinary Zoological Society (BVZS) meeting held at London Zoo where I also acknowledged Olympus Cameras, who lent me their camera for this life-changing expedition. Though I was extremely nervous during my first-ever presentation to veterinarians, so much so that I had to drink a glass of wine to calm my nerves, I was deeply encouraged by their compliments, including from Professor Murray Fowler, editor of a book I often refer to, *Zoo and Wildlife Medicine*. I was ecstatic when this research study at Bwindi was eventually published eleven years later in *Primates*,[4] a very prestigious Japanese scientific journal.

Grateful for the relevant training I received to improve the welfare of wild animals in Uganda, I felt compelled to write to the *Veterinary Record*[5] responding to a letter that said that zoos are not needed. It became my first publication in a scientific journal.

Emboldened by my success, I sent my report to Dr. Edroma, telling him that I wanted to become the first veterinarian for Uganda National Parks. To my surprise Dr. Edroma responded that my job would be waiting for me after I completed my studies. I did not expect to get an answer so quickly; it was too exciting! I was going to get my dream job!

I also sent a copy of the report to Dr. George Schaller, who was the first person to study mountain gorillas, even before Dr. Dian Fossey, and had also spent a few weeks in Bwindi Impenetrable Forest. Dr. Schaller introduced me to the first vet for the Wildlife Conservation Society field veterinary program, and author of *Appointments at the End of the World,* Dr. Billy Karesh, who became a lifelong mentor. It appeared as if everything was falling naturally into place. There was only one hurdle left; I needed to pass my final exams.

However, I didn't feel ready. I had not found the time to really prepare for my finals, as so much of my time had been taken up with my experience in Bwindi. I prayed for the best, but was devastated when my name failed to appear on the list of graduates. I had failed the surgery component. I recall calling my mother in tears. As always, my mother's belief in me motivated me to keep going. I returned to Uganda for a holiday, where I also arranged to gain work experience with Dr. Johnson Acon, a renowned small-animal veterinarian and excellent teacher at Makerere University. I learned so much from him, and returned to the UK more confident in sitting the exams which I, thankfully, passed.

It had been a long road but a worthwhile one. Finally, I was ready to return home as Uganda's first wildlife vet.

PART II

Becoming a Wildlife Veterinarian

Chapter 5

A Dream Is Born—Creating a Job for Myself

Now that I had secured this new role, the real work began. Though I had a choice of first gaining experience in a small- or large-animal clinic in the UK, I felt strongly that this was the right time to return home and set up the veterinary unit in the Uganda National Parks. I was so anxious to start my dream job that my sister cautioned me not to get too excited. She too had returned to Uganda very excited to start work in her first job at the Ministry of Finance, Planning and Economic Development, as a fresh graduate after four years studying electrical engineering and computer science at Princeton University. Though she enjoyed the work and being back home, she found that she had to adjust to the more laid-back work ethic.

Dr. Liz Macfie took me out for a coffee at the Kampala Sheraton Hotel to congratulate me on the new job. She also informed me that she was on call for the Mountain Gorilla Veterinary Project (MGVP) based in Rwanda because their clinical veterinarian had gone on Christmas holiday in the United States. A few days later I got a call from Liz that she had been called to rescue an infant gorilla from a snare in Rwanda. She asked if I would like to come along. Because Liz was living in Kabale, a six-hour drive from Kampala, I got on a public bus to meet her at their offices before we drove ten kilometers to Gatuna at the Uganda and Rwanda border. The bus ride was so overpacked I had to carry a stranger's baby. When I got to Kabale, Liz collected me from the bus station, and we crossed the border to Rwanda. These were the green undulating hills where the late Dr. Dian Fossey had set up a long-term study of the mountain gorillas. Though the director of the Office Rwandais Tourisme Parc Nationale (ORTPN) mainly spoke French, I was able to pick up his comment that I looked too young to be a veterinary officer, and the British had done better in training the nationals of the countries they colonized, unlike the colonizers of his country, Rwanda. We stayed in Kigali, the capital city of Rwanda, and the following morning got up early and collected the MGVP Rwandan vet Dr. Tony Mudakikwa from his home. He was tall, gentle, and soft-spoken and delighted to meet a fellow African wildlife vet. Tony was to become a great pillar of support for my veterinary work in Uganda.

It was my first veterinary intervention with wild gorillas. I had been involved in treating captive animals at London Zoo, but not in the wild. When we got to the park headquarters at the base of the Volcano National Park, we gathered together some rangers, trackers, and porters to carry the veterinary equipment. This included a dart pistol and blowpipe with carbon dioxide cartridges to power the pistol, pliers to cut the snare, and a vet kit containing thermometers, stethoscopes, darts, syringes, needles, anesthetic drugs, anti-inflammatories, and antibiotics along with cotton balls, surgical kit, suture material, masks and gloves. We started to hike up the mountain. After one hour, we found the gorillas. Immediately the trackers started to make the comforting grunts with which I had become familiar in Bwindi. The Virunga mountain gorillas were slightly larger than the Bwindi mountain gorillas and more habituated, enabling us to get much closer. The trackers showed us the snared infant gorilla, about four years old, that had a rope cut into his lower arm, a devastating effect of poaching, even if the snare was not intended for the gorillas, but for duiker and bush pigs that people like to eat. Liz and Tony prepared the dart while I passed on to them the ketamine anesthetic, with a needle and syringe to draw up the drug. We walked in single file toward the gorillas, with Liz and Tony leading the team. When the gorilla was within three meters, Liz took this opportunity to fire a dart through a blowpipe attached to a pistol, into the juvenile gorilla, aiming for the thigh muscle. It was so silent that you could not hear the sound of the charge going off, and the dart found its target in seconds. We put on masks and gloves and watched the gorilla until the anesthetic took effect within five minutes and he lay on his side. This youngster was about the size of a four-year-old child. As we moved toward the infant, the silverback of the group came swiftly toward us and my legs started to become wobbly. I had to fight against my instincts, when I saw that everyone was standing still and I remembered that we were not supposed to run. The trackers clapped and made loud humming noises that kept away the protective father. I was assigned the role of holding the infant gorilla, which had a strong grip on my hand even under anesthesia, and watched Liz and Tony removing the snare, cleaning the wound, and injecting him with long-acting antibiotics. After thirty minutes the young gorilla started to move his legs and arms, and within forty-five minutes he was fully awake. The trackers returned him safely back to his family, who immediately accepted him, which was so heartwarming to see. It was one of the most exciting days of my life.

On January 2, 1996, after not having had much sleep the previous night because I was so excited to begin my first job, I got up early and reported for duty at the Uganda National Parks headquarters in Kampala. To my surprise, after the security guard let me in, I found that I was the first and only person in the office that day. That night I went out for dinner with my family and friends, and when my sister asked how my first day was, I could not hide the truth. She laughed and told me to be patient. On the second day, a few more people came to work, and by the end of the first week most people had reported back to work from the Christmas holiday. The director of Uganda National Parks, Dr. Eric Edroma, introduced me all around and brought me to the office I would share with the internal auditor. I was officially a Veterinary Officer for the Uganda National Parks.

I soon realized that even though I had got my dream job, there were no funds to support it. At the time that I was recruited, conservationists believed that wild animals should not be interfered with and natural selection should always take its course. I had to spend a lot of time explaining to others within the parks service why exactly I'd been hired and what vets can do to support conservation efforts, and the need to carry out an intervention when it was human-related or life-threatening in a species as critically endangered as the mountain gorillas that were only about 650 in number at the time. Kenya Wildlife Service (KWS) has a veterinary unit with which I was sent to gain experience. I worked at their animal orphanage in Nairobi where I learned from the other vets, attending to a wide range of captive wild animals, from impalas to lions. I saw firsthand how human intervention is essential to solve human-caused crises. We also attended to semi-captive rhinos in the Masai Mara that needed to be moved to another protected area, and I was particularly fascinated when they were given just enough anesthetic to be hypnotized to walk into a crate to be transported to another place.

I got a lot of support from my immediate supervisor, Captain Otekat, the Deputy Director of Uganda National Parks. Though I had no darting equipment at the beginning, I asked him if I could go and check on the gorillas. While we were there, we visited the Katendegyere gorilla group. I was delighted to see how much the baby gorilla I had named Kawere had grown over the past year and a half, but I was surprised to discover that Mugurusi, the fifty-year-old lead silverback of the gorilla group, was not with the rest of his family. We eventually found him walking slowly while foraging on the Muzabajiro loop trail toward the DRC border. The rangers told me that he was growing old and could not keep up with his group anymore. I told them that they should call me whenever a gorilla like Mugurusi is not behaving normally, and explained to them my role as a veterinarian who had been hired to treat sick gorillas because we can no longer assume that they are dying of "natural causes." Not having any darting equipment, I tried to make a pole syringe by attaching a syringe with a dose of long-acting antibiotics to a stick, and managed to inject Mugurusi from a meter away, which was only possible because he was so lethargic. Seeing how weak Mugurusi was, I told the rangers that if he died, they should call me immediately to come and do a postmortem, because it was important to find out what he died of and to also determine whether the other gorillas in the group are being affected by the same disease so that we can treat them before it is too late. I returned back to Kampala and three days later, received a message on the radio call that Mugurusi's body had been found in the forest that morning. Saddened by his death, I also realized that we did not have much time to conduct a useful postmortem before his body decomposed, yet it was going to take at least a day before I could get a vehicle and driver from the park headquarters to take me to Bwindi to carry out a postmortem. Then I thought of Dr. John Bosco Nizeye, a Rwandese vet from MGVP who was based in Uganda and working at Makerere University's facility of veterinary medicine As a Hutu, he could not work in Rwanda anymore—his ethnic group had been overthrown by the Tutsi in the bloody genocide. I asked John Bosco if he would join me to conduct a postmortem on the gorilla and also teach me how to do one. I had only done postmortems on domestic animals as part of my training at vet school. We arrived in Bwindi ten hours later at night. The following morning, we assembled a few rangers to assist us also as an important learning opportunity, together with a Peace Corps volunteer who took notes. And we did it at the park office where the old silverback's body had been carried to, by the trackers. The postmortem was a six-hour process because John Bosco took time to patiently explain the gorilla's anatomy and procedures. I was fascinated by the very large intestines, due to the heavy roughage diet of leaves, shoots, and stems, and it reminded me of a horse's large colon and other sections of the intestines. If I had not been with John Bosco, I would have thought that this was abnormal. I was also intrigued that the gorilla and the horse had the same tapeworm species, *Anoplocephala,* not found in other species. We found that Mugurusi was emaciated and had abnormalities in the kidney and heart. Our preliminary finding was renal failure and mild heart failure, which was later confirmed on histopathology. Fortunately we did not see any signs of an infectious disease on postmortem that could affect the other gorillas in his group.

I was pleasantly surprised to see the story among the first pages on the nation's main newspaper, the *New Vision*. Condolence messages from family, friends, and colleagues came in about the loss of the old man, "Mugurusi." People hadn't expected a gorilla to have a detailed postmortem, but they were fascinated that the old gorilla died of the same causes as humans. This article raised the profile of gorillas in Uganda and made the general public care more about them. A few years later, Ndyakira Amooti, who wrote the story, won the prestigious Goldman's Environmental Prize for his fearless reporting on wildlife issues in Uganda and was later knighted to become a "Sir."

Shortly after, I was asked to attend to an adult male chimpanzee called "Big Brown" in Kibale National Park that had a wire snare on his wrist, attached to a ten-foot pole. This forest park suffered from heavy poaching for duiker and bush pigs, leading to accidental snaring of chimpanzees, several of which had missing arms or feet. By the time we got hold of all the necessary equipment and a vehicle to travel for five hours to Kibale, it was dark and too late to find the chimpanzee. So we slept overnight at the Makerere University Biological field station at Kibale National Park and made plans to carry out the intervention on the following day. However, this was the first time that a chimpanzee was going to be darted, and everybody was nervous. We had to also get the "buy in" from Professor Richard Wrangham, a well-known primatologist from Harvard University who founded a long-term research project, the Kibale Chimpanzee Project. This particular chimpanzee was among those he had been studying for more than a decade and was very dear to him. He was concerned that once the chimpanzee was darted he would go up the tree where he felt safer, and then once the anesthetic had taken effect, he could fall. So, we came up with the idea of getting a tarpaulin that people would hold under the tree. We were not able to dart the chimpanzee even on the next day because he had isolated himself in another part of the forest. Big Brown returned a few weeks later without the pole on the snare and later managed to remove it himself, though his arm was maimed forever. This attempted intervention made me understand how difficult it was to remove snares from wild apes and how important it was to prevent them in the first place.

Following this incident, UWA Veterinary Unit received a donation from the Dian Fossey Gorilla Fund Europe (which later became the Gorilla Organization) to buy darting equipment. Jillian Miller, the director of DFGFE, then went on to convince Care for the Wild in UK to donate a secondhand four-wheel-drive Suzuki vehicle. I excitedly put the UWA logo on the vehicle, and was so thrilled that the veterinary department was becoming functional. Debby Cox, who started the Jane Goodall Institute office in Uganda to look after orphaned chimpanzees rescued from the bushmeat trade, generously got her former employer, Taronga Zoo, to donate anesthetic drugs, which could not be found in Uganda. I was beginning to see how funding and support worked: it took a substantial network.

The Budongo Forest Project invited me to a conference on forest conservation, and so I returned to the place where I first conducted research on wild animals—the chimpanzees—at the age of twenty-two. On my way back from the conference, I saw a man casually walking along the road holding the hand of a three-year-old chimpanzee that had a rope around the waist. It was like an illusion. I realized that I had to arrest this man and asked the person driving to stop. I introduced myself as an officer of Uganda Wildlife Authority and asked him what he was doing with the chimpanzee. He agreed to enter the car and took us to his home explaining that he was working for a general in the Ugandan army. When we met the general, he told us that whenever they go to neighboring DRC they often get pestered to buy infant chimpanzees, so he eventually bought one. It was obvious that the general had grown attached to the chimpanzee, which he was feeding the same food his family ate. I noticed that unlike other infant chimpanzees that are rescued from the bushmeat trade, this chimpanzee looked healthy, well-fed, and not traumatized or withdrawn, he was in fact very playful and sociable. I explained to the army general that getting a baby chimpanzee involves killing the mother who is very protective, and buying the chimpanzee encourages the seller to go back and capture others. I also added that chimpanzees don't make good pets because at five years old, they often become aggressive and difficult to control, and, most immediately pressing, it is illegal to have them as pets in Uganda. He willingly, though sadly, handed over the chimpanzee.

The infant chimpanzee clung to me all through the three-hour journey to Kampala, and when they dropped me off, we immediately had to get him to the rescue and rehabilitation center at Entebbe Zoo. Luckily the Congolese researcher who traveled with us from Budongo offered to carry the chimpanzee, while I drove. But the little chimpanzee only wanted me to hold him, and even bit us. My companion didn't drive, so with the opinionated baby chimpanzee on my lap, I drove them to Entebbe. I realized just how dangerous this was when he thought he'd like to try driving and grabbed the steering wheel as I was driving. He was so intelligent, so like a human child, that I understood on an even more visceral level how unethical it was to separate them from their mothers. When we got to the zoo, Debby exclaimed that this chimpanzee was actually overweight and relaxed around people in contrast to the many emaciated and traumatized chimpanzees she had rescued in Burundi and Uganda.

The chimpanzee was put on a diet of fruits and vegetables, and was eventually taken to the Ngamba Island Chimpanzee Sanctuary. I was honored when he was named "Kalema" after me. Perhaps because he was not mistreated in his early childhood, Kalema grew up to become a confident and handsome second-highest-ranking alpha male and the favorite of the keepers and visitors who came to the island. This confirmed what I had read in Jane Goodall's *In the Shadow of Man*: that, much like humans, chimpanzees that are treated well as infants are more confident and rise faster in the ranks to become alpha males. I hoped that the army general would not purchase any more chimpanzees and, more importantly, tell others why they shouldn't. I knew, too, that the trade in chimpanzee infants was the result of poverty: people were so desperate they resorted to such trade to survive. Having been involved in the capture and translocation of Kalema, my Congolese colleague vowed to convince his community not to capture chimpanzees, gorillas, or other primates. It gave me hope for the future of great apes that more of my fellow Africans were becoming empathetic and willing to protect these precious endangered species that are part of our natural heritage. Ngamba Island Chimpanzee Sanctuary and Wildlife Conservation Trust, now called the Chimpanzee Trust, to this day still takes in infant and orphaned chimpanzees who are victims of the illegal wildlife trade. Because they sustain their operations through donations and fees from local and international visitors, twenty-one years later, when tourism ground to a halt due to the COVID-19 pandemic, they struggled to feed the chimpanzees and though we were also struggling to sustain our work with gorillas, I felt compelled to give a donation to keep Kalema and his fellow chimpanzees thriving.

Chapter 6

The Wandering Gorilla

Three months into my job, I received a strange but urgent radio message from Ignatius Achoka, the Chief Park Warden of Bwindi Impenetrable National Park, to come and translocate a gorilla that had settled on community land. I pondered this bizarre request, which had never been considered before in managing free-ranging gorillas. Moving gorillas from their home range greatly disrupts their natural behavior. I asked John Bosco to join me, and we headed to Bwindi in his car, where we met his counterpart from Mountain Gorilla Veterinary Project (MGVP), Jonathan Sleeman, at the Rwanda and Uganda border, and proceeded south to Nkuringo, another sector of Bwindi that I had never been to before.

I was amazed at how much steeper the hills were in Nkuringo compared to Buhoma, the only tourist site of Bwindi Impenetrable National Park at the time. When we arrived, Ignatius explained to us in more detail why he had made this drastic decision to carry a gorilla from its natural home range to a place it has never been to before. A semi-habituated mature adult male gorilla, a silverback, had broken off from his group and because he had lost his fear of people, decided to settle in community land. The chief warden had been called by the community when this silverback scratched a man with his sharp nails and bit his ankle and also scratched his wife. The man had been so badly injured he had to be taken to the hospital, and Bwindi Park management had to pay the hospital bills as well as deal with the tension that this was creating in the community. After further consultation, the community admitted that when the gorilla came to the garden and found the woman digging, she got very frightened and called her husband for help, and he then chased the gorilla with a hoe.

Having heard that a vet had been hired at Uganda National Parks, Ignatius seized this opportunity to move the gorilla to save him from being set upon and killed by the angry community members.

That evening we looked for the gorilla and found him settling in his night nest thirty meters from the road. As soon as we were within a distance of ten meters he charged us; though it frightened me, it was not unexpected. We quietly walked away so as not to startle him into moving somewhere else, as it would take us more time to find him the following day. We discussed with the warden and his team of rangers and volunteers how best to capture him in the morning. Jonathan and I planned to dart him, and we asked the community stretcher society to make a larger stretcher than they normally would for a human, to carry the gorilla out of the forest. Jonathan insisted on a mattress as well to make it more comfortable for the gorilla. When the local ambulance team got to the road, they would put him on to the back of the pickup truck and John Bosco would drive the gorilla along with the rangers and community volunteers to a location above the narrow neck of the forest park to be released 120 kilometers away. I decided to name him "Kalambuzi," which means "Explorer" in Rukiga, the local language.

This sector of Bwindi had no hotels, lodges, or motels where we could stay, so our best option was to spend the night in our sleeping bags on the mud floor of Nteko Primary School in Kikobero Village. We discovered that the sheet-iron roof leaked when it rained heavily in the night. We got up in the morning not having had enough sleep and soaked to the skin. With a banana and water for breakfast, we got ready for the intervention.

I was extremely nervous about this operation, but also encouraged by the willingness of the local communities to get involved in solving the problem. Jonathan made up the dart with the standard dose of ketamine anesthetic for habituated gorillas. We walked to where we had found Kalambuzi the previous evening, and within ten minutes, Jonathan had managed to dart the gorilla. To our surprise the three-hundred-pound gorilla got so frightened that he immediately started running, and we had to keep up with him as he briskly walked down the steep hill. After twenty minutes, Kalambuzi started to slow down as the anesthetic took effect, but did not stop moving. When we realized that the anesthetic was wearing off Jonathan concluded that the gorilla should have been given a larger dose possibly because he was not fully habituated, meaning that he had greater fear of people and more ketamine was needed to counteract the higher levels of adrenaline. We hurriedly made up another dart and attempted again. However, we never got close enough to get another dart into the gorilla because he sped up as the anesthetic wore off. After four hours of running up and down the hills of Nkuringo, Kalambuzi ran back into the forest. Though not where we'd intended to release him, we had translocated him on foot!

Ultimately, we found ourselves at the bottom of a very steep hill. We had run out of drinking water and decided to drink the water from the running stream, ignoring the dirty feet of our assistants who were cooling off in the water upstream. It was a choice between dehydration and cholera or any other infectious disease. The water was clear-running and delicious. However, after four hours of running up and down hills, I was completely depleted. I'd run out of energy and adrenaline and my muscles were so sore that I could not imagine climbing the steep eighty-five-degree slope to get back to the road. Though it was midday, I said I'd spend the night at the edge of the forest much to everyone's surprise, and that I was sure I'd feel stronger in the morning. Jonathan tried to convince me to start walking again, but I was simply too tired to climb back up the slope in the baking sun. He left me to head back to get more water and urged me to try. As I attempted to slowly drag myself up the hill, a barefooted woman in a dress came down with a bottle of water and without saying anything to me, grabbed my hand. With her strong grip, she slowly but steadily pulled me up the hill. I was amazed at her strength. I also felt that I had something in common with this angel who had overcome whatever her society thought she ought to be doing as a woman to come to my rescue. When we got up the hill, two hours later, everyone clapped.

I thought often about this female angel, but it was not until twenty-four years later, when we hosted a community workshop in Nkuringo, that I learned her name. I mentioned her that day and one of our Village Health and Conservation Team volunteers reconnected me with her. Her name was Peace.

It was an emotional reunion, two decades later, when I visited Peace at her semipermanent mud thatched home and our children met. Peace remembered being as amazed as I was that day. She was so captivated that a fellow Ugandan woman would go down their steep hills to rescue a gorilla that she wanted to help me when they told her that I was too weak to walk back up. I too had never seen the women at Bwindi get involved in tracking gorillas. All the rangers, trackers, and porters I'd met were men.

The problem of the habituated or partially habituated gorilla entering the community was one that needed consideration. Though Ignatius's ambitious plan to translocate the adventurous gorilla Kalambuzi to the northern part of the park didn't quite go as planned, it was successful in that he never came back outside the park.

Following the incident we decided that it was the partial habituation that was the problem. After habituating the Mubare and Katendegyere gorilla groups in the northern sector, which you could reach from Buhoma, Uganda National Parks decided to habituate other gorilla groups in the southern sector. It takes at least two years to fully habituate a gorilla group. However, after spending one year habituating a group that was close enough to the main road to go out and return on the same day, they soon found that this sector was too steep for tourists to comfortably trek. They decided to stop the habituation process halfway, which proved to be dangerous because though the gorilla had lost most of his fear of people, he was not comfortable enough for people to get within a few meters to dart him without becoming aggressive and charging.

Bwindi Impenetrable National Park is a 321-square-kilometer forest island surrounded by a dense human population of more than three hundred people per square kilometer almost dividing the park into two sectors, with a narrow neck in the middle. Once gorillas became habituated they started to leave the safety of the park to forage on land where their family once ranged before, but had been taken over by people. Ignatius had arranged for us to take the gorilla where he would not get into competition with other gorillas or people, north of the neck in an area that gorillas had not been sighted before. As vets we could not question what the warden had decided because he had much more experience than us in managing wildlife.

Some of the conservationists felt that we should not have rushed to move the gorilla without finding out why there were no gorillas in that sector of the park. Dr. Liz Macfie, having seen that chasing the gorillas rather than translocating them had proven to be an effective way to get wandering gorillas back to the safety of their forest habitat, strongly felt that they should not be chased by vets or rangers who were supposed to be protecting them, because it would send conflicting signals to this highly intelligent species.

A Peace Corps volunteer, Francine Madden, suggested that the local communities should be the ones to herd the "problem gorillas" back to the park, giving them control over the problem. This led to the establishment of Human and Gorilla Conflict resolution teams—HUGOs, a network of community volunteers trained to safely chase gorillas back to the park. It was agreed that for sustainability and ownership of this solution, the "gorilla chasers" should be volunteers who would be given incentives, such as livestock rather than staff who are paid a salary.

Four years later, the Mubare gorilla group in Buhoma sector spent several days eating the banana stems in the garden of Mzee Bigirwa and he got very angry. While showing me the damage they had made, I plucked up the courage to ask him if he liked the gorillas.

He told me that gorillas were important because some of his children were employed by the park, and money from tourism was being used to build schools, clinics, and roads in his community; however, the individual farmer like him was not getting compensated when gorillas damaged his crops and yet tourists were paying Uganda Wildlife Authority to see gorillas in his garden. This seemed very unfair to me, and I felt compelled to give him what money I had in my pocket (equivalent to two dollars) and relayed his complaint to my supervisors at UWA. Mzee Bigirwa later became one of the first HUGO members and his son, Medard, who is a park ranger, was made the main supervisor of the HUGO teams at Bwindi.

This approach to conservation where community members are empowered and engaged in solving the conflict between people and wildlife has gone a long way in reducing the tension between the community and the park management. The HUGO members have not dropped out after twenty years, and are a source of pride in their community. This model was expanded to other national parks and wildlife reserves in Uganda and around the world.

Little did I know that a few months later I was going to engage community members in handling a much larger endangered species of wildlife in another part of Uganda.

Chapter 7

Saving Elephants
That Lost Their Way

One day Dr. Eric Edroma called me into his office for another urgent task. Hon. Moses Ali, the Minister of Tourism, Wildlife and Antiquities (MTWA), had received distressing news from the First Lady of Uganda, Mrs. Janet Museveni, that two elephants were destroying the banana plantation of her cousin, Geoffrey Kagyenzi, a few kilometers from Mubende town. It was strange to find elephants there, because, unlike the case of Kalambuzi, the wandering gorilla who strayed just outside the edge of the national park, Mubende was 150 kilometers away from any protected area.

Usually the only option was to kill "problem animals" that were destroying people's property and sometimes even injuring or killing people. Dr. Edroma said, "Now that we have a vet I want us to move the elephants instead of killing them." I looked at him and wondered,

"What have I gotten myself into?" How do you move a 5½-ton animal from one place to another? I had never been taught this at vet school in London, but I assured him, without fully believing it myself, that we could do it.

My first step was to assess the situation. We traveled with the legal officer of Uganda National Parks, Innocent Ngobi, who was a woman my age, also new to the organization. On the way, we compared notes on what it was like being surrounded by male colleagues who sometimes didn't understand us. As soon as we arrived at Geoffrey Kagyenzi's home, he showed us where the elephants had destroyed his garden, complaining bitterly about this lost banana crop. They had flattened about thirty trees in his banana plantation, but also left quite a lot of it untouched. The elephant footprints fit ten of my own prints within them. We learned that there used to be a much larger herd, but sadly only two elephants remained; the community had most likely poisoned the others.

On our return, we weighed the options of two locations and two routes to move the elephants by road. The shorter distance would involve territory now controlled by the Lord's Resistance Army headed by warlord Joseph Kony. We chose the longer but safer route to the Queen Elizabeth National Park (QENP) end of their migration route.

The first thing we did was recruit rangers from QENP to be part of this exercise so that they could follow the elephants after the translocation. We made plans for two of their most experienced rangers to locate and keep track of the elephants in Mubende while we prepared the mission.

Marcello Onen, a thin man in his fifties, was dedicated to wildlife conservation and had taught many researchers from Uganda and all over the world how to identify mammals and different species of birds in the national parks. Emmanuel Kaheru was a few years younger and equally dedicated to wildlife conservation. They set up camp for two weeks, reporting the movements of the elephant pair. One elephant was bigger than the other, suggesting that they were male and female. Kagyenzi also noticed that they didn't appear to have any babies, which was unusual. Our only conclusion was that they were too stressed to reproduce due to harassment by the local community who likely killed their family, leaving them as the only surviving members.

While our plan to translocate them to QENP had the support of the MTWA, not everyone agreed with the plan. Dr. Eve Abe, the only Ugandan with a PhD in elephants, having done extensive research on elephants in Queen Elizabeth National Park, worried that we could be transferring a problem from one place to another. She echoed the concerns of Henry Busulwa, head of the Uganda Institute of Ecology, who had written to me insisting that more studies needed to be done before we attempted to move the elephants. But my immediate supervisor, Captain Otekat, defended the decision that Uganda National Parks had made to translocate instead of kill the elephants. The media got more excited about this bold decision and reported extensively on it.

But first, I had to learn how such an operation was conducted. I flew to Kenya to participate and learn from Dr. Richard Kock who was heading an operation larger than the one we were planning. The Kenya Wildlife Service (KWS) brought in Clem Coetzee, an animal capture expert from Zimbabwe who had developed the technique for moving adult elephants, which had not been possible until he devised the use of heavy-duty rubber conveyor belts fastened to shipping containers. They assembled an aerial team and a ground team that included vets, an animal capture team, and researchers who measured the elephants and collected ticks and other important biological samples. The media also accompanied the Kenyan team on this exciting and dangerous mission.

A light four-seater aircraft spotted the elephants, after which Clem got into a helicopter with Richard and darted a family of five elephants headed by a matriarch, the most senior adult female. The aerial team radioed the ground team to tell them where the elephants were. It was a military-style operation where the stakes were animal and/or human casualties. When the elephant family was darted with etorphine, I drove with the capture team to the first elephant that went down. She lay on her chest, which meant that her lungs were being squashed so she couldn't breathe properly. The capture team headed by Mr. Kinigi immediately started digging the ground around her to flatten it so that she could lie on her side. We took blood from the elephant's ear vein; it was on the surface and so large that it was a great place for me to gain confidence in taking blood.

Richard trusted me to monitor the elephant on my own. His only words to me were "Here is the drug to reverse the anesthetic if the elephant stops breathing." Because this was the first elephant to be darted, the media stayed with me to capture the moment.

The rest of the vets went on to check on the other elephants, leaving at least one vet per elephant, with Richard moving around to check on all of us.

After thirty minutes, my elephant lifted her head. I froze, because in my pocket I only had the drug for waking her up if she was having difficulty breathing! I scrambled in the vet box to look for the drug that put her to sleep. Mr. Kinigi sprang into action to keep her head down. It seemed like everyone was holding their breath until I found the etorphine and then had to quickly figure out how much to give this giant. I decided to give half the dose that she had been darted with, drew up one milliliter of the drug, and injected it in her ear veins, conscious of the fact that if I accidentally injected myself I would have died in minutes. After five minutes she stopped struggling and went back to sleep, breathing regularly. I'd gotten the dose right.

Richard returned thirty minutes later and said, "I heard that you managed to stop the darted elephant walking away, well done." This apparently was Richard's way of training people: throwing them in the deep end and allowing them to sink or swim. It was the fastest way to learn, and I needed it because I was soon going to be in charge of the operation back home in Uganda.

When Richard revealed that this was the largest elephant, and therefore the matriarch, the team decided to put a collar on her so that they could track the herd's movements to keep them out of trouble. Five people were needed to lift her head to fasten the thick black leather radio collar round her neck.

The next part was pushing this elephant into a twenty-foot shipping container that was modified with the roof raised to hang her trunk outside—a highly complex process. Ropes were fastened on the elephant's legs and tusks, and she was pulled onto the conveyor belt, which had been modified to have a channel iron and chain attached to it. A winch from a tractor was attached to the channel iron, which pulled on the conveyor belt wrapped around the elephant while people pushed her up a wooden ramp into the container, which itself was attached to a truck. Once the elephant was in, we had to reverse the anesthetic. Within two minutes, she stood up and was ready to travel along with her family of five elephants that were put into a second shipping container, for the ten-hour-long journey to Tsavo National Park.

As soon as we arrived, the elephants were released. They walked majestically out of the crates to the safety of their new home. Our first elephant reunited with her family, including an adult female and three youngsters. That night, when I returned to my Uncle Semu's home in Nairobi, I was both shocked and humbled to see myself on Kenya Television Network talking about traveling from Uganda to learn from KWS how to translocate elephants. It was the first time in my career I was on national TV.

On my return to Kampala, I contacted Clem Coetzee, who directed us on how to modify the shipping container, which was donated by the ROKO construction company. Kakira Sugar Works donated a conveyor belt. I approached Peter Moeller, a German warden engineer working in Kidepo Valley National Park, to arrange for the right trucks for the shipping container and all the mechanical aspects. Peter also succeeded to obtain funding for the translocation from "Save The African Elephant" in Germany. I returned to Mubende to plan the ground operation with Mr. Kagyenzi.

The day before the operation began, I went with the two rangers from Queen Elizabeth National Park into the Kasambwa Kisombwe Forest Reserve on foot to track the elephants, and we managed to see them at a distance of one hundred meters. It was far scarier than checking on semi-wild gorillas from only ten meters. We decided not to scare the elephants so we could find them easily the next day. Our challenge was finding a capture team. We had no money with which to recruit. Our only option was to reach out to the local community. In the end, the community members were so excited that they helped to push the elephants for free. In contrast to the large team in Kenya, we had one vet, one warden engineer who was operating the vehicles, one capture expert, Clem, three rangers, and the local community. We also had two people from the media, Adam Shand and Mick Purdy, who came from Zimbabwe to video this momentous event. That evening Clem showed footage of an elephant translocation he had led in Zimbabwe to help the team prepare for the considerable task ahead.

We camped at Kagyenzi's home and arranged that after putting the elephants on the truck, we would have dinner at his place before traveling to Queen Elizabeth National Park. Much like the operation in Kenya, the plan was for Peter to fly in a light aircraft with Clem to locate the elephants, and then for Clem to go up with the helicopter pilot to dart them. I was in charge of the ground team. However, as the light aircraft came in to land on the main highway of Mubende town in Uganda, a huge crowd of people began running toward it. I had to chase everybody off the road because the police who had been told to stop traffic were too awestruck to send them away. It was the Mubende residents' first time seeing an airplane. When the plane landed, everyone wanted to touch it. I had to frantically keep them away from the rotating blade. When the helicopter landed it became even more chaotic. I was relieved when Clem quickly jumped in and took off to locate the elephants.

Within minutes the enormous female elephant had been spotted and darted from the helicopter, and she was on the move. Clem radioed and directed us to where she was running. When we reached her, she was down. I worked with Onen and Kaheru to put a radio collar on her. Luckily, she had fallen on her side in a valley close to the trail. After giving antibiotics for the dart wound and eye ointment to prevent her eyes drying out, I took a blood sample and bathed her in water to prevent her from overheating in the hot sun. However, we were soon joined by a large crowd of over six hundred people who skipped the Sunday church service and walked up the hill to see the elephant. They were led by the Resident District Commissioner, Zeridah Rwabushagara, who headed Mubende and who I had requested to get the local community to cut trails to transport the elephants out of the forest. Having gotten so close to the elephant, a few people wanted a souvenir and to my dismay, plucked off the hairs on her tail. Nevertheless, only one person was not happy, an old woman, a traditional healer, who complained that we were taking away her source of medicine, the elephant dung, and started collecting the last remnants for her medicine cabinet. After an hour, the loader and tractor arrived. Clem roped the elephant onto a conveyor belt, and another crowd of people excitedly helped push her into the container. She stood up two minutes after the anesthetic had been reversed, which was a relief. With one elephant successfully loaded for the journey, I flew in the helicopter with Onen and the farmer Kagyenzi to go and monitor the second elephant, which had fallen on top of a hill, two kilometers away from the first one. When we got to the elephant, we realized that we had put the radio collar on the wrong animal. This one was also a female, but larger and was therefore the matriarch, the group leader. I thought to myself, *No wonder they were not having babies!*

It took the tractor pulling the container four hours to get up the steep hill to us so I had to give her several doses of additional anesthetic to keep her asleep. Several people took photos with the elephant. When the tractor finally arrived another eager crowd helped to push the elephant up a ramp into the container. After reversing the anesthetic, Clem and I jumped out of the container before she got up. However, to our shock, she didn't get up, not even after three minutes, which was the expected time of the reversal. The only safe way to inject more of the reversal anesthetic into her was in her thigh muscle through a space in the container. When she still didn't get up, Clem climbed on top of the container and passed me a rope, which I fastened on her tusk to pull her trunk out from beneath her head so she could breathe more easily. We waited anxiously for another ten minutes; however, she still wasn't moving. With the light of day fading and night closing in, we decided to start our journey, praying our unconscious elephant would recover. When the tractor accelerated over an anthill and the container tilted, my heart skipped a beat. Thankfully, this sudden movement woke up the elephant, and she miraculously stood up and waved her trunk outside the container.

This time round the local print media, *Bukedde*, featured me in the paper bending over an elephant with the words "Akamega enjovu kenkanawa" which means "how small is the one who brings the elephant down," a Luganda proverb about a rat bringing an elephant down by going up its trunk.

The plan to have dinner at Kagyenzi's house was almost thwarted by Peter, who impatiently said that we had to get going to QENP. However, having experienced the long journey in Kenya with nowhere to stop over to eat, I insisted that we all had to eat first and not offend the person who had kept these elephants rather than poison them. His wife had prepared a delicious traditional meal, which turned out to be a lifesaver. The journey that started at 9 p.m. took fifteen hours, longer than expected because of three tire punctures on the trucks carrying the elephants. Kagyenzi, at the last moment so excited that this problem was finally going away, joined us on the journey to the park to make sure that these beasts arrived in their new home (never to return to his).

When we finally arrived at Queen Elizabeth National Park, the big moment had arrived to release the elephants into their new home. Much to my surprise the elephants did not rush to get out of the container like the Kenyan elephants had. They needed a lot more encouragement. After fifteen minutes the first elephant came out and then the second one followed almost immediately after. As they reunited, we clapped and cheered. It was a moment I'll never forget.

We arrived to a warm welcome at the Queen Elizabeth National Park headquarters. However, it was spoiled when Peter made a comment that Ugandans lacked initiative and nothing happened without a white person getting involved. I got so upset by this comment, knowing that, without all the hard work I had put in, this operation would not have happened. I burst into tears and immediately told Peter how untrue his statement was—it had been a team effort this time round, led by a Ugandan—me. The German vet Dr. Siefert apologized on behalf of Peter, and seeing how tired I was, the chief warden Abdullah Latif got me a private room in the only hotel at the Mweya park headquarters. Peter spoke to my supervisor Captain Otekat and apologized for upsetting me. I quickly forgave him, knowing how much work he had put into making the translocation a huge success, and we continued to work together to translocate animals.

Elephants can live up to over fifty years, and I was so glad to have given them a second chance. These two females didn't get into any trouble again. And we successfully demonstrated that elephants, an endangered species, are important enough to Uganda that they can be translocated instead of being killed.

When I returned home, my mother greeted me with a long hug and congratulated me. She reminded me of how my paternal grandmother, Jaaja Nalubowa, who I was named after and who'd died a few years after my father was murdered, was so brave that she used to chase elephants from her garden in the same district of Mubende, and perhaps we had just translocated the same herd. I smiled, hoping that it was true.

The success of this operation paved the way for translocations of wild animals in Uganda large and small. A few months later I was tasked to move another species of wildlife for a different reason. But before I could do that I had to deal with a mysterious disease in giraffes.

Chapter 8

Restocking Giraffes to Prevent Extinction

Giraffes with a mysterious skin disease were spotted in Murchison Falls National Park. The location was particularly concerning because the park had become the stronghold of the infamous Joseph Kony rebels, who were known to mutilate their victims by cutting off their lips and buttocks. I knew there wasn't a moment to lose and insisted on going. Captain Otekat tried to talk me out of my decision, but I was adamant that I needed to get to the giraffes as quickly as I could.

My first hurdle was finding transportation. Thankfully my old mentor, Professor Vernon Reynolds, who I'd met during my university days in the UK, happened to be in Uganda and would be traveling to Budongo Forest Reserve, which was on the way to Murchison Falls National Park.

Vernon and I traveled together to Budongo Forest Reserve. I got up early the following day to visit the chimpanzees, one of the few remaining strongholds with an estimated population of five hundred. It was encouraging to see that they were more relaxed than they had been when I had studied them four years earlier. After breakfast, I waited eagerly for the Murchison Falls National Park vehicle to collect me, but it took several hours. Vernon reminded me to be patient by relating a saying I will never forget, "Africans have the time while Europeans have the watches!"

The army-green pickup truck finally arrived at 6 p.m. in the evening packed with staff and their wives who were standing in the back. I was given a space in the front. Vernon cautioned them to drive carefully and wished me all the best. We proceeded to Paraa, and drove in the night to the park headquarters at the south bank of the river Nile. The Chief Park Warden, John Bosco Nuwe, warmly welcomed me and led me to the camp I'd be staying in. It had bandas, small cottages, made out of mud with grass thatched roofs like the huts of the local Acholi tribe. Though I was the only guest, I was comforted that the warden's house was only one hundred meters away, and I was too excited to feel lonely.

While having dinner, John Bosco described how the disease was affecting the giraffes and he arranged for a vehicle and ranger to take me to see them the following day. As I settled into the banda under a net, I heard mosquitoes buzzing loudly; the only way to get some sleep was by blocking out the sound with music from my Walkman.

The next morning, I was taken to the guard station, where the rangers showed me the dried skin of a giraffe that had died with the skin disease. I could see crusty patches of gray on the skin. An hour later, the only functional vehicle in the whole park arrived to take me; it was a pickup truck with a missing door on the passenger side. Though I felt exposed, I climbed into the truck and prayed that we would be protected against the Kony rebels and any dangerous wild animals. We drove back toward the edge of the river Nile and crossed on a ferry to the northern bank. It was very hot on the ferry, and hippos kept bumping it, making for a stimulating ten-minute ride. When I got to the northern bank, we drove toward the giraffes. My patients were a bit shy, but let us get as close as fifty meters. They all looked healthy and were walking gracefully. I noticed from a distance that a large darker male giraffe had gray crusty lesions on the skin similar to what I had seen on the dried skin at the Quarter Guard. I asked the ranger for his binoculars and was able to observe more giraffes with these unsightly lesions, but only male giraffes were affected, which was notable, but not a big cause for concern because they all looked healthy.

We continued out of the park to Pakwach, the nearest town, to get groceries and other food for the park staff and the camp, and luckily while we were on high alert, we encountered no rebels. When we got back safely to the camp, I gave the warden a report about my visit to the giraffes, and he explained that the vegetation had changed over the past two decades as a result of the heavy poaching, which could be contributing to such new diseases because of a higher density of certain flies in the environment.

Murchison Falls National Park is one of the oldest national parks in Uganda; it was established in 1952. During Idi Amin's reign, he encouraged the hunting of elephants in all the parks. Former Ugandan chief warden Paul Naluma Ssali recounted to me how he was almost killed by President Amin when he openly opposed his decision to invite the Libyan president Gaddafi to hunt elephants in Murchison Falls National Park. Paul's courage helped to protect the elephants and he was in turn protected by the rangers when Amin sent people to kill him. Paul was an outstanding warden who trained and mentored many Ugandan wardens including Captain Otekat and Abdullah Latif, the Queen Elizabeth National Park chief warden. Paul was featured in the 1972 documentary *Two Men in Karamoja—The Wild and the Brave*[6] when Iain Ross, a white Ugandan-born British citizen and chief warden of the Kidepo Valley National Park was handing his park over to his mentee, Paul Ssali, a black African warden, ten years after Uganda gained independence from the British. However, Amin eventually got his way, and national parks lost their purpose as animals became hunted everywhere. Elephant populations were further strained when the Tanzanian soldiers who were brought in to Uganda to overthrow President Amin resorted to killing the wild animals for food. The situation did not improve during the successive regimes, and over time the vegetation became bushier in the northern and southern sectors of Murchison, favoring the proliferation of certain insects, which included parasites that caused diseases. Nothing in an ecosystem functions in a vacuum. As we drove back to catch the ferry, George Atube, one of the oldest rangers present during those days, took me to a place that was in ruins, and told me how it was the former Pakuba lodge destroyed during Idi Amin's era. Northern white rhinos used to graze just outside the lodge, but were poached to extinction in Uganda. I became inspired to bring back the rhino. I was following my father's dream to restore Uganda to its former glory, by reestablishing wildlife populations. I later became a founder member and served on the first Board of Rhino Fund Uganda in 1998.

Back in Kampala, I got on the phone to Richard Kock, who had seen a similar skin disease, called filariasis, in the black rhinos in Zimbabwe. It was caused by flies laying eggs in the skin, which then hatched into larvae and caused the skin to thicken and become crusty. He also advised that treating the affected animals with an antiparasitic drug such as ivermectin helped, but it would only last for one or two months. There was no long-term solution if the flies remained in the environment and continuously laid eggs.

A few months later I took the opportunity to ask Clem Coetzee (of the elephant translocation project) to help me dart an affected giraffe, so I could take samples. I sat in the front directing the driver, and Clem was in the back with his dart gun. He darted an adult male giraffe with etorphine, which took longer than expected to go down; after fifteen minutes the giraffe came toward the truck salivating. The local Acholi driver raised an alarm warning me not to let the giraffe get close to us because once the saliva gets onto our skin, we would get leprosy. When I told him that giraffes didn't carry leprosy, he stared at me in disbelief because he could not let go of a local cultural belief that easily. Later I realized that local belief was also the reason why there were several giraffes in Murchison Falls National Park and only a handful in Kidepo, where boys had to kill a giraffe as part of the initiation ceremony into manhood.

As this dazed giraffe kept running we grew concerned that he was getting too hot, and Clem darted him with an additional half dose of the anesthetic. The giraffe finally went down within three minutes with a big thud. Because of its long neck, the blood pressure in a giraffe's brain is at a different level to the rest of its body, and if the giraffe keeps its head down too long—more than twenty-five seconds—the blood pressure to the brain can drop significantly. Clem directed the rangers to quickly lift and hold his head up, while I took skin samples from both the affected areas and unaffected areas for comparison, and Clem took a blood sample from the jugular vein in the neck. After we had completed all the procedures, Clem gave diprenorphine to reverse the anesthetic in the giraffe, who, once awake, quickly ran away to rejoin the rest of the herd. Back at the Veterinary Pathology Laboratory in Zimbabwe, a diagnosis of filariasis was confirmed. After discussing this information with Captain Otekat and John Bosco, we jointly made a decision not to treat the giraffes with ivermectin, but to get the rangers to continue observing them and that I would only treat a giraffe that was losing body condition as a result of the filariasis.

This intervention plan was invaluable, particularly a few months later, when the mountain gorillas became sick with an even more serious skin disease that threatened their very existence.

The trip to Murchison had long-lasting effects personally as well. It led to monthly bouts of severe malaria that, together with the quinine treatment, left me too weak to walk. Realizing that I had lost my immunity after five years of undertaking veterinary degree studies in England, on my brother William's advice I took malaria prophylactics for six months, after which I stopped having symptoms.

★ ★ ★

Dr. Edroma was a very busy executive director and rarely called me into his office, but when he did, it was often to handle something very big. Having been encouraged by our success in translocating the elephants, he asked me to restock giraffes in Kidepo Valley National Park. Kidepo was down to six Rothschild's giraffes: one female and five males. It was a huge concern that if anything happened to the female, this would be the end of giraffes in Kidepo that was once a stronghold for this rare subspecies of giraffes. It was not an option to restock giraffes from Murchison Falls that had viable herds of Rothschild's giraffes, because we didn't want their skin disease to spread. But also, the Kony rebels made it too dangerous an undertaking. However, Dr. Edroma had received news from Kenya Wildlife Service, who wanted to reduce the large giraffe population who were debarking and killing the trees in Lake Nakuru National Park.

It was complicated enough moving animals from one part of the country to another, let alone from one country to another. We had to get permission from the Kenyan government to donate six giraffes to the Ugandan government. This involved me going to the Ministry of Foreign Affairs office in Kampala to obtain a letter to seek permission from the Minister of Foreign Affairs in Kenya, which I carried by hand to Nairobi. I could not imagine that as a vet I would be having meetings with such high-ranking government officers. Nine months and many meetings later, permission was given, and we could plan the next stage in this mammoth task, which was to find funding for the project. With thanks to Peter Moeller, we received enough funding from the Frankfurt Zoological Society for our project.

There was one problem with moving giraffes: They are much more fragile than elephants and could easily collapse on long hot journeys. Furthermore, the journey between the two national parks involved nomadic pastoralists in Karamoja armed with AK-47s who often attacked vehicles, a chance that we could not afford to take on a twenty-four-hour road journey from Lake Nakuru to Kidepo Valley National Park. The only option was to fly the giraffes from Kenya to Uganda. However, giraffes are so tall that their babies reach a height of two to three meters, so we could only translocate baby giraffes in a military Hercules cargo plane. I wondered where I would find such a cargo plane. Peter, being a pilot, managed to locate one.

The giraffe transport would involve capturing the young giraffes in Lake Nakuru National Park, then driving them to Eldoret airport, and then flying them to the Kidepo airstrip. Around this time, Jane Marie Franklyn, an independent film producer with Franklyn Films, approached me about making a film for the BBC. She asked me so many questions about the challenges I was facing in my work that I almost declined her invitation. She decided that I was the right subject for her film to tell the story of the great efforts being made to restore Uganda's wildlife back to its former glory after decades of civil war and unstable leadership. Together with the mountain gorillas, the giraffe translocation became a major part of the BBC 1 documentary film *Gladys the African Vet*.[7]

We decided to carry out the translocation in March 1997 and selected two rangers, Patrick Owele and Paulino Lokwar, from Kidepo who would learn how to translocate giraffes and look after them in their new home. Peter and I had a debate about bringing the Ugandan rangers for training; he said "rangers (in Uganda) are stupid and useless." I argued successfully that we needed to build their skills and confidence so that they could become more useful. For training, I invited them to Lake Nakuru. UWA was able to give me a driver, Tom Amanya, and an old Land Cruiser that barely made it there and back. We were joined by a young French student in her early twenties, Marylise Lefevre from *Terre Sauvage* magazine, who wanted to gain work experience with me as her supervisor. She was highly motivated and ended up taking phenomenal black-and-white photos providing precious memories of this historic event.

After three hours, I crossed the Uganda border into Kenya with Tom and Marylise and drove on to Lake Nakuru National Park, where we set up our tents together with the translocation team from Kenya Wildlife Service (KWS), who regaled us by the campfire with stories of previous translocations. We ate posho maize meal, a staple food in Kenya, with delicious beans, and most people spoke Swahili, which I understood only a little because it was a language of terror in Uganda during the Amin regime. I shared a one-man tent with Marylise. The Franklyn film crew traveled separately.

The following day we woke up early and assigned roles to everyone on the team, much like we had done with the elephant translocation. This time the vet in charge was Dr. John Wambua, a Kenyan who had been trained by Richard Kock. I drove with John to locate the giraffes and he taught me how to dart using their gun with charges that could shoot farther than my air gun, with which I'd learned how to judge distances by target shooting my teddy bears at home. John was a very patient teacher. Though I missed the first two giraffes, which he ended up darting, we were both so excited when I finally got the dart into the third giraffe. Out of the four giraffes which were captured, the first one was injured during capture because she was too large for the crate, which damaged her spine, so very sadly she had to be euthanized. After this calamity, the bar on the top of the crate was removed and the others were safely captured. Much to our disappointment, we found very few young giraffes that fulfilled the requirements for transport. I found it hard to take them away from their mothers, but had to focus on the bigger picture, where it was more important to have them bring back a giraffe population in Uganda from the brink of extinction. Kenya was much drier than Uganda, and was so dusty in the dry season that my braids were dyed brown.

Having had experience with my first giraffe in Murchison Falls National Park, I was not so much out of my depth when we captured these giraffes, and working with a larger, more experienced team put my mind at ease. However, this time we did not reverse the anesthetic until we had blindfolded the giraffes and tied a harness around them attached to three ropes to steer them into the crate. After which we hand carried the crate onto the back of the truck and drove them blindfolded to a boma, a holding pen, before removing the cloth. I called the first giraffe Nakuru. She was later joined by a younger male and female giraffe. The following day I went to check on them, and decided to call the second female giraffe Kenya and the only male giraffe Hercules. Though we had planned to capture six female giraffes, we were not able to find enough young females that could fit in the military Hercules plane so we decided to capture a male giraffe that could also add to the genetic pool at Kidepo. It was going to take at least three weeks for the giraffes to become calm enough to transport them to Uganda without being sedated, so we returned back home and prepared for their arrival in Kidepo. We left the new Ugandan rangers, Patrick and Paulino, in Lake Nakuru National Park to learn from the rangers in Kenya how to look after giraffes in semi-captive conditions.

Back in Kidepo, Peter Moeller built a boma six times larger than the one in Lake Nakuru, for the giraffes to have more space to move around because they were going to stay longer in this boma as they got used to being in a new national park. After three weeks, we returned to Kenya to collect them. However, this time UWA could not spare a vehicle to take us to Kenya, so my mother generously offered her four-wheel-drive Land Cruiser. The small four-wheel-drive Suzuki donated to UWA Vet Unit could only carry four people with very little space for luggage and equipment needed for this huge exercise.

On my way to Lake Nakuru National Park, I stopped at my old primary school, Greensteds, which looked so much smaller than it had when I was a student. There, I met a seven-year-old Kenyan girl who reminded me of myself. Her eyes grew wide when I told her that we were moving giraffes from Kenya to Uganda.

The next morning, we coaxed the three young giraffes out of the boma and back into the wooden crates. They were surprisingly cooperative. We then started the journey to Eldoret airport, which was two hours away. However, after we got to Eldoret I received disappointing news that the military Hercules plane could not take the giraffes that day. I was extremely stressed because it was dangerous to keep the giraffes in the transportation crates all night. The Franklyn Film crew also had to pay for two flights from Eldoret to Kidepo, so this change in plan was becoming an additional expense for us all. Our fears were confirmed when the oldest giraffe, Nakuru, collapsed in her crate. We decided to let her out of her crate and allowed her to move around in a shed, while the other two giraffes were driven around the grounds every two hours. Peter Moeller and the rangers watched over them all through the night.

The following day, the aircraft landed in Eldoret. Nakuru had to be restrained using ropes and put back into the crate on the truck. When we arrived with the giraffes at the aircraft, the pilot pulled me aside and anxiously asked what I would do if the giraffes got excited and started to eat the wires of the plane. I had not thought of that, but realized that whatever I answered would determine whether we would complete the mission. I assured him that I had the drug to sedate them. I also hurriedly explained that I had the drug to revive them. Understandably, the pilot was more concerned about the safety of the humans while I was more concerned about the safety of the animals. Once we had loaded the giraffes into the plane, Dr. John Wambua, the KWS chief vet, admitted that he had forgotten his passport and therefore could not travel with me to Uganda. However, he added that he had great confidence that I would manage. I was shocked. I had never monitored any animal in a plane, and giraffes were particularly sensitive. Peter sat with the rangers in the cockpit, talking to the pilots, while I sat on a wooden crate in the cargo section with the giraffes, watching them intently, and declined the Coca-Cola that the pilots offered. It was a very long hour, where I had the drug in my pocket to revive the giraffes lest any collapsed in the crate and the drug to sedate them if they got too excited. I prayed to God to keep me calm in spite of my fears. Soon we started descending to Kidepo Valley National Park, and when I looked outside, I became very emotional to see the rangers lined up in a parade with their families on the sidelines ready to receive us.

The chief warden, Angelou Ajoka, greeted us with a very wide smile on his face, and the rangers, Paul and Paulino, assisted by other park staff, got the giraffe crates off the plane into a truck that had been arranged. The final leg of the giraffes' journey was only a twenty-minute ride to their new boma in Kidepo. Once we drove into the boma and placed the crates on the ground, we opened them one by one and the first two younger giraffes walked out without a problem. Nakuru, however, fell down and collapsed. I immediately rushed to hold her head up. After two minutes, she slowly got up, and stood shakily on her long, graceful legs. I closed my eyes and said a silent prayer of relief. She then walked to join the others. It was so lovely to see through my tears.

The giraffes settled down well in the boma, which had a water hole and many acacia trees to get them used to their new environment, and the six local giraffes came to check on the new giraffes the following day. Kidepo Valley National Park has many lions and not enough prey. The lions often targeted baby zebras, so the giraffes were very vulnerable. Six weeks later I returned to Kidepo to witness the release of the giraffes from the larger boma. The six adults were slowly driven to them and when they were within one kilometer of the boma, Peter and the rangers broke part of the wall to encourage them to meet. However, the six giraffes ran past the boma. We then chased the three new giraffes toward them and they soon joined the resident giraffes, with Nakuru leading them. For a moment it was lovely to see nine giraffes running in a straight line over the flat golden savanna of Kidepo, where they stopped briefly to nuzzle the newcomers, then continued running until they all disappeared farther into the Naroth Valley. It was a special memory I will never forget. Though tragically, six weeks later I received a radio call with terrible news that Hercules, the only male giraffe, had been eaten by lions, a very expensive meal.

Three months later I received a call that the only resident adult female giraffe was having difficulty. We rushed to Kidepo and found that sadly she had just died. When we did a postmortem, it revealed that she died in childbirth pushing out a baby girl, a double tragedy.

Fifteen years later when I returned to Kidepo to approve their new ten-year general management plan as a board member of Uganda Wildlife Authority, and chairperson of the board planning and research committee, I was elated to find that the number of giraffes had grown from six to thirty-five just from the two females we brought in from Kenya. This conservation success story proved the value of translocating animals as a means of restoring wildlife populations.

Chapter 9

A Fatal Skin Disease in the Mountain Gorillas

Nine months into the job, I was presented with another strange skin disease, this time in mountain gorillas, which was to completely transform my approach to conservation.

Dr. Liz Macfie called me from her office at Bwindi to tell me that Karen Archibald, the Peace Corps volunteer working with local communities had been up to see the Katendegyere gorilla group and discovered that they were losing hair and developing white scaly skin.

I was perplexed, and decided to contact Dr. Jonathan Sleeman, the field veterinarian working with the Mountain Gorilla Veterinary Project in Rwanda. The mountain gorillas in the Virungas had been habituated and monitored since the 1960s by the late Dr. Dian Fossey, who had established the Karisoke Research Centre, and on her request the gorillas in Rwanda had been receiving veterinary care since 1985 to treat snares and diseases. Jonathan told me that they had never seen such a skin disease in the Virunga mountain gorillas.

We asked Karen to obtain additional information from the rangers on when the disease began while I started to make preparations to travel to Bwindi.

In the meantime, I thought back to the key principles I was taught at the Royal Veterinary College. Common things occur commonly, so when you are faced with a sick animal and are trying to determine what could be the cause of their illness you start with the most likely cause of disease and not the rarest. Acknowledging that people and gorillas are so closely related that we can easily make each other sick, I thought of starting with the common diseases in people. I decided to visit a family friend, Dr. Catherine Sozi, who had done her medical degree in the UK and had practiced there before coming back to Uganda to work in the Victoria Medical Centre.

She had a busy practice, so I made an appointment to see her and when I entered her examination room and she asked how I was feeling, I told her that I was not sick, but had come to consult about some gorillas that were sick in Bwindi. I explained to her that gorillas can easily catch diseases from humans, then described their symptoms, and asked what the most common skin disease was in people. She told me that it was scabies. I was surprised because during my veterinary training in the UK, scabies or sarcoptic mange as it is commonly known in animals, was a disease that most often affected cats and dogs and rarely affected people. Though people sometimes contracted it from their infected pets, they quickly healed once their pets had been treated. This gave me some ideas about what the mountain gorillas might be dealing with.

She shared that people from low-income groups in Uganda tended to have high incidence of scabies because of poor hygiene. The people in Bwindi were among the poorest in Uganda. I'd noticed that they did not have adequate hygiene, but had never actually taken the trouble to understand why. I silently hoped that it was sarcoptic mange as I knew it would be relatively easy to treat with just one injection of ivermectin. I was so grateful to Catherine for her insight and help, and was eager to start my journey to Bwindi and the mountain gorillas. I went ahead with my preparations to travel to get a closer look at the situation. Captain Otekat speedily authorized my travel to Bwindi, but the office vehicle broke down fifty miles into the journey. It took three more days to get a four-wheel-drive vehicle in good working condition.

I traveled with Richard Kock, who had been contracted by the World Bank to conduct a needs assessment for wildlife veterinary services in Uganda and was tasked to travel all over Uganda to carry out his assignment. I was grateful for his company, and we had plenty of time on the ten-hour journey to discuss the potential causes of the skin disease and treatment options.

When we got to Bwindi, we were welcomed by Dr. Liz Macfie, and over dinner we received more information about the skin disease in the Katendegyere gorillas, which had worsened over the past few days. We all felt that it was most likely to be scabies, but kept our minds open for any other disease. We also noted that the Katendegyere group had been reduced to just four gorillas as three of them had left a few months ago possibly to create a bachelor group of lone silverbacks in the forest. This was troubling, and Liz was concerned that these gorillas may have been stressed by having too many people visiting them; often the tourists outnumbered the gorillas by six to four. Richard told us of how a pride of cheetahs visited by too many vehicles in the Masai Mara Reserve in Kenya developed sarcoptic mange, which was not afflicting other cheetahs that did not receive as many visitors.

My relief that Liz would be with me on this operation was short-lived. In the morning she felt unwell and consequently would not be able to accompany us on the operation. I felt a great weight of responsibility. Yet Liz assured me that I would do a great job, especially with Richard Kock, a highly experienced wildlife veterinarian, with me. Karen Archibald, who had originally alerted us to the problem, also accompanied us.

We decided to observe the gorillas during a tourist visit and then carry out the treatment after they had left. We drove down to the park office with the veterinary equipment and supplies, and as we were waiting for tourists to arrive for the briefing, I informed the park rangers and trackers what was going to happen and selected porters to carry the darting equipment and veterinary supplies.

To my surprise just before the briefing of twelve tourists scheduled to visit the gorillas that day, two of them, a tall man and woman with an American accent came to greet Richard. Dr. Eric Miller was an American veterinarian, heading the veterinary department at the Saint Louis Zoo and had traveled with his partner, Dr. Mary Jean Gorse, a small-animal veterinarian. They were staying at Mantana tented camp. Richard invited them to come to the Katendegyere gorilla group.

After a four-hour hike, we eventually got to the top of the hill and the Katendegyere gorillas.

I went in first with Richard to see how the gorillas looked. The clinical signs were obvious. I first noticed that the mother, Nyabitono, was carrying an eight-month-old emaciated infant called Ruhara, who was the most affected and had lost three quarters of his hair. We could even hear him moaning. I knew from reading Dr. Dian Fossey's book *Gorillas in the Mist* that crying in gorillas was almost unheard of, even in baby gorillas. I realized how much this infant was suffering and it broke my heart. Nyabitono had also lost hair where she carried the baby on the side of her body.

The second-worst-affected was the juvenile, Kasigazi, who had lost one quarter of his hair and had developed white scaly skin where the hair had fallen off his body. He also scratched a lot. His mother was the third-worst-affected, followed by his father Kacupira, who was only scratching, but had not lost hair. It was clear that we had to quickly intervene if we were going to save them. We left the tourists and started to prepare the darts, sampling equipment and drugs. Even though Ruhara, the infant, was in the most critical condition, we decided to dart Kasigazi, because Ruhara's mother Nyabitono was shy and we could not approach her easily. Far better to get the samples from Kasigazi to confirm the presence of scabies as it would help us develop an effective treatment for the rest of the gorilla group.

We waited for the tourist visit to end before we started working on the gorillas. As they departed, I nervously loaded the dart; I hadn't had much practice with a dart gun and I was also aware that it was the first time an anesthetic procedure had been used on a gorilla in Bwindi. I aimed the dart gun at Kasigazi's thigh and missed. Thankfully, Richard had plenty of experience and offered to dart the gorilla, and when the anesthetic took effect we slowly approached him. This was a dangerous stage in the operation and we tried to be as careful as we possibly could. However, the silverback, Kacupira, was not taking any of this. Accommodating as he was, he realized that it was not the normal routine interaction with humans and walked toward us downhill, which was even more frightening. I then had to master the knowledge I had acquired when Liz took me to Rwanda to assist with removing a snare from an infant gorilla.

I found myself giving the trackers a crash course in scaring away a silverback gorilla. It involved a lot of clapping and creating a barrier between what we were doing and the great silverback who weighed between 330 and 350 pounds. Although I got the trackers to surround us, it resulted in him moving only about fifteen meters away, where he could still see what we were doing. I had not anticipated that the park staff would be so scared of the silverback, nor appreciated their lack of experience in scaring away a silverback, and was relieved to have Richard with us, as he could focus on examining Kasigazi while I trained the park staff.

While I was busy keeping the gorillas at bay, I asked the porters to go and call Dr. Eric Miller and Dr. Mary Jean Gorse to join us while we were examining Kasigazi as I valued their insight as experienced veterinarians.

After a thorough examination with four vets including a small-animal vet who saw many cases of skin diseases, we concluded that the gorillas most likely had scabies and proceeded to treat Kasigazi with one dose of long-acting ivermectin and antibiotics for the secondary bacterial infections to treat the wounds brought about because he was scratching himself so much. This was evident when Kasigazi continued to scratch himself even when he was fully anesthetized with ketamine anesthetic. When it came to collecting a sample, it was nice to be able to conduct the same procedures I had seen many times with small-animal cases that came into the Royal Veterinary College small-animal clinic in London. The whole procedure took forty-five minutes, after which Kasigazi began to wake up. I had been holding his hand as we conducted the procedure and was amazed at how strong his grip was even at the tender age of six years old. When the anesthetic had worn off and he was finally able to get up and move, we watched him for another thirty minutes until he joined his father and his mother, who was carrying his baby brother. I felt elated by our success and ability to anesthetize and treat our first Bwindi mountain gorilla, with a great silverback poised on the brink of attack.

Our success brought with it some important insights. Richard reflected that, increasingly, the link between human health and gorilla health would be important, especially as the gorillas were vulnerable to human diseases. And our work had not yet finished with the scabies outbreak. The next day, Liz went to check on Kasigazi to make sure he had recovered from the intervention and also to check on the Mubare gorilla group, which was the other group of gorillas who lived in the vicinity. Gorilla groups sometimes have interactions as they move through the forest especially when their ranges overlap. When silverbacks fight, females may transfer from one gorilla group to the next. This is when diseases can easily spread from one group to another. Fortunately, these two groups did not meet during the scabies outbreak.

A few days later, I returned to Bwindi after we had examined the skin scrapes at Makerere University and confirmed that it was scabies. This time round I went up with Liz and we managed to treat Nyabitono and Kacupira with one dose of ivermectin though with greater difficulty because now they were more aware of what we were doing. However, the following day, when the park staff went to check on the gorillas, they found a dead baby at the night nests. It was Ruhara, who had been dropped by his mother. This was very rare because gorilla mothers usually held on to their babies in mourning, and even as long as one week after they have died. It was a devastating outcome and it affected me deeply, but at the same time, I was also relieved that he was no longer suffering and that at least the other gorillas had a better chance of recovering with the treatment. Liz also pointed out how lucky we were to be able to do a postmortem on an animal that has not decomposed, enabling us to more accurately determine the cause of death. At eight months Ruhara only weighed four pounds, which was the weight of a newborn baby gorilla. When the rangers brought little Ruhara back to the office of the International Gorilla Conservation Programme, we wrapped Ruhara in a black polythene bag and took his emaciated body to Kampala, where I immediately took the carcass to Makerere University. More samples were taken, and we found that the mites were still alive even after the gorilla had died. It was a truly severe infection and he hadn't stood a chance.

The postmortem also revealed that Ruhara had severe pneumonia brought on from the loss of most of his hair due to the scabies and being exposed to the cold damp environment of the forest. I gave the biopsies to Makerere University to have more tests done so we could get as much information as possible. To my horror, when I went to collect the results a few weeks later, I discovered that the technician had thrown them away. I was furious and was not shy in expressing myself. Unfortunately, the technician had been used to dealing with domesticated animals where samples could be collected any time if needed. Little did he realize that collecting samples from a critically endangered powerful wild species with the ability to charge you at any time was a totally different ball game from getting samples from a docile goat! Thankfully we had given Dr. Eric Miller some biopsy samples of Kasigazi for a second opinion and at least these were in safe hands.

When I returned to Bwindi a month later to check on the progress of the remaining Katendegyere gorilla group members, with the intention of giving them one more dose of ivermectin, I was in for a shock. Kasigazi had wised up and would not allow me near him whenever I had a dart pistol and blowpipe. I tried to hide it behind me and cover it with a raincoat, but whenever he saw me, he would walk backward so that I could not dart his back or thighs. Furthermore, his father, Kacupira, kept mock charging me, to the extent that I would ignore him, and this annoyed him even more. I was again reminded of how intelligent these amazing beasts were and struck by their similarity and closeness to humans. One time, Liz commented how brave I was when the silverback charged and I stood my ground while the trackers moved back. I asked Liz if the

Bwindi gorillas were smarter than the Virunga gorillas, which were easier to dart a second time round, and she smiled, further confirming my belief about the mountain gorillas. Nyabitono remained too shy to approach again. We eventually gave up on trying to give them a second dose, because they continued to improve and Kasigazi's hair coat grew again, and so did Nyabitono's.

Life for the gorillas returned to normal and one year later Nyabitono had a baby, a great blessing, more so because this baby was born during the one-hour tourist visit. It was the first time that such a birth had been witnessed and a deeply moving experience for all those present. William Betunga, the head ranger, described how Nyabitono became restless, and then leaned on the silverback, Kacupira, who supported her back; she then squeezed her stomach and pulled out her infant, and licked the afterbirth off it, and showed it to Kacupira, who fondly stared at the newborn baby. Kasigazi tried to come close, and they sent him away. This baby was called Magoba, meaning "profits" because the rangers received large tips from the tourists that day. To our dismay, after four months this baby died. In the Virungas at least 25 percent of gorilla infants do not make it to their first birthday; in Bwindi, where the altitude was lower and not as cold, fewer gorillas die in infancy, but it still happens. Magoba's death seemed still more mournful because this was the first baby to be observed being born in the history of Bwindi Impenetrable National Park. However, to lose any infant of such an endangered species was a blow that affected us all.

How did this group of gorillas contract the scabies in the first place? We concluded that they must have been exposed when they left the forest to forage for banana plants and the bark of eucalyptus trees on community land, where people put out dirty clothing on scarecrows to scare away wild animals including gorillas, baboons, and birds. Naturally curious, the gorillas may have touched clothing from severely infected humans and the mites burrowed under their skin, and when they groomed each other the mites quickly spread through the group.

Dr. Richard Kock also noted how close the gorillas were ranging next to the local communities because of the deforestation that had occurred before it became a national park. Little did I know that I was going to start an NGO seven years after this disease outbreak that would address human health and seek to find a solution where the human and gorilla community could live in harmony, side by side.

Perhaps this was a foreshadowing of things to come, but toward the end of the year, there was a severe shortage of funds and the Uganda Wildlife Authority was considering to let some staff go. I found myself having to justify my position as the only wildlife veterinary officer in Uganda. Thankfully, by sharing the fatal scabies outbreak experience with the American financial adviser and the impact losing the Katendegyere gorilla group would have had on the UWA (over half a million dollars a year), he realized how essential my position was, and I remained on the team.[8]

Sadly, the Katendegyere gorilla group disintegrated, and the group members were never seen again. To this day I hope that they did not end up in the Democratic Republic of Congo like their fellow group members, and are instead living in Bwindi Impenetrable Forest enjoying life integrated in the unhabituated gorilla groups.

Chapter 10

Controversial Surgery on a Mountain Gorilla

I received a call from the Bwindi chief warden to check on a female gorilla in the Mubare gorilla group that had a fresh wound on the finger. The group was ranging along the main road leading into the forest, only two hundred meters from the park office at Buhoma, and fifty meters from the luxury Gorilla Forest Camp owned by the travel company Abercrombie and Kent, putting them into close contact with humans who could easily spread diseases to them. I was concerned that she may have a snare injury and invited Dr. Ken Cameron, an American veterinarian working with Mountain Gorilla Veterinary Project based in Rwanda, to assist me. When we checked on her, we found that her finger was not constricted and the wound was healing. We concluded that thankfully the wound was not due to a snare, but probably due to a natural form of trauma.

As we were checking on the other gorillas in the group, I saw something very surprising. Up in a tree, a juvenile gorilla about six years old had a strange-looking pink tube hanging out of his backside. It looked like a rectum. However, the gorilla did not show any other signs of illness and was swinging off the branches and playing normally. I turned to Ken and asked him what he thought and he exclaimed that he had never seen this before. We asked the ranger if he had seen this condition before and to our surprise he nodded his head. I asked him why he had never reported it, and he elaborated that he had also seen this condition in two other gorillas of the same age. However, he didn't think it was serious enough to alert anybody because the pink tube would come out and the gorilla would push it back with his hand, and it would eventually return back inside the body. I had seen this condition in kittens during my veterinary training. I explained to the rangers that the pink tube was a rectal prolapse, which is an unusual health condition that they should report.

Internet had not yet reached Bwindi, so Ken made a phone call to his boss, Dr. Mike Cranfield in the United States, who advised that though it was unlikely this condition was human-related or life-threatening, we should intervene because it was abnormal.

The next day we got ready to dart the juvenile gorilla, but could not find him in the Mubare gorilla group. We spent an hour counting the gorillas in the group to make sure that we had not missed our patient, and saw that all seventeen gorillas were there, which confirmed what the rangers had said about the prolapse returning to the body. So, I asked the rangers if they could show us the gorilla that had had the prolapse the previous day, and they could not recognize which one it was. This made me realize that the time had come for the rangers to get formal training in how to identify the individual gorillas and how to look out for clinical signs and report in a timely manner. They also needed to learn how to assist the vets if the gorillas had to be treated or a postmortem had to be done.

This was going to be the first training of its kind in Uganda, and when I got back to my headquarters in Kampala, I spent several days preparing the training content. I realized that I needed additional expertise to be able to give the rangers a more detailed and useful training of this kind. So I called upon Mountain Gorilla Veterinary Project vets Dr. Ken Cameron and Dr. Tony Mudakikwa, and Dr. Liz Williamson, a British primatologist working with the Dian Fossey Gorilla Fund as Director of the Karisoke Research Centre, to assist me with the training. We trained thirty tourism ranger guides in Buhoma, Bwindi's main tourist site and Ntebeko at Mgahinga National Park, which is part of the Virunga Volcanoes mountain range.

Though as vets we could easily explain the clinical signs of gorillas and how to help a vet during an intervention, we needed Dr. Liz Williamson to teach the rangers how to identify individuals and provide other important information about their behavior and ecology. Gorillas are identified by noseprints, and other unique marks on their faces and head. Just like humans, they can also be identified by their personalities where for example some gorillas are friendly, others are shy. Liz admitted that the Virunga gorillas were easier to identify because the noseprints were more pronounced and each family had unique noseprints. The Bwindi mountain gorillas did not have distinct noseprints that could easily be identified, so we had to rely on other marks on their faces or head such as a scar or cut ear, a flat head or browner shade of hair, and if we were lucky, some gorillas had more obvious features like Binyindo with very wide nostrils, which means "big nose" in the local Rukiga language. It is easier to identify adults that have developed some scars, and when new babies are born we often identified them by their mothers. By the time they become juveniles at four years old, we'd have to start to look out for other marks and blemishes on their faces to identify them.

I also prepared exams for the rangers, and one of their answers thoroughly amused and scared us. I asked what they would do if they found all the gorillas coughing in a group, and one of them said that he would do nothing, because it would be too late. We all laughed nervously and I explained why he should report immediately so that they can all be treated (before it is actually too late!) and, more important, we should prevent this happening by making sure that the tourists don't get too close to them. It was a rare opportunity for me to hear about the challenges the rangers faced, including the dangers of confronting poachers in a dense forest, and it was also a time to bond while sitting by the campfire.

A few months later, senior ranger Richard Magezi came running to me with news that another gorilla, a six-year-old juvenile in the Mubare group had a prolapse. This time it had not returned to the body. I was getting ready to travel to Mgahinga for a meeting hosted by International Gorilla Conservation Programme (IGCP). The next day, while at the meeting, I got reports that the prolapse was still outside her body and the gorilla was becoming much less active. The chief warden, Chris Oryema, grew particularly anxious also because the tourists demanded a veterinarian come and attend to the suffering gorilla. He sent a vehicle to collect me, and I had to excuse myself from the meeting.

This time round I was going to be on my own with the rangers. I'd taken the opportunity while at the IGCP meeting to discuss the case with the vets and other conservationists. It seemed straightforward that I had to intervene because it was becoming more apparent that the case was life-threatening. However, I was still unclear whether this could be human-related. It was possible that the gorilla had picked up a parasite from humans since this group ranged close to the park office and the lodges, which may have caused her to strain when defecating and resulted in the prolapse. Nevertheless because the case was so unusual, it generated a lot of debate among the conservationists who were at the meeting. Some pointed out that we may be interfering with nature if I attempted to treat this gorilla. Others, including Dr. Liz Macfie, believed that the prolapse may be due to bad genes and by intervening I would be promoting this trait in a tiny population of an already critically endangered species. Inbreeding had been seen among mountain gorillas in the Virungas, which numbered about 350, where some of them had partial or full fusion of the digits, a condition called "syndactyl" in humans. However, I had not seen this condition in the Bwindi gorillas.

I thought about all these arguments on the five-hour drive from Mgahinga to Buhoma. When we finally got to Buhoma, I found that the gorillas were ranging so close to the park office that I was able to check on her that late afternoon and see that the prolapse had started swelling outside her body and she was moving very slowly, not even able to play with her age-mates. However, I was encouraged that this time round the rangers knew who she was; her name was Kahara, which means the girl who likes to take care of others, and they gave her this name because she liked to babysit her younger brother, Kanyonyi. Additional reports from the park staff indicated that she had grown worse over the past two days, and they wondered why Kahara's prolapse did not return to her body. Even if I was terribly nervous, I had no choice but to prepare to carry out an intervention the following day. This time I had no other vets to support me, and yet I had to deal with a new condition that had never been seen before in mountain gorillas, which made me extremely uneasy. However, I was comforted by the fact that we had just trained the rangers on how to monitor sick animals and assist a vet during an intervention and this was the time to put it into practice. I called Dr. Tony Mudakikwa for tips on how I should conduct the surgery to correct the prolapse. Having been a large-animal vet, he had attended to many cows with prolapses of the uterus after giving birth, and told me how he used sugar to absorb the water that had been retained causing the organ to swell, making it easier to return it back to the body. I made a note to find some sugar to pack among my supplies.

I had a sleepless night reflecting upon all the arguments for and against intervening in this delicate and complicated case. Clearly, her condition had become life-threatening.

When Liz had cautioned me about the danger of promoting bad genes in an endangered population of only a few hundred, I had responded that perhaps the option of euthanizing the gorilla could be considered, just like with pets. She said, "Do you want to become the first vet in the world to euthanize a mountain gorilla?" Of course, I didn't, but if the gorilla was in so much pain I might feel I had to do something to put her out of her misery. With all these conflicting recommendations, I realized that the final decision rested with me, the attending veterinarian. I decided to intervene to save the gorilla's life, possibly gaining insight into the cause of the prolapse and enabling us to prevent it from happening. The fact that Kahara was female made her even more valuable to conserving the mountain gorilla population at Bwindi, as she was likely to have at least six babies in her lifetime, which is a great addition in a population that was numbering only about three hundred at the time. Most male gorillas did not have a chance to mate. If they are not strategic enough to become the dominant silverback, there is no guarantee that they will have offspring to carry their genes to the next generation.

We checked on the group early the following morning at 7:30 a.m. I went with two of the most experienced rangers, William Betunga and Stephen Mugyisha, to first check on Kahara. We found the gorillas still sleeping in their night nests at 8 a.m. The tourists were taken to visit another group so that we could attend to Kahara in private. Once the gorillas saw us, they got up. Kahara also tried to keep with the family routine, but was very weak. When she finally left her nest, we saw a swarm of flies. Her prolapse had become gray and white with maggots. An American volunteer who had come with us took several photos during the intervention. I prepared a dart with ketamine anesthetic, and William cautioned me to be as relaxed as possible so that I didn't scare the gorillas. This worked, and I was able to successfully sneak a dart into her thigh muscle without the protective father, Ruhondeza, or other gorillas noticing. When Kahara fell asleep, the rangers formed a barrier between me and the silverback. My main instruction to them was to tell me if her respiratory rate fell or if she stopped breathing or if she started waking up. Once the anesthetic had taking effect, I examined her body and the prolapse. The maggots would have reached her body wall if we had waited another day, and she would have died. I cleaned the prolapse and then took out the surgical equipment and amputated the rotten portion while preventing her from bleeding too much. I started to clean the healthy-looking section, but it was too swollen to return to her body. I retrieved the bag of sugar I'd brought with me from breakfast and emptied it on the prolapse, which magically shrunk within minutes. With a sigh of relief I was then able to push the rectum back into her body and then sutured it to the body wall. I was elated when that part of the operation had ended successfully. I also took a blood sample to better understand what was going on, and asked the rangers to collect fecal samples from her nest. I injected her with long-acting antibiotics for her surgical wound to heal quickly. We also took photos of her hands and feet, and saw that the digits of her feet were partially fused, an indicator of inbreeding. Almost immediately, she started waving her arms and tried to get up as the ketamine anesthetic began to wear off. The rangers and I helped her to sit up, and held on to her for ten minutes until she was steady enough to walk on her own. The bravest ranger then carried her to the rest of the group, which had moved only a few meters. This time round there was no aggression from the silverback, Ruhondeza.

I was euphoric that the operation had been successful. The rangers didn't believe that she would get better, but they called me a "witch doctor" which may have been a compliment. The next day, Kahara was still weak, but had started to eat, and two days later she started to play with her younger brother, two-year-old Kanyonyi. It was a joyful moment to see them reunited. By the end of the week, she was able to join the other gorillas and climb the trees.

After the success of this operation everyone congratulated me including those who had discouraged me from intervening. After all, saving the life of a gorilla always created a warm feeling in our hearts. When the samples were analyzed a few days later, no human parasites were detected, but we found that she had a larger-than-normal parasite burden, which could have contributed to her straining to defecate, and her blood sample also indicated an infection. The rotten portion of the prolapse was analyzed and confirmed to be necrotic. I was elated to have this case report published in a scientific journal.[9]

Four years later when Kahara became ten years old, she naturally left the group to find a mate and transferred to a wild group that was not being followed. I always keep an eye out for her every time we conduct a census, about every five years. I hope that from the genetic studies done on all the fecal samples, we may be able to locate Kahara, and know which part of the forest she is in, but have not yet been able to. However, I am gratified that if she has added to the number of mountain gorillas at Bwindi, it's because we saved her life that day. The first census of mountain gorillas at Bwindi took place in 1997. It was led by Dr. Alistair McNeilage, who headed the Institute of Tropical Forest Conservation (ITFC) affiliated with

Mbarara University. Gorilla censuses are now routinely conducted every five years because their interval between births is typically four to five years.[10]

It is difficult enough to find the gorillas you know, but how does one find the ones you don't? Two factors enabled wild unhabituated gorillas to be counted. All adult gorillas build a nest. Babies sleep with their mothers until the age of four years old.[10] They also leave a trail of damaged vegetation in the forest as they move from one day to the next within their range. To count gorillas, you have to follow a trail of three consecutive sets of the same number of night nests to confirm that it is the same group. The census teams are given different areas of the forest and have to set out at the same time to avoid counting the same gorillas twice.

On my first gorilla census, we were divided into six groups of about five people each who would camp in the forest for six weeks. These also included wardens and rangers from Rwanda and DRC. After an early start, every one hundred meters we stopped to take GPS readings and count every animal we came across including signs of blue monkeys, black and white colobus monkeys l'Hoest monkeys, red-tailed monkeys, chimpanzees, elephants, duiker, bush pigs, and illegal activities such as snares and unauthorized trails.

After six weeks the six teams had combed every corner of the forest, and three hundred gorillas were counted. Knowing that very young infants may be missed because their dung was too small to be detected in the nest of their mothers, this was factored into the final figure. Fecal samples collected from the night nests of gorillas, and other species, enabled genetic studies to be done. It is rare to come into contact with unhabituated gorillas, and the census was the only opportunity to take samples from their night nests.

During the following censuses, fecal samples were also collected to detect parasites and other pathogens in gorillas that are not habituated to humans. Genetic studies by Max Planck Institute for Evolutionary Anthropology started to reveal more and more information, showing that some gorillas may build more than one nest each day, and so censuses may count too many gorillas. Another surprising result was a group's silverback is not the only male who sires offspring; the younger adult males also sometimes mate with the harem of females when the silverback isn't looking (which I have managed to observe myself). This helps to increase the genetic diversity and reduce inbreeding in such a small and endangered population of gorillas. I hope that through genetic studies, we will one day reveal the whereabouts of Kahara and other gorillas that have transferred from habituated to wild groups.

Chapter 11

The Bwindi Massacre

When I first came to Bwindi in 1994 to conduct research, I thought it was the most remote and peaceful place on earth; however, this illusion was shattered in 1999.

After Idi Amin was overthrown in 1979, the freedom and rejoicing was short-lived because he had destroyed government structures, including abolishing the Parliament, and ruled by decree. This gap led to seven years of civil war and unstable leadership, until in 1986, a guerrilla war led by President Yoweri Museveni resulted in long-term stability. I was old enough to remember most of the instability and rejoiced that the country was regaining its stability. This was one of the reasons I opted to return to Uganda after veterinary college in London to follow my father's dream and develop this country, through restoring the wildlife to its former glory; the mountain gorillas became an integral part of it.

But on March 1, 1999, during a staff meeting at the Uganda Wildlife Authority Headquarters in Kampala, we received the shocking news that Bwindi had been attacked. We all looked at each other in shock and disbelief as the UWA Executive Director Saul Kaye told us that rebels had taken over the park. The meeting immediately ended.

I rushed to the radio to try and speak to the Bwindi chief park warden, Chris Oryema, but the radio transmission had been cut off. I managed to make a phone call and got through to the nearest police and ranger post at Kanyantorogo where I was able to get more details of the attack. The attack came from Hutu rebels, the Interahamwe, who had been forced to flee Rwanda during the genocide that took place in 1994. As a result of their displacement, they had been consigned to refugee camps in neighboring Democratic Republic of Congo. The rebels had attacked in the early hours of the morning, coming in from the nearby trading center, Butogota, and had burnt all vehicles including the Deputy French Ambassador's car and tragically killed the law enforcement warden Paul Wagaba while he was fighting to protect the tourists. His body was burnt beyond recognition along with the cars. I realized that the rebels had strategically cut off all communication and felt a sudden strong urge to go to Bwindi to see how everyone was faring and how I could help.

It was an additional shock because I had planned on being there to check on Ruhondeza, the lead silverback gorilla of the Mubare gorilla group, who had severe fighting wounds. Recognizing that fighting in gorillas was part of their natural behavior and his condition was not life-threatening, I had postponed my trip to Bwindi by two days so I could travel with a photographer, Chris Renty, and his wife, Felicity. I had met Chris when he was the soundman for the film *Gladys the African Vet*.

Jillian Miller from The Gorilla Organization called me after hearing the devastating news, which was already circulating in the international media.

I contacted mountain gorilla conservationists Dr. Ken Cameron and Dr. Martha Robbins and we all traveled to Buhoma together to assess the situation and discuss what we could do to help the park staff. On arrival I met Phenny Gongo, a head ranger, who greeted me with a big shaky smile and said, "Doctor it was terrible, but we managed to survive, and sorry we have not been able to check on the gorillas, but we hope they are fine." I told him that this time round I had come to check on him and the other park staff, having heard what they had been through. He narrated his ordeal to us. The rebels had come to his home in Buhoma, and he had shot at them until his bullets ran out, and in the process managed to actually kill one of them, then he'd run out of his house under a shower of bullets, and narrowly managed to escape into the thicket of the nearby forest.

Ranger William Betunga told us how the rebels had come to his room and captured him and then asked for clean underwear. He had no choice but to surrender his clothes to them, and then walked with them until he found a thorny thicket on the side of the road and dove into it. Though he endured the agony of being gashed by thorns, they could not follow him, and he survived. Stephen Asuma, who was the Tourism Warden, had a difficult kind of ordeal, because the rebels planned to take all the senior officers. They knocked on the door of his house, asking for him. His wife had insisted that he hide under the bed. She bravely told them that her husband was not around and they slapped her several times to try and get her to give them more information on his whereabouts, but she stood firm and told them that she had not seen him for a few days. Stephen told me that he had to fight the urge to leap out of hiding to protect her from the rebels. When the rebels left, he resigned from UWA. The other wardens, including Grace Kyomuhendo, the accounts warden, managed to run into the forest thicket and American researcher Dr. Elizabeth Garland stayed hidden in her one-man tent at the bottom of the community campground close to the edge of the forest, which saved her because the rebels avoided the forest. She was particularly lucky because in addition to senior park officials their main target was to capture American and British citizens.

After killing Paul Wagaba, the rebels went to the different lodges capturing tourists and then gathering them all up at the Abercrombie and Kent luxury tented camp. They singled out British and American tourists, as well as two Australian women. The rest of the tourists, including the deputy French Ambassador to Uganda, and her teenage daughter and niece, and Germans were put in a different group. The Ambassador pleaded with the rebels not to kill her driver who was Tutsi, an ethnic group that was also a target of wrath, and succeeded. They ordered the first group to take off their shoes and move with them in the forest and got the Bwindi national park driver, Masinde, to lead them to DRC. On the way up the hill an American tourist faked an asthma attack, and they let her go back with an escort. As they continued up the steep hills toward DRC, seven other tourists also asked if they could return because they felt too tired to continue walking and were escorted back by some of the rebels. When the remaining tourists got to the border of Uganda and DRC, the rebels let them go, including a well-known American tour guide, Mark Ross, who said that his fluency in the Swahili language enabled him to keep up a friendly banter with their captors. The tourists thought that their ordeal was over, but as they walked back down the hill, they saw the eight tourists who had turned back, all dead. Pinned to the eight bodies were notes explaining that they had been killed in retaliation for the help British and Americans had given the Tutsi to overthrow the Hutus who were being supported by the French. It took Masinde, who led the surviving tourists down the hill, two days to find his voice and recount in detail what happened.

Having got this shocking news from Phenny and William, we visited the chief warden, Chris Oryema, who was in the most sensitive position as the head of the national park. His paramilitary training had enabled him to narrowly escape. When the rebels came looking for him at his house, he ran to the back of the house and forced himself to squeeze through the window, and when they called him, he answered as if he was in the house. While they proceeded to break down the door, he stealthily crawled through the grass to the nearest bush and hid there. Once they had entered, he took the opportunity to flee into the forest. Chris was blamed for this horrific attack, and explained that when he heard that rebels had attacked Butogota trading center, twenty miles away, he sent the rangers to reinforce the police there. But this had been a deception by the rebels. Once most of the rangers had been sent to Butogota, they attacked Buhoma in the early hours of the morning, when it was least expected and least protected.

After the massacre, an army barracks was set up at Buhoma to ensure that it would never happen again. Ironically, this led to the park becoming the safest place in Uganda. To this day, when tourists trek the gorillas, they are accompanied by an armed soldier from the Uganda army, dressed in the same uniform as rangers. Furthermore, an advance team goes out to find the gorillas and make sure that it is safe for tourists to come in and see them. To show the world that it was safe, two months after the attack, President Museveni visited Bwindi Impenetrable National Park himself for the first time and trekked the gorillas together with the US Ambassador to Uganda.

Nevertheless, the attack left the lives of many park staff and their families forever changed. William left UWA to pursue further studies and achieved a degree in environmental studies. Stephen left UWA and joined the International Gorilla Conservation Programme. Grace the accountant, who narrowly escaped by running into the forest, transferred to the park headquarters in Kampala. A scholarship fund was put together in memory of Paul Wagaba at Mweka Wildlife College in Tanzania, for students who wanted to become wildlife managers and engage communities in conservation, a fitting way to continue his legacy. However, Paul's family was not provided for. Sadly, this is very common, where wildlife authorities do not have enough resources to protect the wildlife or those who devote their lives to the mission. For several years, Solome Ntongo, who was a secretary at UWA, and I tried our best to support his lovely widow, Margaret Wagaba and her three children. Ten years later, an Australian park ranger, Sean Wilsmore, founded The Thin Green Line to provide for the families whose spouses have lost their lives while protecting wildlife.

The park was closed to tourists for two months. During that time, I checked on Ruhondeza, the silverback gorilla of Mubare group, and though his battle wound smelled so rancid that the stench made the rangers vomit, I decided not to intervene, because he was improving, and fighting is a natural part of the life of gorillas. He fully recovered without treatment, which was ultimately the best way for him to heal, without human intervention.

★ ★ ★

Having narrowly missed being involved in the horrific massacre, I had an accident on my way to a meeting with Makerere University to address the concern that diseased impalas might be used for human consumption. The practice of sport hunting for impalas was a source of revenue for some communities. I had mixed feelings about hunting impala for sport and was totally opposed to slaughtering of wild animals at the entrance of the park. The meeting was specifically called to discuss setting up an abattoir next to Lake Mburo National Park to check the health of animal corpses.

I traveled with Karl Karugaba, the chief warden of security, in an African Wildlife Foundation (AWF) pickup truck, driven by Isaac. About two hours into the three-hour trip, a boy about twelve years old suddenly dashed across the road right in front of us. Isaac slammed on the brakes so hard, the truck flipped. I panicked as I didn't have a seatbelt on in the back and instinctively braced myself against the roof with my arms, to prevent myself from falling out of the open window. For a second, the truck righted itself, then kept rolling over. I felt a sense of peace come over me, accepting that these may be the last moments in my life, and said a silent prayer. When the truck finally came to a standstill upright there was a tragic silence. The child had been struck and died on the spot.

After the accident, the UWA legal officer, Jane Anywar, heard that no one had survived the wreck. She gave the news to my mother who broke down, and went with her to the central police station in Kampala. I returned by public transport in a minivan to my mother's home where I lived, and the housekeeper told me to call her immediately. She was so relieved that I was alive.

But no such happy reunion happened for the boy's family. It is a practice that when a child is killed by a car, the driver gives money to the child's family. Weeks later, I was both shaken and depressed to learn that the person who had come to the truck had lied to us that he was the boy's father and managed to extort money from AWF. This was not discovered until the boy's grandmother, who was his legal guardian, asked for support.

★ ★ ★

There are inherent dangers even beyond rebels and car accidents in working with wild animals. I had another near-death experience with an elephant. I received a radio call that an elephant was limping in the Naroth Valley near the park headquarters of Kidepo Valley National Park. I contacted German vet Dr. Ludwig Siefert, assistant professor at the Makerere University veterinary faculty, to assist me, and Peter Moeller offered to fly us to the park. When we arrived at Kidepo that morning, we found a team of rangers assembled and waiting for us, and we all got into the truck and drove slowly toward the elephant. Dr. Siefert and I both loaded our dart guns so that whoever got the best opportunity to dart would take the shot. We reached the elephant within thirty minutes of a bumpy ride with many warthog holes in the vast savanna plains. The rangers pointed to the lone elephant bull. When we got within one hundred meters of the elephant, the darting team disembarked and we started to walk slowly toward him. Though I was scared for our safety I felt comforted that I was with a senior vet and two rangers with armed rifles. However, when we got within fifty meters of the elephant, he started to charge us. I immediately started running, and did not even feel the weight of my dart gun. Fueled by adrenaline, I outran the three men. When we finally made it back to the truck, we took a deep breath to figure out how to handle this patient who was chasing away his doctors!

We decided to dart the elephant from the truck, and he was unconscious in minutes. We found bullet wounds on his upper front leg near his shoulder. It was no wonder he chased us, he must have thought that the people who shot at him on foot while he raided their crops in the garden on the outskirts of Kidepo had returned to finish him off. We cleaned the wound, but could not locate the bullet in his very thick skin. After a shot of antibiotics and a shot to reverse the anesthetic, we jumped back onto the truck. A few weeks later, the rangers brought me a photo of the team treating the elephant with the report that he was fully recovered. I was so excited that we had healed him and relieved that we'd done so without being trampled until the rangers said, "We wished we had a video camera when you were all running because the distance between you and him kept getting smaller and smaller until he stopped." My heart skipped a beat. I could not believe how we narrowly avoided being crushed and vowed to never tell my mother about this incident.

A few years later, we were not so lucky. Having been encouraged by the success of the first elephant translocation in 1996, I immediately started to make plans to translocate to Murchison thirty elephants that were posing a threat to people grazing their cows in the savanna grasslands of Luwero, a district adjacent to Mubende, where the first two elephants were translocated from. I contacted United States Fish and Wildlife Service, but was not able to raise the funds. USFWS refused on the grounds that there was still a lot of poaching in Murchison and that without testing the animals before moving them, we could transfer diseases from one location to another, which were valid points. Other conservationists argued that the elephants should not be translocated because one day the local community will be able to earn a living through tourism, an idea that has started to take shape in Uganda two decades later with the establishment of conservancies. I took these arguments into consideration and invited Clem Coetzee, the Zimbabwean animal capture expert, to do a feasibility study of the area in Luwero. We spent a night camping in one-man tents. I spiked a high fever for several days, and wondered what could have bitten me while camping that first night. Thankfully we were able to confirm the presence of a herd of eighteen elephants that the local pastoralists were keen to get rid of.

A year later, Dr. Eve Abe, the Ugandan elephant researcher now sold on the conservation benefits of translocating elephants, raised funds for the operation. Having gained experience from the Mubende elephant translocation, I anticipated that this time it would be easier to arrange everything. However, though the team of technical people was much larger, they were inexperienced, and because UWA was not in charge of the exercise, I was not allowed to lead the team. The new team leader this time round decided to hire the Pancom construction company to modify the containers that carry the elephants instead of ROKO, whose containers we had used in 1996. The new company had no experience designing containers for carrying elephants, and did not make them robust enough, which led to additional repairs and modifications in Kampala in the middle of the operation. Though Peter Moeller led the ground team while Clem darted them from the air, the rest of the team had never been engaged in an elephant translocation.

Dr. Jonathan Arusi, a thirty-five-year-old large-animal vet working with the Mukono District local government and doing a master's in wildlife management, took a keen interest in translocations, having heard me give a talk about them at the East African Wildlife Society. Jonathan had asked me if he could join us for this elephant translocation. I asked him to send me an email that I would share with my supervisors at UWA, which stated "I will be eternally grateful if given this opportunity to join the elephant translocation." He was granted permission. I allowed him to join our team though this time round I was not leading it. Dr. Josephine Afema, the only vet at the Uganda Wildlife Education Centre, also joined the team along with Dr. Joseph Okori and Dr. Siefert from Makerere University. When I joined the team one week into the project I was shocked to find that there was no clear leadership and the team was disorganized and demotivated.

Before I arrived, an elephant had died. He'd fallen on his trunk, compromising his breathing, and the vet who attended to it did not know that he was supposed to reverse the anesthetic and it died. I was outraged and gave a briefing to everyone about what should be done should it happen again. However, I was relieved that Jonathan had managed to fit in with the team. Another tragedy followed my arrival, after one darted elephant was put in the container, and Dr. Siefert and I wanted to translocate him that night, but it was decided that the cost was too great to move one elephant. Unfortunately the elephant died the following day when a second elephant was being translocated with him and stepped on his trunk.

Shortly after that, I took a day off to attend the Royal Wedding of Buganda Kingdom in Kampala. As I was getting ready to return to Luwero, on August 28, 1999, I received a distressful phone call from Eve asking if I was the one who invited Jonathan to the translocation. When I affirmed this, she relayed the tragic news, that he had been killed by an elephant that morning. She asked me to travel with the ambulance to collect his body from the hospital in Kiwoko. I could not believe it when I saw him lying peacefully. I said a silent prayer for God to give him an eternal rest. I traveled back to Kampala with the warden and the veterinary volunteer, who had flown with him to the hospital. They told me what had happened. I listened in stunned silence.

When Clem darted the first two elephants from the helicopter, the ground team was supposed to wait for instructions from the aerial team who had a bird's-eye view of the darted elephants. Clem tried to tell the ground team to wait until they'd located the second elephant before they ran to the first one. Instead, the ground team did not wait and ran to where the first elephant had fallen and after checking her, left Jonathan with a ranger and went in search of the second elephant. The second elephant, partly anesthetized, found Jonathan and the ranger. The ranger shot in the air and told Jonathan to run, but he tripped and fell while running, and the second elephant squeezed his chest with his trunk, leaving him unconscious. By the time he had arrived by helicopter to Kiwoko Hospital, he was dead.

Everyone on the team was distraught. Clem tried to console us by telling us not to blame ourselves or each other because working with elephants is inherently dangerous work for vets and capture experts like him. I had to break the news to Jonathan's lovely wife, Eva Arusi, while she held her five-month-old baby girl, Elizabeth, their first and only child. When I spoke at Jonathan's funeral, it was very difficult for me to explain how he died. Eva, who had such a generous spirit, told me not to blame myself because he really wanted to be at the translocation. I was touched by her courage at such a traumatic time.

Back in Kampala the UWA Executive Director, Robbie Robinson, sent me a memo, asking who was responsible for inviting Dr. Jonathan Arusi. I first consulted with Margaret Cooper, a renowned environmental lawyer and wife of my mentor, Professor John Cooper, who happened to be in Kampala giving lectures at Makerere University. Margaret told me that in law an accident such as this is considered to be an act of God and nobody is to be blamed. Armed with this legal advice, in my statement, I admitted that I was responsible for inviting Jonathan, but I was not responsible for his death. This was backed by his email indicating that he came voluntarily to participate in the operation. I learned from this tragedy the importance of safety and designing indemnity forms when engaging people in dangerous wildlife operations. I also learned that clear leadership is critical for such complex operations.

A few years later, we tragically lost another colleague, Dr. Zahir Kashmir, in the same way while he was treating elephants in a national park in Ethiopia. He was an experienced wildlife vet.

I became emotional and cried after reconnecting with Dr. Jonathan Arusi's family when writing this book. Tragically his wife, Eva, had died the previous year of cancer. Elizabeth, now twenty-one years old, answered my call on her mother's phone. She was shocked to hear from me and told me that she grew up hearing about her father who was killed by an elephant while working as a vet. I felt a particularly strong bond to her also because I was too young to remember my father and grew up being told that he was killed by President Amin. We have both grown up with this big gap in our lives, and I promised myself to support and encourage her to also continue her father's legacy.

Chapter 12

The Beginnings of One Health

It was 2000, a new millennium and a turning point in my life. I was invited to a workshop about tourism at Bwindi, which enabled me to understand that ecotourism is not only about treading lightly to prevent people from making gorillas sick, the main reason why I was hired in 1996, but also about engaging local communities in earning a meaningful living from tourists. When the burning issue of gorillas being exposed to human disease came up, I reminded everyone that the local communities were putting dirty clothing on scarecrows to chase away gorillas, baboons, and other wild animals, which may have led to the Katendegyere gorillas getting scabies. Stephen Asuma, who narrowly survived the attack by Interahamwe rebels at Bwindi in 1999, suggested that health education workshops would be helpful. People were not covering their rubbish heaps and, worse still, some were openly defecating in their gardens, putting the gorillas at serious risk from common diseases in the community such as cholera and typhoid. Everyone then turned to me as the only veterinarian in the organization who had the expertise in disease prevention, to lead these health education workshops.

Years earlier, I had read a book called *Where There Is No Doctor: A Village Health Care Handbook*, by David Werner. In the absence of physicians in remote locations around the world, such as Bwindi, anyone can be called upon to treat a person, and veterinarians were the next best solution because, after all, a human is just a more sophisticated animal.

I had been requested to give a quinine injection to an eleven-year-old child with malaria. His father, warden Pontius Ezuma, called me to attend to a snared elephant in the Ishasha southern sector of Queen Elizabeth National Park. Pontius had no vehicle in his sector to return the child for a second injection, so the local health center gave him the quinine drug in a syringe for him to find someone to give his child the injection. Faced with a wounded elephant and a gravely ill child, there was no way I could say "no" to the warden. Though I really did feel out of my depth then, I was reassured that I was with another veterinarian, Dr. Ludwig Siefert, who had come to assist me with the elephant. However, we were both not sure of where to inject the child on the bum, and the main advice he gave me was to avoid the nerves in the middle, as the child could become paralyzed. Though I had now become used to injecting animals of all shapes and sizes, I was completely petrified about injecting the child, and when he screamed immediately after the stinging injection, I was convinced that I had indeed damaged his nerves forever!

Over the years, Pontius, who became the chief warden of Bwindi, kept updating me on the progress of "my patient" who has since graduated from university and started working.

Having been given the important duty of conducting health education workshops, I set about designing brochures with the messages that we needed to get across to the local communities so that they could change their habits. I had no existing program to refer to, because this was going to be the first health education program with local communities in Uganda linking the health of people and wildlife, and they were going to be the first brochures printed for local communities about preventing disease transmission between people and gorillas. I found a talented artist in Kampala who I gave the script to and he drew the images. Then I got Uganda Wildlife Society to design and print over one thousand brochures in both English and the local language—Rukiga—because most people in the region cannot read and write in English.

The communities targeted for the workshops included eight villages in four Bwindi parishes and one parish in the Democratic Republic of the Congo (DRC), because the Katendegyere gorilla group often went there after crossing the border through the Bwindi Impenetrable National Park. Crossing the border to treat a sick gorilla, I was once mistaken for a spy in DRC and almost got arrested.

Finally, in January 2000, I traveled to Buhoma, Bwindi's main tourist site, this time not to attend to an emergency in a gorilla, but to hold the first health education workshops about the risks of human and gorilla disease transmission.

We started with Mukono parish and set up a flip chart stand next to the playground shared by the Anglican church and the primary school. The Mubare gorilla group often ranged on the hill above the church and sometimes came down into people's gardens, and so did the newly habituated Rushegura gorilla group. A crowd of over one hundred people trickled in and sat on the grass under the shade of a big tree. We started the workshop by introducing ourselves, with me as the team leader and conservationists warden Benon Mugerwa, ranger Johnson Twinomugisha and Stephen Asuma from IGCP. We also had a health professional on our team, who I met for the first time that day, the Kayonza subcounty health assistant, Robert Sajjabi. Coming from Buganda, the central part of Uganda, I did not speak the local dialect of the Bwindi communities in southwestern Uganda and asked Johnson to do the translation while Benon and I jointly facilitated the sessions. I started off by asking the communities how many people liked gorillas, and most people put up their hands. When I asked them why, they said that the gorillas brought tourists who gave them money, which helped them have a better standard of living and reduce poverty in their community. Only a few months earlier the massacre of tourists by rebels had led to a suspension of tourism.

The villagers were feeling the pinch, but seemed hopeful that tourism was beginning to pick up again.

I spoke about gorillas being closely related to humans and sharing over 98 percent genetic material, which meant that we could easily make each other sick. I talked about the Katendegyere gorilla group contracting scabies from people and losing an infant and having to treat the mother, brother, and father with ivermectin to get better, and how this prevented us from losing the whole gorilla group. I also revealed to them that gorillas are very curious like human children, and will likely play with dirty clothing they find on a scarecrow, potentially infecting the whole group while grooming each other. The community nodded their heads in agreement. So far so good.

Just as I was getting ready to go to the next item on the agenda, which was to tell the community how to prevent this zoonotic disease transmission, Johnson touched my arm, and whispered to me that we should let them come up with the solution. I was a bit taken aback because as a veterinarian I was used to solving problems, and believed that I had come up with the perfect solution, but knowing that he often engaged communities, I reluctantly followed his advice. I turned to Benon to lead that session and put whatever they suggested on the flip chart.

It turned out to be the most interesting and important part of the whole workshop. The communities came up with very good and varied suggestions of how to improve the situation. I was so thrilled that they understood what we had taught them. I was also astonished by their solutions, which were much better than any I had developed for them. It was a truly humbling and enlightening moment for me. It was also a huge eye-opener for me on the power of Participatory Rural Appraisal methods in getting people to understand a problem and propose solutions, which are more likely to work because they are not imposed on them by outsiders. Their solutions included bringing health services closer to them. I had not realized that most people lived twenty miles away from the nearest health center, and when they got sick, some of them just never made it to see a modern doctor and only went as far as the traditional healers in their villages, who could not cope with ailments like infectious diseases that could also affect the gorillas and were a major cause of death in people. The second main recommendation was around improving their hygiene through continuing to hold health education workshops like the one we had given them that day to reduce such dangerous infectious diseases. The third recommendation was to give more support to the Human and Gorilla Conflict Resolution Teams that herded gorillas back into the park when they ranged in community land, by giving them more rubber boots, rain gear, and food rations. Though most of the people talking were men, one woman in particular really impressed me with her very-well-thought-out solutions. I also realized that having a workshop with a female leader among a team of men was having additional results, when I heard people whispering that they should educate their daughters.

I asked Robert if as a health professional, he found it difficult to convince people to adopt good hygiene and he said that it was difficult to convince people to even simply wash their hands. However, he was excited that this workshop had given people an additional reason for wanting to be healthy and hygienic so as to prevent the gorillas from getting sick or even dying, because tourists want to see healthy gorillas, which in turn brings in money. Most of them were aware that a portion of the revenue paid by tourists goes to support community development projects and some community members interacted with tourists directly, earning a living through selling crafts, food, and accommodation and working as guides and porters who carry their bags when they trek the gorillas. I came away from the workshop exhilarated about this new approach to conservation.

The next two workshops in Kyumbugushu and Nyamishamba villages in the northern sector of Bwindi also had encouraging results. However, in Nteko Parish, in the southern sector, people were not as excited to see us because they had not yet started to benefit from tourism. That was where four years earlier, we had gone to deal with Kalambuzi, the half-habituated gorilla who eventually ran back into the forest. Since that time a whole gorilla group had been habituated called "Nkuringo," and spent over 50 percent of its time in community land. The community was willing to tolerate this if they could gain some money from the gorillas. You could see the desperation in their eyes. They were eagerly waiting for tourism to begin and benefit from gorilla-trekking tourists like their fellow community members in the northern sector, but it hadn't happened yet. The reasons for the delay was because the gorillas were spending so much time in community gardens that the Uganda Wildlife Authority preferred to first solve this issue as it would heighten the conflict if tourists were drawn to see the gorillas on community land.

Our last workshop was in the Democratic Republic of the Congo. The chief warden, Chris Oryema, and Helga Rainer who was heading IGCP country office in Uganda joined us for this workshop. Chris led the team, where this time, we crossed the official border of DRC in a vehicle, escorted by soldiers for protection. The communities of Sarambwe Game Reserve where Bwindi gorillas sometimes range, were mobilized by Mbeki Sylva, an energetic Congolese woman, working for IGCP in DRC.

I immediately noticed that the Congolese were poorer than the communities in Uganda, mainly living in tiny temporary houses made of mud and wattle with grass thatched roofs. After introducing ourselves, I asked the standard question of how many people liked gorillas and to my surprise, nobody raised their hand. I asked them if they had seen gorillas and the response was the same and not only that, an old man in his seventies stood up and vehemently stated that in all his life, he had never seen a gorilla. I was so confused that I stopped talking and then asked the chief park warden to take over the workshop. Realizing that this community appeared to have no idea about conservation, he instead started to talk to them about the importance of conserving the forest, a source of water and a home for wildlife. We never even got the opportunity to talk about preventing disease transmission between people and gorillas because they claimed to have never seen them. Though it was obvious that this community was not welcoming and did not trust us, I handed out the brochures anyway. I asked Mbeki why she mobilized this community for the workshop if they had no contact with gorillas and she laughed nervously and told me that they were lying to us, they see gorillas often, but were worried that we had come to arrest them for the loss of some of the gorillas from Uganda. I shook my head and realized that coming with uniformed armed guards had made things worse.

By the time we had completed the eight workshops and met over one thousand people, I was convinced that you couldn't keep the gorillas healthy without improving the health and well-being of the people with whom they shared their fragile habitats. My approach to conservation had changed. I started to think of setting up an NGO that improved the health of wildlife and people together. I invited former Bwindi Chief Park Warden Keith Musana to become a founder member. Around this time, Dr. Richard Kock asked me to work with him to investigate rinderpest, also known as cattle plague, in buffalo, and the vet technician we worked with from the Ministry of Agriculture, Animal Industry, and Fisheries, Stephen Rubanga, also joined this new entity, which we called "Wildlife Vet and Community Conservation Association." Many of the ideas that the Bwindi communities proposed during the participatory rural appraisal workshops were used to start this association, which never took off but later evolved to become another NGO.

Meanwhile, the chief warden called to tell me the shocking news that Kawere, the five-year-old gorilla I had named when I was a veterinary student, had been abandoned by his mother and he had taken him to a room in the park office. I was perturbed because this had never happened before. I advised him to give the gorilla plenty of water and keep him warm, but sadly by the time I arrived, the baby gorilla had died. I traveled with a highly motivated young vet, Dr. Innocent Rwego. I gave him an opportunity to assist me during the postmortem. The gorilla showed signs of starvation and had aspirated milk in the lungs, which was the likely cause of his death. The gorillas I had met were very devoted to their infants and juveniles, so it was sad that the mother did not think that her infant stood a chance of surviving and abandoned him. I started dreaming that this NGO could set up a center that enabled more proactive management of the gorillas' health, including a room to house abandoned gorillas like Kawere.

Shortly after, I was called to attend to an adult male chimpanzee whose arm was caught in a foothold trap. He died right before

I arrived. The trap weighing about ten kilograms had been set for other species in the forest pocket of Kasokwa a few kilometers from Budongo Forest Reserve. I was horrified when we conducted the postmortem with Julia Munn, a researcher from Budongo Forest Project. The chimpanzee's hand, trapped in the jaws, had become rotten before death and it was horrifying to think of the intense pain he must have been in. These types of traps are typically set in agricultural fields and more deadly than snares more often set within forests. Julia and I published the case to raise awareness about this emerging issue.[11] This incident prompted me to think that the Kasokwa community also needed to benefit from living next to wildlife like the Bwindi communities, so that they could see the connection between conservation, improved health, and enhanced livelihoods through tourism.

During my years in UWA, I raised funds for the UWA Vet Unit and was getting better at convincing donors to support our work including World Society for the Protection of Animals, which later became Wild Animal Protection, the International Federation for Animal Welfare, and the Born Free Foundation. Through the Born Free Foundation, I got to meet Rachel Hunter, the former supermodel and wife of Rod Stewart. The Born Free Foundation arranged for Dr. Ian Redmond, who was Dr. Dian Fossey's first research assistant, to bring Rachel and her sister, Jacqui, to trek the gorillas at Mgahinga National Park and asked me to take her to see them. The experience was both memorable and emotional. Rachel cried, and it was the first time I saw someone shedding tears when first meeting the critically endangered mountain gorillas. It reminded me of the first time I had met Kacupira, the silverback gorilla. I admired Rachel's courage to openly express her emotions. Rachel and Jacqui also loved being with the local children, who they allowed to draw pictures on their feet. I asked Rachel if she felt tired after the long hike and she said, "I want to make the most of my time here, there will be plenty of time to rest in the grave." This visit was featured in *Hello Magazine*, and my twin cousins Nakato and Babirye Kiwana excitedly sent me a copy from London when they saw my photo. This publicity resulted in more donations to the UWA veterinary unit.

I was learning the value of publicity for fundraising. I also learned how to raise funds from individual donors. Our family friends the Woodsfords donated one thousand pounds toward drugs and supplies for the UWA veterinary unit. Sadly, once the money was handed in, it was used for administration needs and not for veterinary purposes as was intended, which hurt. When the Franklyn Films crew donated eight hundred pounds toward the UWA veterinary unit after filming our work for Animal Planet and instead it was used for a Board meeting, I felt so demoralized that I decided it was time to leave UWA. As if by fate, I received a phone call from Dr. Felicia Nutter, who I had met when giving a talk at North Carolina State University about setting up a veterinary unit at UWA, the previous year. She told me that they would like to offer me a zoological medicine residency where I would be able to conduct research, get a Master's degree, and also get more clinical experience, which I felt that I badly needed. Having taught myself as much as I could without constant supervision from a more experienced veterinarian, I jumped at the chance and handed in my resignation.

I was excited about starting a new life, but also apprehensive about leaving my baby—the Uganda Wildlife Authority Veterinary Unit—behind. However, I had the next leg of my journey waiting for me in North Carolina. As I headed home to pick up my luggage and rush to the airport with my mother to see me off, I didn't realize that my personal life was also going to change drastically.

PART III
One Health

Chapter 13

One Health Research and Marriage

Though I was excited to work in the United States, the land of opportunity, I was also apprehensive about what lay ahead in this next phase of my life. I stopped off in London for two days and visited my sister, Veronica, who had gone to college in America, for her insight.

One evening she held a dinner for me, inviting my cousins Nakato and Babirye. Nakato's husband, Moses Zikusoka, also came along. It was a lovely evening, although my fears grew when they told me to be prepared for a culture shock in the United States, which would be unlike anything I'd experienced before.

It was the second time I heard about Moses's nephew Larry. I learned he was also in North Carolina doing an internship at Nortel Networks in Research Triangle Park and would be a good contact.

Moses scribbled his number down on an old envelope as I vaguely remembered dancing with a charming young man at their wedding in Uganda two years earlier. I was part of their entourage as a bridesmaid and Larry was a groomsman.

All too soon I found myself boarding the plane to my new home. I was already homesick by the time the flight landed. I was also devastated because I forgot my Walkman on the plane with an audio recording of my presentation on becoming Uganda's first wildlife vet. But I looked forward to the next phase of my journey—adding public health to my wildlife veterinary portfolio, having applied for funding to conduct "One Health" research in Uganda as part of my master's studies in Raleigh, North Carolina.

I was collected at the other end of customs by one of my supervisors, Dr. Mike Stoskopf, who surprised me with a $4,000 interest-free loan to buy a used car, explaining to me that there was hardly any public transport in North Carolina. He handed me over to Dr. Craig Harms, who helped me to buy the car and took me to the apartment where he used to live. My first impression of my new home only heightened my fears about the United States. When I was introduced to my landlord as "Gladys from Uganda," his response was "Is that in India?" Even the fact that I couldn't open a bank account until I acquired a social security number only made me long for home. My apartment wouldn't be ready for a few days so in the meantime I stayed with a third-year resident student, Dr. Beth Chittick. However, I made the most of things and was grateful for Beth, who made me feel welcome and showed me around the university.

I decided to call Larry and was disappointed when a loud American voice on the phone assured me, "There's no Larry here!" Puzzled, I asked if anyone from Uganda lived there and breathed a sigh of relief when he said, "Oh, you mean Lawrence!" Lawrence immediately remembered me and was only a five-minute drive away. He was keen to see me then and there, but as I had a 5 a.m. start the following morning, I suggested we meet a few days later. Perhaps things were looking up after all.

My first day at North Carolina Zoo, where 30 percent of my time would be spent, was exciting. I was given an orientation on my tasks which included diagnosing and administering treatments for all the animals in the collection, whose size ranged from a few grams to a few tons. My colleagues were warm and friendly, and I was comforted to meet Geisla, an African American vet tech and the only other person of color at the Hanes Veterinary Hospital, and the receptionist, Judy Hunt, who was extremely welcoming and always looked out for me.

A couple of days later, Lawrence came to Beth's apartment and took me out for dinner to the Jamaican Grille restaurant, which ended with a cake saying "Welcome Gladys to North Carolina." I immediately warmed up to this thoughtful man. I eventually met Brian, Lawrence's energetic flatmate, who had almost stopped us from meeting each other. A few days later Lawrence helped me move into my apartment and taught me how to drive on the right side of the road.

Just around the corner was a coffee shop called Cup of Joe, where Lawrence introduced me to the strong coffee-drinking culture of the United States. (Perhaps this foreshadowed that one day Lawrence and I would develop a global coffee brand to save gorillas.) Lawrence took me to the university church on Sunday, where I met Kelly, a white American, and her husband, Francisco Ojeda, a software engineer from Colombia, whose parents had worked for the United Nations Interim Force in Lebanon. Coincidentally, a few years later, Lawrence's parents served as peacekeepers in the same UN mission while living in Nahariya, Israel. The Ojedas had two beautiful daughters, three and four years old. They often invited us for lunch after church on Sunday, and became lifelong friends. I introduced Lawrence to my cousin Eleanor and her husband, Peter Nsubuga, who lived in Holly Springs, a forty-five-minute drive from us. The two families became my pillars of support in North Carolina.

I had always fantasized that when the right person came along, it would be love at first sight, yet when it happened, it took me by surprise. After only four days of dating, Lawrence proposed to me. I said "yes," and off we went to the closest Walmart to buy commitment rings. Then Lawrence left to spend a few weeks with his mother who was working as a peacekeeper for the United Nations in Kosovo (UNMIK).

I'd resigned from Uganda Wildlife Authority with three months' notice, hoping that would give them time to hire a replacement, but they had not yet done so when they contacted me three weeks after leaving Uganda. I received an anxious email from my former supervisor, Dr. Arthur Mugisha, saying that giraffes were getting skin diseases and worse still the gorillas in Nkuringo gorilla group had also developed scabies where the infants were losing their hair and like Katendegyere group, all sixteen gorillas were scratching and many were developing white scaly skin. I wanted to jump on a plane and return home, but resisted the urge. If they could depend on me coming back with every crisis, why would they need to hire anyone else? But I was uneasy until UWA hired Dr. Joseph Okori, the young energetic veterinary intern who had worked on the second elephant translocation. Once he was on board, I could comfortably focus my energies on my life in North Carolina at the top zoological medicine residency program in the world. Here I was exposed to all aspects of veterinary medicine that were important for wildlife conservation, including anesthesia, pathology, and clinical medicine on captive animals at the North Carolina Zoo as well as presenting at seminars and zoo rounds at the North Carolina State University. My supervisor, Dr. Suzanne Kennedy-Stoskopf, taught me how to give better oral presentations by projecting my voice. The learning culture in the United States was so different than in Uganda or the UK. Here, it was more playful, and I was amused that we were given treats for answering questions correctly or having the best group presentation.

Lawrence returned from Kosovo and moved to upstate New York to complete his Master of Science in Telecommunications at State University of New York Institute of Technology.

My mother visited me in North Carolina and Lawrence came down from New York for the weekend to meet her. A few weeks later I went to visit Lawrence in Albany to meet his parents. His mother had just flown in from Pristina, Kosovo, for a two weeks' rest and relaxation. Before we were to meet them, Lawrence and I went to the movies, and *Meet the Parents* just happened to be the film playing! It put me in the right frame of mind to respond to Lawrence's parents' probing questions to see how serious we were about each other. Though we were going to have a long-distance relationship for most of our first year of engagement, we spent every break we could together.

As part of my residency program, I was posted to work at the red wolf recovery program facility at Manteo in the Alligator River National Wildlife Refuge in coastal North Carolina in the Outer Banks. It was a three-hour drive from Raleigh, and I stayed alone in a cabin in the forest that had an outside toilet. I welcomed this opportunity to look after another endangered species. My job was to feed the endangered red wolves and clean their cages, where they were being kept to prevent them also breeding with the more common coyotes. However, alone at night, thinking of the black bears lurking around as I went out to tend the wolves, freaked me out a bit. I was used to living in remote locations with wildlife, at Bwindi and other national parks in Uganda, but always had people to talk to. Here, I was very isolated. It made me appreciate that in Africa the local communities who share their habitats with wildlife are an integral part of nature conservation.

That fall, the one-hour program aired on Animal Planet featuring me, entitled *Saving Uganda's Wildlife*. It showed footage of me working with the mountain gorillas at Bwindi and chimpanzees at Ngamba Island Chimpanzee Sanctuary and Uganda kob (a medium-sized antelope) at Queen Elizabeth National Park with researchers from the Makerere University genetics department. I felt nostalgic for my early days as a vet at UWA. My nephew Willie Kalema, who was based in the United States, commented that it was rare to see films on Animal Planet featuring black people as the main subject.

Never one to rest on my laurels, before being offered the North Carolina State University residency program, I had applied to the African Wildlife Foundation Charlotte Conservation Fellowship Fund to conduct master's research on tuberculosis.

A few weeks after arriving in North Carolina, I received word that my application was successful. I was elated because this meant that I could return to Uganda in the summer holidays, this time as a researcher where I was conducting a study on TB cases where people, wildlife, and livestock lived in close proximity to each other at two national parks, Bwindi Impenetrable National Park, and Queen Elizabeth National Park. A study conducted in QENP by Dr. Mike Woodford, a British vet, in the 1960s, found TB only in buffalo within the northern sector of the park where they mixed with cattle and concluded that they likely got the TB from cattle. Dr. Roy Bengis, the state veterinarian at Kruger National Park in South Africa, wanted to find out how the buffalo had fared in the park since Woodford had done his study thirty years earlier. I invited them both to Uganda in 1997 to help me conduct a follow-up study on the buffalo. Our findings would help to address the rapid spread of TB from the southern to the northern sector of Kruger National Park. We found that buffalo in all sectors of the park apart from the south of Maramagambo Forest still had TB, and concluded that they had now become maintenance hosts for this chronic bacteria. When I shared the news of funding to continue this study, my supervisors were excited also because they wanted me to maintain ties in Uganda.

On Valentine's Day, Lawrence and I arranged to have a phone call at exactly 5 p.m., half an hour before my Research Ethics class. A few minutes before 5, I ran up the stairs to the office. As I opened the door, I almost collapsed. There he was. He had driven twelve hours from Utica to Raleigh to surprise me. I took him to my Ethics class. We went for dinner to our favorite Jamaican restaurant where he had taken me on our first date. One month later, in March 2001, we got officially engaged. We started to make plans for the wedding to be held in Uganda in August.

I had more to plan than just my wedding. I also planned for the summer of TB research and ordered a new dart gun and tuberculin reagents for the gamma interferon test, a technique developed by South African scientists to investigate TB in wild animals because it requires handling an animal only once to take one blood sample instead of twice, as the skin test requires. For cows and people, the standard test requires checking the skin after three days to see if there was any swelling of the skin. But that would be impossible with wild buffalo living in herds within a national park.

Just before traveling back to Uganda in May, I went for an elective course at the Marine Mammal Center in Sausalito in San Francisco,

California. Here I learned about the care of elephant seals, harbor seals, sea lions, and porpoises, all of which I was seeing for the first time. This research and rescue center was led by two veterinarians and employed two veterinary technicians in addition to hundreds of volunteers, which saved on costs, as well as involved the local community. Here was an example of involving communities in protecting wildlife, a concept that would become a guiding principle of my life for the next decade.

One day, I was left in charge because the vets were off for the weekend and a porpoise was found dead at the shore. I conducted a postmortem and was amazed at how big their testes were in comparison to other animal species. I felt the same when I first conducted a postmortem on mountain gorillas—their large intestines were much bigger than those of humans and other primates.

After returning from the West Coast, between wedding dress shopping and wedding plans and my studies—I had so little time to think, let alone pack, that Lawrence ended up packing for me. This was the first and only time I traveled light! It was just as well because I had to get special permission from the airlines to travel with two pieces of hand luggage, my wedding dress and a dart gun!

On arrival at the airport in Uganda, I found the new UWA Veterinary Officer, Dr. Joseph Okori, waiting for me with the special ammunition import permit for the dart gun and helped me to go through customs. I immediately made plans with the first two new veterinary interns at the Ngamba Chimpanzee Island, Dr. Peter Apell and Dr. Richard Suuna, to assist me while learning how to anesthetize buffalo. African Wildlife Foundation lent me their vehicle, a black pickup truck, to conduct research in the national park. We took turns driving on the way to Queen Elizabeth National Park where we also traveled with Stephen Rubanga, a vet tech from Ministry of Agriculture, Animal Industry and Fisheries. We stayed in rooms at the Mweya Hostel on the Mweya Peninsula at the Kazinga Channel, where lakes George and Edward meet. It was magical to be back in the wild and wake up to waterbuck and mongooses coming to the verandah and sleep to sounds of roaring lions and chomping hippos eating grass just outside the window.

In the two weeks that we conducted the research, we were able to dart and take blood samples from fifteen buffalo and incubate them to send to Onderstepoort Veterinary Institute to look for TB. My darting skills had drastically improved after one year of the residency program in North Carolina where the head veterinarian there tactfully trained me by saying that I was not allowed to miss any animal. My clinical skills and knowledge of anesthesia had also greatly improved, making me much more confident to train my fellow researchers.

However, when it came to taking samples from cattle, it was a different story. Queen Elizabeth National Park is a UNESCO Man and Biosphere Reserve made up of eleven fishing enclaves. The local community, who are both pastoralists and fishermen, would not allow us to touch their cattle. They said that I was from the wildlife authority and had come to kill their cattle because they were competing for resources with the wildlife. They claimed that a veterinarian had come and deliberately injected their dogs and cats with the canine distemper virus and they had all died. Though I was shocked, I realized that they could die if injected with a bad batch of vaccine or if their pets had underlying conditions. I tried to explain that I was a veterinary doctor who cared for all animals, but they kept coming up with excuses and never honored our appointments to meet them.

I asked the District Veterinary Officer, Dr. Godfrey Kalule, who was their main animal doctor to try and convince them. We drove to the leader's home, Mzee Eliphaz, who complained that I had been paid by foreigners to get rid of their cattle and that is where I got my "American" accent. He then told Dr. Kalule to come back the next day, which really meant that he did not want to see us again. Realizing that we needed to employ a different tactic, and knowing that I would return the following summer to complete the research, we decided to give up on taking samples from cattle and instead conduct questionnaires in the local community to help us understand their issues better. I had not realized that they had so much resentment toward the Uganda Wildlife Authority, my former employer.

While that seemed to be an enormous hurdle, something else was more encouraging. I was particularly touched when people undergoing treatment for TB would point to their next-door neighbor or friend who was watching them taking medication every day to make sure that they finished the eight-month dose. They'd employed a buddy system that seemed to be working well. This revolutionary system was called Community Based Direct Observation of Tuberculosis Treatment Short Course Therapy (CBDOTS), and was the brainchild of Dr. Francis Adatu, a dynamic medical doctor heading the Uganda TB and Leprosy Programme. It was first piloted in Kiboga district, where my father came from and where my mother was a current member of parliament.

When Lawrence arrived in Uganda one month later, toward the end of the first phase of the TB research, I felt strongly that he should meet the mountain gorillas to understand my work before we got married. He caught a bus from Kampala to Mbarara. We drove for five hours from Mbarara to Buhoma, Bwindi's main tourist site to introduce Lawrence to my second home, and it was even more special taking him to meet the mountain gorillas, where we tracked Mubare gorilla group. We stayed at the Buhoma Community Rest Camp, which enabled him to meet the community members working with wildlife. After Lawrence went back to Kampala, Stephen and I remained in Bwindi to conduct community surveys asking the local communities what experiences they had with TB. It became clear that in Bwindi, villagers had not employed the CBDOTS model. I met two people who had just been discharged from hospital after two-month stays for TB and were now solely responsible for making sure that they took the tablets themselves. Sadly, when I returned to complete the research one year later, these two people had died.

I reconnected with Robert Sajjabi, the Subcounty Health Assistant who had joined us for the first health education workshops with the local community one year previously. He suggested that we go into the villages that came in contact with gorillas when they wandered out onto community land to conduct verbal questionnaires about TB symptoms. We asked people we spoke to if they knew anyone who had been coughing for more than three weeks. Then we tracked down those people and asked them to cough in a tube to collect sputum samples. We then asked them if they knew anyone else with similar symptoms. This convenience sampling focused on people with clinical signs suggestive of TB rather than a random sampling method.

Stephen and I also checked on Rushegura gorilla group, energized to see them again, we walked for four hours through the forest to check on the Nkuringo gorilla group. That particular day we arrived at night using the moonlight to guide us to the ranger camp, where we spent the night in very basic tents, and ate posho maize meal and beans, as well as matooke—savory banana that the ranger, Sylva Mbonigaba's mother kindly made for me. The following day we visited Nkuringo gorilla group, who were all fortunately beginning to recover from the scabies, including *Posho* the infant gorilla who had been the worst affected and had almost died. Building upon the experience from the first scabies outbreak a few months into my first job, the gorillas had been treated with ivermectin by Dr. Okori. We then walked cheerfully back to Buhoma through the forest arriving in the evening, this time before dusk.

★ ★ ★

On July 28, 2001, Lawrence and I had a traditional ceremony in my ancestral home in Kiboga, in Central Uganda, where his family, relatives, and friends traveled in a party of around forty people to participate in a traditional ceremony called a "Kwanjula" where the groom's family gives the bride's family valuable items in exchange for her hand in marriage. The women put on gomesi or busuuti—brightly colored floor-length dresses made of silk with a square neckline and short, puffed sleeves tied with a thick sash below the waist and over the hips. I wore a sky-blue gomesi with white flowers; blue is my favorite color, representing hope. Lawrence and all the other men put on kanzus—white floor-length garments that were introduced to Uganda by the Arab traders in the nineteenth century, with a black suit jacket on top and trousers underneath. The ceremony was conducted in Luganda and a spokesperson from either side of the bride and groom carried out the negotiations. The most important part of the ceremony was clarifying our clans—a group of people with a common ancestral origin and unique totem of an animal or plant. People in the same clan are not allowed to get married, primarily to prevent inbreeding. Fortunately, I was from the lion clan and Lawrence from the civet cat clan!

I was traded for only a "goat," a "rare East African coin," and a "rocking chair," a symbolic gesture that greatly amused everyone. After negotiations, the guests brought additional gifts including beautiful gomesis and kanuzus to the hosts. It was attended by family and friends from Uganda and the UK.

One week later on August 4, 2001, we got married at All Saints Cathedral in Kampala, the family church for both our families, where I was baptized. The church ceremony was followed by a big garden reception at "Ranch on the Lake" at the shores of Lake Victoria and attended by about four hundred people, an average-size wedding in Uganda, including family, friends, and colleagues in wildlife conservation.

On top of the emotional speeches from our parents, it was also memorable because we received a message of congratulations from the President of Uganda and King of Buganda, which were read out by their representatives. We changed into traditional Ghanaian kente cloth for the final part of the ceremony that included cutting the cake. The oldest person on the dance floor after the main wedding reception was the lovely energetic eighty-year-old mother of Sue Woodsford.

We honeymooned in Zanzibar, an island off the coast of Tanzania, a generous gift from my brother William. We visited Zanzibar's Prison Island, home to some of the oldest Aldabra tortoises in the world.

Three weeks after swimming in the Indian Ocean with bottlenose dolphins, we were back in North Carolina, and I was taking samples from a mandrill, a monkey from Nigeria, when planes flew through the twin towers of the World Trade Center. We were all stunned with disbelief. My niece, Rhoda Nabaada Kalema, was living in New York City, and I called her to make sure she was okay. She told me that, luckily, she did not go into work that day. Lawrence turned twenty-eight the next day.

When my schedule changed, requiring me to spend more time at the zoo, my commute became too inconvenient. After spending a number of nights sleeping in the cramped resident's office on an air mattress, Lawrence and I decided to move closer to the zoo. We found a mobile home on an isolated farm next to a creek, in the beautiful countryside, which reminded me of the rural areas of Uganda and Bwindi in particular. It was owned by a veterinary graduate from NC State University, Dr. Karen Jordan, and her husband, whose family owned Brushcreek Dairy Farm with around seventy cows in Siler City. To earn money while he completed his master's thesis, Lawrence milked the cows. We quickly adjusted to the convenience of living in Siler City because it was thirty minutes' drive from the zoo and one hour's drive from the university.

Nonetheless, I was a bit taken aback to find that the white and black community was completely segregated in rural North Carolina. We decided to look for a local church and the first church we came across was Brookdale Baptist Church. Though we were the only black people in the church, they welcomed us with open hearts. We also decided to go to a church that had only black people, who also warmly welcomed us; however, their service went on for over two hours every Sunday whereas Brookdale Baptist Church service was not quite as long. Because Sunday was a sacred day for both of us, it was my only day off from working at the zoo, and Lawrence's only day to play soccer with the Mexicans who were working at the nearby chicken factory, we opted for Brookdale Baptist church. The congregation were so kind that they raised $400 for us when we were particularly short of money, and we sometimes had lunch with the pastor and his wife after church.

During the second summer of the residency program, I returned to Uganda to complete the TB master's research. This time round, I conducted the research with two other highly motivated young vets from Australia, Dr. Annie Cooke and Dr. Liz Dobson, who came to gain work experience and were also of great assistance.

We darted thirty buffalo and I enjoyed teaching the vets how to capture and take samples from them. When it came to community work, it was Annie who had something to teach me. She had a different perspective on working with the local communities. Based on her experiences with the Aborigines in Australia, she felt that I needed to be more understanding of the fact that the Basongora pastoralists had been evicted from Queen Elizabeth National Park when it was created. I eventually agreed with her. By the end of this study the local leader, Mzee Eliphaz had warmed up to us, and my perspective of local communities surrounding protected areas had completely changed. I began to empathize with them and started to understand that education and delivery of essential services to them had potential to change their attitudes to wildlife conservation. I was lucky that by the time I had come to Bwindi in 1994, the local community was already beginning to benefit from conservation and had started to become partners in protecting the critically endangered mountain gorillas. I realized the great need to get the QENP community to also become partners in conservation. In 1952, when Queen Elizabeth National Park was created it was an era where wildlife conservation was about fences and fines, and the British colonial government hired people from northern Uganda who were better at warfare to come and fight the local poachers in western Uganda, not realizing that they were not providing jobs for communities living around that park, which generated great resentment and conflict that was still very intense fifty years later.

This second time round we got the senior veterinary officer, Dr. Tumushabe to speak to the local pastoralists. He told them that he would not lift quarantine for a recent Foot and Mouth Disease (FMD) outbreak until their cattle had been tested, which meant that they could not move them. We were finally able to sample seventy-five cattle, which we found in the middle of the national park, where they were not allowed to be grazing them.

During the research, we planned to not only test for TB, but also for Foot and Mouth Disease, brucellosis, and other diseases that could affect livestock, wildlife, and people.

The findings proved valuable. It was the first time we had been able to compare buffalo and cattle, and results suggested that though thirty years ago, cattle had spread TB to buffalo, they had become maintenance hosts of TB and could potentially retransmit it to cattle. One quarter of the people with chronic coughs who had a sputum sample taken had TB. Close to half of the people interviewed drank unboiled milk from cattle, whereas others were willing to eat meat from an animal that had died of unknown causes, putting them at risk of getting Bovine TB.

We needed to control TB in both buffalo and cattle to reduce the risks of transmission to people, as well as educate them on the risks of drinking unboiled milk and eating meat from diseased animals.

To assess the risk of people giving TB to the mountain gorillas at Bwindi Impenetrable National Park, humans living in the area were also interviewed and tested for TB. The first group from the local communities had chronic coughs and the second group had people working with gorillas. Just like at Queen Elizabeth National Park one quarter of chronic coughers sampled had TB. Five percent of staff sampled had TB, though they did not have a cough, highlighting the need for an occupational health program to regularly test employees and minimize the risk of disease transmission to gorillas. Fifty-eight percent of people interviewed from the local communities had seen gorillas in contrast to 97 percent of staff. If TB was to get into a gorilla group, it would be impossible to treat them every day for eight months, which made me realize how urgent this issue was.

While finalizing the field research at Bwindi, I attended a meeting to establish a Public Health and Conservation Technical Support Unit (PHCTSU) to address zoonotic diseases following the scabies outbreaks in the two mountain gorilla groups that range in community land. The International Gorilla Conservation Programme wanted the local governments surrounding Bwindi Impenetrable National Park, from Kanungu, Kisoro, and Kabale Districts, to take a lead in this issue. It was perfect timing for me to launch the NGO that addressed the One-Health approach I wanted to bring to the area. The TB research I'd just completed underscored the need to have a holistic approach that integrated human, wildlife, and livestock health. At the meeting I reconnected with colleagues in the wildlife sector and met new people within the human public health and livestock health sector among the local government. Back in Kampala, I met with Anthony Ratter who had facilitated workshops I had held to determine veterinary needs for UWA to tell him about my idea for the NGO. He said "that sounds like Conservation Through Public Health." A light bulb went off in my head, it sounded just right. I was excited to return to the United States for my final year of the residency program with a name for the new NGO!

Chapter 14

Conservation Through Public Health

"You're black, so you won't be able to raise the money." I was shocked by the response from African colleagues after I shared my excitement about setting up an NGO to protect the lives of gorillas in Bwindi Impenetrable Forest by improving the health of the local community. Of all the responses I could imagine, this definitely wasn't it. But I also felt the truth of what they were saying. In Africa, conservation was dominated by people from the Western world who had developed a certain brand of conservation in Africa that proved popular with international donors. Also, the world of conservation was dominated by white people and there was a perception that Black Africans had no interest or expertise in this area, which was far from the truth. In Uganda, during those years of terror under Idi Amin, who had chased all the white and Indian Ugandans out of the country, as well as foreigners, the task of conservation fell to those Black Africans who remained behind and it was they who had begun the process of rebuilding conservation back up again.

I felt a dark cloud descend as I wondered: If this was the resistance I faced why was I even bothering? The answer was quick and simple: this was bigger than me. It was about protecting the critically endangered gorillas and supporting local communities—it was about building Uganda back up again from the devastating impact of Amin's rule. My parents had not given up when they had come up against even tougher obstacles to build a better Uganda: my father had given his life and my mother had endured many hardships. I also carried that legacy within me, and it was this that supported me in digging deep to find my courage. Yes, I knew I would have to work twice as hard, being a Black Ugandan, I knew I would be judged as an African woman, an even greater rarity in the world of conservation, but I was determined to succeed. I had never let my color or gender stop me from accomplishing what I wanted to do, and I wasn't about to start now. I had become Uganda's first wildlife vet. I had successfully raised funds to set up the veterinary unit for the Uganda Wildlife Authority (UWA). I had put up with derision and prejudice over the years, of people's lack of belief in me because I was a woman and I was black. But in all those tough years, I had never lost faith in myself and it was my self-belief that gave me the strength to move forward with plans to set up Conservation Through Public Health.

I returned to North Carolina State University that fall, fueled with determination and excitement about setting up my new organization. Addressing the health of people and wildlife together was unusual in the conservation world. Most conservation projects at the time only addressed the issue of animals and did not see the connection to humans. And those that had started to engage local communities in conservation did not consider public health. But my research and experience as a wildlife vet clearly showed the health impacts humans and animals had on one another. I realized that to be successful, conservation could no longer be seen as either/or. Everything was interconnected, and I wanted my organization to address this. I was not prepared for how consuming this path would be for me, nor did I realize that it would be one I continued to walk and learn from for the next two decades and that Lawrence would walk with me.

I was in my final year of study in North Carolina and my supervisors, Professor Mike Stoskopf and Dr. Suzanne Kennedy Stoskopf, were thrilled by my bold decision to set up my own NGO and also gave me permission to spend my final year gaining a certificate in nonprofit management at the nearby Duke University. The NC State University even gave me financial assistance of $500, which was available to all students who had to attend conferences linked to their area of study. I used it to immediately sign up for a course in nonprofit management. I also had a meeting with another of my supervisors, Dr. Mike Loomis from North Carolina Zoo, who probed further and asked what I wanted to accomplish with the NGO. I shared the urgent need to address the health of people, gorillas, and other wildlife in Uganda, who shared the same habitat. My personal experiences during UWA and the residency program clearly showed the impact of disease transmission between humans and wildlife and the need to reduce it to protect the gorillas. He thought that it was an important and innovative idea and offered to give as much support as possible. Soon we were introduced to the Director of North Carolina Zoo, Dr. David Jones, and together with Lawrence, we began to flesh out the details of our new, exciting venture.

Dr. Jones introduced me to Shana Kinnard Stockton, the dynamic and brilliant grant writer for North Carolina Zoo. If what my African colleagues had said was true about getting donations, then I would need to develop my skill and expertise in this area.

Our initial idea was to include the health of humans and wildlife, as well as my husband's field of expertise, information and communication technology, which would support local communities in accessing education and opportunities, meaning they would not be so dependent on the habitat they shared with the gorillas. However, Shana pointed out that too much diversification would confuse donors who would already struggle with getting to grips with our two programs of conservation and public health. So, we decided to downplay the communications tech element and concentrate on the first two. Funnily enough, however, it turned out to be the third element that really won the support of the local Bwindi community. But I'm getting ahead of myself. Shana also taught me a valuable lesson as a scientist, that to write a successful grant, I needed to not only present facts, but to also win the hearts of donors.

At the same time we were setting up the NGO, Lawrence was also making plans for his career and was accepted for an internship in India with United Nations Information Technology Service (UNITeS) to set up telecentres that could help rural farmers in Orissa, one of the poorest states in India, to access information to enable them to get a better price for their produce.

Before he went to India, Lawrence and I registered CTPH as a legal entity. We met with the US Senator John Edwards from North Carolina and on December 31, 2002, CTPH became recognized as a corporation. From there, it was a simple step to open a bank account with Lawrence being the first donor, depositing $100 into the account, while I deposited another $100. Seven months later, I was overcome with joy when CTPH became a 501(c)(3) nonprofit, which meant that we could more easily raise funds through tax-deductible donations from the United States.

During those four months he was away, between February and June 2003, I missed him terribly, feeling the isolation of North Carolina more acutely. I called him often. But Lawrence's experience in India proved invaluable in the early days of CTPH and in winning the hearts of the Bwindi local community when he adapted the telecentre model he had used in Orissa to set up a similar one for the local community in Bwindi.

Lawrence's trip to India also proved to be fortuitous in another way. The Zoo's graphic designer, Diane Olson, offered her pro bono assistance to develop the CTPH logo. The logo design had a red cross symbolizing health, with the people inside the cross defining our focus on engaging communities and the gorillas above the people representing a critically endangered flagship species that we are working to protect. The first draft of the logo had a defined crest and a cross, which Lawrence's Hindi colleagues in India found to be provocative because they saw it as emphasizing Islam and Christianity. This valuable perspective enabled us to adjust the logo and replace the crest with a circle that better symbolized our message that the health and well-being of people and wildlife is a connected cycle.

With Lawrence in India, I could focus all my attention on the nonprofit management course. One of the most useful classes was called Diversifying Your Fundraising Portfolio. We did not fit into a neat box because we encompassed both human and animal categories, and most people found this strange. Consequently, it was even more important that we were able to describe the work we did and its impact in a way that was simple and easy to grasp. By the time I had qualified and got my certificate, I had perfected my two-minute elevator pitch about CTPH, and this in turn helped to craft our mission and vision. I learned that to have a stable nonprofit, it was critical to build a solid base of individual donors, and, where possible, to generate revenue from the programs.

Next, we needed a website and we reached out to a black student, Demarcus Williams, from the North Carolina State University School of Design to design our website To this day, Demarcus still runs his company, Freshdesignz, and I like to think that we helped each other to get started.

I had a steep learning curve when it came to applying for funding. I first called, then applied to the Bill and Melinda Gates Foundation, which had an interest in preventing the spread of TB, something CTPH was also interested in. But after applying, I received the response: "We had several applications and while your work is important, it does not fit with this round of applications, and we are not able to fund your project." I had been so sure that the response would be positive. As I absorbed the news, I remembered that I'd learned it was acceptable practice to ask a donor why they did not fund you, so I immediately sent them an email requesting feedback on our application. They got back to me a couple of days later, and explained that they were not interested in funding animal health programs. Although disappointing, this was also very helpful as it made me realize that our concept was totally unique in that it put equal emphasis on people *and* animals, and the Bill and Melinda Gate Foundation's main focus was people. It seemed we didn't fit into any neat category. I realized that most donors offered single-sector funding, and we were asking them to fund two sectors at once. It became clear that the funding route was not going to be straightforward, and evident that CTPH was disrupting the clearly defined categories conservation had traditionally come under. We were trying to do something new, something that connected the dots and could have a long-lasting impact on both human and animal communities. I recognized that I would need to get creative in educating donors about our new innovative approach.

My first port of call was to reach out to the African Wildlife Foundation who had supported my research on TB, and whom I was due to give a presentation to in Washington, DC. I really hoped they could advise me on how best to reach donors who were still used to thinking one-dimensionally.

I also gave a formal presentation at Conservation International where I met a Ugandan conservationist, Kaddu Sebunya, who gave me tips and explained that Washington, DC, was the capital for donors who gave funding to organizations in Africa, and that I needed to spend more time in DC.

It was like following a set of bread crumbs and I was grateful for each crumb that came my way. Every person I contacted introduced me to someone else. Through Dr. Lynne Gaffikin, I became aware of donors who also took a holistic view of conservation and saw the value of combining programs that addressed poor human health, destruction of the environment, and high human population growth, through an approach commonly known as Population, Health and Environment (PHE). The only problem was the focus on family planning. At the time, I could not envision us promoting the use of condoms among the Bwindi local communities. Even so, I met the United States Agency for International Development (USAID) population officer Tom Outlaw. Although Tom was sympathetic to our cause, their focus was primarily on promoting family planning rather than preventing zoonotic disease transmission. Declining funding for a family planning program was a defining moment for me and CTPH. It meant standing firm about what I had set out to do rather than drifting away from the mission. (Years later we would embrace family planning as a part of our public health mission, but I wasn't ready for that yet.)

I drove from DC back to Raleigh, more determined to look for the right funds to realize CTPH's mission. It was a long drive back to North Carolina and even longer when halfway through my journey late in the evening, my car ground to a halt in Virginia, luckily next to a motel.

It was too late to find a mechanic and I had no choice but to spend the night in the motel. The next day I was scheduled to present at the North Carolina Zoo where they were starting a new collaborative program with schools around Kibale National Park in western Uganda called UNITE—"Uganda and North Carolina International Teaching for the Environment." Next to the motel was a gas station, where the staff directed me to a nearby garage, which was not yet open by 8 a.m., so I was advised to go to the owner's home nearby. I knocked on his cottage door, and a short energetic old white man with a hardened wrinkled face came to open it. He asked me to come inside and lowered his voice and said, "This is a redneck area, if your car breaks down again do not get out, you will be lynched as a single black woman on her own in this part of America." I was gripped by fear, and it was the first time in my life I had ever felt scared in America. I thanked him for his fatherly advice and then after the car was fixed, drove as fast as I could to North Carolina. I realized I needed to get a mobile phone for the long journeys I was making on my own around the United States. It also pointed to a sad truth about the great divide between Black and White in America.

Back in North Carolina, I set about finding donors who could help us and I soon found my mark. I remembered that Dr. Steve Osofsky who was the first Wildlife Veterinary Officer of the Botswana Department of Wildlife and National Parks and often gave me advice on setting up the UWA veterinary unit, was now working at the Wildlife Conservation Society (WCS) headquartered at the Bronx Zoo in New York. He and the head of their field veterinary program, Dr. William Karesh, had recently started to support organizations addressing the transmission of disease between people, livestock, and wildlife through a new program called Animal Health for the Environment and Development (AHEAD). When I spoke to Dr. Osofsky about the new NGO, he invited me to join a convention, for the International Union for the Conservation of Nature (IUCN) in Durban, South Africa, that September where AHEAD was hosting a workshop with support from the Wellcome Trust, on diseases shared between people, wildlife, and livestock. This was my chance! He asked me to prepare a presentation, and obtained funding from the Education for Nature Fund of the World Wide Fund for Nature (WWF) in the United States for my participation at the conference. Steve also asked me to present at an earlier session in the conference on "Building support for conservation from other sectors" where my talk focused on our One Health approach to mountain gorilla conservation, and introduced CTPH. It was even more exciting to be on the panel with two of my mentors, Dr. Richard Kock and Dr. Mike Kock, his brother, and another vet, Dr. Tom Demaar. It didn't strike me then that I was the only woman and only black African on the panel. At this conference I was also able to have a meeting with Richard Ruggiero from the United States Fish and Wildlife Service (USFWS), one of our first donors at CTPH.

During all this excitement, my zoological medicine residency program in Raleigh came to an end. I now had a master's degree in Specialized Veterinary Medicine. I had not only become a more well-rounded wildlife veterinarian, but had gained essential experience on giving public presentations, publishing peer-reviewed scientific papers, and even setting up an NGO. There was a dark side of my experience, too. North Carolina had indeed been a culture shock. Though I enjoyed the warm Southern hospitality of the people I met and worked with in grad school, I noticed how differently I was treated, as the first and only Black African on the course, from the other residents. When I made a mistake, I was berated much more severely than white students who were treated with more understanding. Even though I had more experience in working with wildlife than other vets on the course did, I was never given the opportunity to lead in veterinary procedures while the other vets were often invited to lead. The only time the opportunity presented itself was when the other vets weren't around and I was the only vet available, and on this one occasion I felt a great sense of achievement and relief that the procedure went so well. The lack of confidence they had in me sometimes made me feel that I was incompetent. However, I fell back on the fact that there were many procedures I had carried out back in Uganda that the vets at North Carolina had never done, and that gave me the confidence and courage to keep going.

On my exit interview, I was invited to share my experience and did so in the hope that others from a different cultural background and color did not have to experience the same discrimination. However, for now I had so much to look forward to as another new chapter in my life began—it was time to go home to Uganda.

Prior to returning home, Lawrence and I had one final stop to see Dr. David Jones of North Carolina Zoo, a great supporter of our plan. So much so, that when we asked for funding support, the Zoo donated $6,000! This was great news, yet I also knew that we still needed to use every penny wisely. I really wanted to get off on the right foot launching our NGO and from my experiences setting up the veterinary unit at the Uganda Wildlife Authority, I knew it was really important to have all our beneficiaries and stakeholders on board with what we were planning with CTPH. With this in mind, I decided to use the funds to organize a strategic planning workshop in Uganda that fall and invite stakeholders to contribute.

It was late July when we arrived in Uganda. We stayed at Lawrence's mother's house in Kampala. In September I jetted off to Durban. The conference was a great success and an opportunity to build relationships that would support CTPH in the future. Then, it was back to Uganda and the stakeholder workshop. Stephen Rubanga joined us as our third Founder. He'd been my research assistant two years previously when conducting tuberculosis research. With me as president, Lawrence as treasurer, and Stephen as secretary, CTPH was all set.

The big day of the workshop arrived at the Institute of Tropical Forest Conservation (ITFC), Bwindi Impenetrable National Park's research station. This was where I had spent many days in the forest six years earlier counting gorillas during the census. Now the room was packed with forty-one stakeholders. These were community members living around Bwindi Impenetrable Forest as well as representatives from the local government, Uganda Wildlife Authority, conservation NGOs, universities, schools, and tour companies.

The workshop facilitator, Anthony Ratter, enabled us to come up with three main strategies to achieve CTPH's goals: the provision of veterinary services, provision of community health services, and education and advocacy. The only question was how we would implement them. And that was a big question. I realized the importance of gaining political support for CTPH and tried to engage the highest level of support in Kanungu, one of the Districts around Bwindi. The District Head, Local Council Chairperson sent the District Health Officer, Dr. Stephen Ssebudde, to represent them. Also in attendance was the ITFC Director, Dr. Alistair McNeilage, and both gave inspiring remarks about CTPH introducing health as a new way to achieve conservation.

What was most exciting about the event was that our stakeholders shared more ideas than I could ever have thought of, demonstrating the importance of tapping into the expertise of the people most impacted by our organization every day. Far too often conservation projects failed to recognize the expertise of local stakeholders and how they could really contribute to the success of a project. They were all invested in and passionate about what we were trying to achieve at CTPH, and embraced our idea of adding health to integrated conservation and development initiatives. They remain steadfast supporters to this very day.

After the workshop, Lawrence and I made our way to the Nkuringo sector of Bwindi, where the UWA had given us permission to track the Nkuringo gorilla group (that had not yet been open for tourism). After three hours of tracking the gorillas, it was great to see that they were all healthy and recovered from the scabies outbreak, and I was reminded of the reason I had begun this journey all those years ago. It was a magical ending to one of the most important days in the history of CTPH, and two decades later the benefits I have seen to both gorillas and people is truly humbling.

On our return to Kampala, we also visited the offices of the United Nations Development Programme, and were advised that we must register the NGO in Uganda in order to access their funding. I realized that we would also need to select a board and I reached out to my contacts who had a level of expertise and insight that would benefit CTPH, including: Alexandra Karekaho, Dr. Ian Clarke, Hon. Dr. Johnson Nkuuhe, Dr. Noelina Nantima, and my good friend from Kibuli Secondary School, Madina Nakibirige. Madina also helped me register CTPH as an NGO in Uganda as we didn't have the funds for a lawyer. We were required to find offices to operate from, which posed a problem because the law stipulated that it couldn't also be our place of residence. Luckily, we had been offered an affordable small office on our arrival in Uganda, by the country director of International Union for the Conservation of Nature.

As we flew back to the United States for Lawrence to defend his master's thesis and to collect our belongings in North Carolina before starting our new life in Uganda, I reflected on this entrepreneurial journey we had started in conservation and the seemingly endless possibilities that lay ahead for us to change the world.

Chapter 15

Improving Community Health Where Gorillas Range

In 2004, the time had come to implement the CTPH mandate. Though it was daunting to set up one of the first organizations in the world dedicated to conserving wildlife through a One Health approach, I did have a reference point. I'd read about integrated population, health, and environment (PHE) projects that had recently been implemented by international NGOs including the Jane Goodall Institute's TACARE project around Gombe National Park in Tanzania to protect endangered chimpanzees and their habitat. I was also inspired by similar projects in Madagascar to protect marine habitat that had been implemented by World Wide Fund for Nature and Conservation International.

However, we needed funding. Lawrence, Stephen Rubanga, and I had to get busy raising funds. To get around town, we needed a vehicle and my mother generously loaned us her pickup truck. She also gave us a grant of $4,000, and so did Lawrence's parents. We recruited an intern who I taught how to enter supporters' names in a database. Though she was hard working, after two months she left because we could not pay her a salary. Reality hit me that it would be difficult to retain anyone for long as a volunteer.

To make it worse, people often asked us "who funds you?" They expected an answer like "USAID" or "European Union" or another bilateral government donor because projects in Uganda were typically being supported in that way. Whenever we told them that we had started an NGO that improves the health of people and wildlife together, with funding from North Carolina Zoological Park, ourselves, and our parents, they didn't take us seriously. Nevertheless I was determined to make our idea a reality.

I also discovered that I was pregnant with our first child, another delight that was going to lead to a complete change in my life. When at the wedding of my childhood friend Arigye Mpairwe, I revealed that I had started an NGO and was expecting our first child, one of her colleagues, who had set up an office for an international NGO in Kampala, cautioned me that it was impossible to have a baby and set up an NGO at the same time. But I was going to make sure that I succeeded with my two "babies" and thought about how lucky I was that I had a companion, my husband, embarking on both journeys with me.

I decided to seek advice from friends and former colleagues working in donor agencies in Uganda to see if we could fundraise locally. A good childhood friend and former next-door neighbor who used to bury my pets with me, Dr. Flavia Mpanga, worked with the Irish Embassy, and told me that they had a small grants program to support healthcare and development among rural communities of Uganda and that the Development Cooperation Ireland liked projects that also helped the environment. I saw how our model would fit into their funding criteria and applied for funds to consolidate CBDOTS (Community Based Direct Observation of TB Treatment Short Course Therapy) in Kanungu District among communities that interact with the critically endangered mountain gorillas.

I had been greatly affected when two people died during my research on Tuberculosis because the CBDOTS program had not yet been established at Bwindi Impenetrable National Park. It was common that when the patients felt better mid treatment, they did not complete the eight-month daily course and then developed drug-resistant strains of TB. I also shuddered at the thought of them spreading the disease to other members of the community who they came into close contact with and then increasing exposure to the gorillas. Having seen the benefits of the CBDOTS program at Queen Elizabeth National Park, I wanted to bring it to Bwindi. The Development Cooperation Ireland liked our concept and confirmed their support after a visit to Bwindi.

This meant working closely with the local health centers, who received these referrals of TB patients. That is when I met Dr. Scott Kellerman, an American missionary doctor from California. He was working to help the Batwa, a hunter-gatherer tribe that had lived in the Bwindi forest until they were evicted by the Uganda government for the creation of the national park in 1991 and then put into settlements. Dr. Kellerman had helped to provide additional funding to the Bwindi Community Hospital that was built by the Church of Uganda Kinkizi Diocese in 2003, with revenue from gorilla trekking tourists. We invited him to join our board. Also on our board was Dr. Ian Clarke, a famous Irish missionary doctor and author who had built Kiwoko Hospital and International Hospital in Kampala.

Our first hire was a woman named Vaster Orikiriza to help us implement the program on the ground. She was the first female college graduate from the Bwindi community and had been inspired to obtain a bachelor's degree in tourism because of the mountain gorillas. When we hired her as our staff, she became the first person to earn a salary at CTPH.

On September 19, 2004, Lawrence and I were blessed with our first child, a baby boy, a true wonder in our lives. Culturally a newborn baby is given a name from the father's clan—we decided to name him Ndhego James William. Ndhego was a name from the civet cat clan that Lawrence also shared. James came from his paternal great-grandfather and William from his maternal grandfather. Ndhego was born in Kololo Hospital just two kilometers from where I was born, and delivered by a family doctor, Dr. Batwala. He was born at 6½ pounds. I was amazed at how small he was and how his fingers were almost as tiny as those of Poncho the vervet monkey, who'd terrorized our pets at home when I was a child. Just two weeks after he was born, I gave a keynote speech on the Uganda Independence Day celebrations at International School of Uganda, where Ndhego would eventually spend some of his primary school years.

When Ndhego was two months old, I received a call from Stephen Asuma of International Gorilla Conservation Programme (IGCP) that they had received funding of $13,000 to support the Public Health and Conservation Technical Support Unit. They wanted to give these funds to CTPH. This was the opportunity we were looking for to put our new idea—Conservation Through Public Health—into practice and though I was exhausted from lack of sleep as a mother of a newborn, we could not turn this down. However, when I mentioned to Stephen that we had just had our first child and I was going to delegate Vaster to hold the meeting with the local government, he insisted that I should be the one to lead the meeting to set the direction for these integrated projects. He made it clear that IGCP did not want more meetings. Enough money had been spent on talking about what could be done, they now wanted *action*. IGCP also wanted their donors to see progress when they visited Bwindi in a few months' time. I had no choice but to take Ndhego with me for his first of many trips to get CTPH off the ground and running.

On my first trip to Bwindi with our four-month-old baby, Lawrence remained behind to look after Ndhego when I checked on the gorillas. He greatly amused the local community by carrying him on his front in a sling because babies are normally carried on the backs of women. We were just beginning the fascinating journey of parenting in the wild.

We decided to hold community drama workshops about how people and gorillas can make each other sick and how best to prevent this. We engaged an existing drama group, Bwindi Conservation Actors, who had been trained by Bwindi and Mgahinga Conservation Trust, set up in 1994 to support the Uganda Wildlife Authority in improving the livelihoods of the communities surrounding Bwindi Impenetrable and Mgahinga National Parks. We gave the theater group the brochures on preventing zoonotic disease transmission between people and gorillas that I'd developed in my last year as the UWA Veterinary Officer. They designed a play that they performed in the local language in Mukono Parish. It drew a large crowd, with many hilarious skits including men dressed as women. I was impressed that they often referred to heroes in their community who everybody knew, and thought how clever they were to include them as role models on their skits.

Six months after the visit of the Irish Embassy director, in December 2004 we received funding of 25,000 euros for the project. We could begin our work at Bwindi, but we would require transport. It was a proud moment when we bought our first vehicle, a secondhand four-wheel drive Land Cruiser and branded it with the CTPH logo. We started off by working in Mukono parish with high human and gorilla conflict where we had gone to conduct the health education workshops with the local communities in my last year as the UWA veterinary officer, and Kyeshero parish, where Vaster comes from. Revenue sharing for tourism income went to the parishes where communities were most likely to affect the gorillas and their habitat, but there were also good arguments for supporting parishes like Kyeshero that don't touch the park boundary, because poachers sometimes came from these parishes. For sentimental reasons I selected Kyeshero so that Vaster's community would be among the first to benefit from CTPH programs and would encourage her to talk her community into warming to our new approach to conservation.

To launch this program, we traveled to Buhoma, Bwindi's main tourism site, and worked with the Community Conservation warden and rangers and subcounty health assistant to mobilize the local council leaders, one from each village, through an efficient system of decentralization that Uganda had set up. I introduced the CBDOTS program. After an intense two months of daily injections, TB patients would be discharged and supported by a friendly neighbor to watch them taking the tablets every day for six months with checkups at intervals of five and eight months. We emphasized that the friendly neighbor was not going to be paid a salary and had to make a commitment to be a volunteer so that the program was not dependent on funding and could be sustainable. Though some people were hesitant about volunteering, Stephen Rubanga managed to convince them that reducing TB in their neighbor's home was also going to protect the health of their families and their community. My research had found that people were at great risk of getting the Bovine strain of TB by drinking unboiled milk or eating meat that has not been inspected. Bovine TB is more difficult to treat than tuberculosis from humans, because though it presents the same, it needs different drugs in the treatment protocol. The subcounty health assistant, Godfrey Katungi, also mentioned that people often shared cups when they went to bars, which caused the disease to spread even more, putting the whole community at risk. Godfrey also reminded the local leaders that the majority of TB patients were coinfected with HIV/AIDS because it was easier to contract when your body had reduced immunity. Consequently, the Government developed a program to comanage TB and HIV, and I was glad that our program was also indirectly helping stop the spread of HIV. Vaster was a fast learner and took detailed notes at these meetings. But she proved to be more valuable than we could have known.

Another element that came along with this program was engaging the traditional healers. Being the most respected and most accessible healers in the village, they were often the first port of call when someone acquired TB or HIV/AIDS, yet their herbs could not heal the patients. Dr. Adatu had managed to convince these healers to be honest about what they could treat and could not treat and refer the patients to the nearest health center, where they would be tested and put on a course of treatment if found to be positive. When the patients returned to their homes, the traditional healer would be the volunteer watching them taking their medication every day and would therefore truly help their patient survive, which is also good for business. This approach turned out to be so successful that it has been adapted by the World Health Organization (WHO) for all the twenty-two countries most affected by TB (including Uganda), which are responsible for 80 percent of the global TB burden.

Traditional healers were not part of my own African culture. My mother had grown up in a family of devout Christians, who condemned "witchcraft." But now, I needed these healers as partners. We held our first meeting with the traditional healers, and to our surprise we saw one impressive man who had a strong resemblance to Vaster. He was putting on a well-worn brown suit with white shirt and feathers both on his headgear and walking stick. Vaster indeed sheepishly introduced him to us as her father and in the meeting, we soon discovered that he was also a senior traditional healer in the community. I could not help but admire her father for having the foresight to educate his girl child to the level of university. Because of this, Vaster had waited until the age of twenty-five to have her first child. In this community, by the age of twenty-five, most women have had five children. Because his daughter was part of the team, these healers were much more open with us about their challenges, frustrations, and suggested remedies.

When we started the workshop, we asked them if they had seen cases of TB and HIV, and then what they did when they saw them. There were a varied number of responses to this question, where some claimed to be able to treat it and others admitted that they could not treat it and had even contracted the disease from their patients. I thanked them for being honest about their limitations and explained to them that TB and HIV often occur together and were infectious diseases that could only be controlled using certain antibiotics and antiviral treatments. I could see some nods in the audience, while others grumbled in disagreement. As I was going to the next item on the agenda, how we could work together to control TB, Lawrence touched my arm to silence me and asked them what diseases they could treat. I was astonished at the number of sicknesses they could treat, including allergies, stomach upset, skin diseases, headache, and mental health. Some of them claimed to also drive out evil spirits. I had no doubt that they had herbs that could treat some of the ailments they claimed to cure, and realized that it was important not to let go of traditional medicine, which our ancestors used before the first missionary came to Africa with modern medicine.

The Community Conservation Ranger, Deus Tugumisirize, told the healers that UWA had a program where registered groups can enter the national park to collect medicinal plants, honey, and basket-making material. However, he encouraged the traditional healers to plant medicinal plants in their gardens to avoid the need to always enter the park. Most of them agreed to this solution though some claimed that the plant does not have "as much medicine" if it is not grown in the forest. It was an eye-opener to me on the importance of maintaining culture in societies and how it could play a significant role in strengthening conservation and public health programs.

When we implemented the program, I quickly realized that we had to spend the first three months of the one year project raising awareness about the dangers of tuberculosis and held several education workshops. In addition to the theater group we used earlier, Vaster suggested that we also work with a a theater group called Rutendere Health Promoters from Kyeshero parish, as they would be readily accepted by that community. It was interesting that in both drama groups, there was the scene of the child getting sick and the mother encouraging the father to go into the forest to poach because game meat was considered the only medicine that could cure their child. Instead the child was exposed to more diseases from wild animals, and the skit had warning that this was not a safe practice. However, one day, two of the women in the group came up to me and said that they had something to say to me in confidence. They told me that in the three months we'd been working with them, they had never been paid and had all been planning to boycott the next show. They were aware that I had given funding to their leader, the only man in the group, and felt that it would be unfair to me if they continued with this protest plan without informing me. I was so shocked that I called their leader for a private meeting and demanded that he pay them immediately. He apologized and we both agreed to change the system so that everyone signed for their money directly from CTPH, which helped to create transparency and motivated the women to work harder.

Nevertheless, when the time came for our funding review after six months, The Development Cooperation Ireland told me that though awareness was important, the Irish government was more interested to know how many people were being referred to the health centers and treated for TB as a result of our efforts. They encouraged us to work more closely with the local health centers owned by the government, and Bwindi Community Hospital owned by the church, and show them how we could increase their numbers through our programs.

In some cases, we were welcome. We learned that the microscope at one of the government health centers was broken. They need this essential piece of equipment to diagnose important diseases like malaria as well as TB. Stephen Rubanga fixed the microscope, which made them warm up toward CTPH.

But not all inroads were as successful. The Bwindi Community Hospital did not fully understand why a veterinary NGO was getting involved in human public health work and became reluctant to work with CTPH. In spite of all these challenges, the program had an impact within one year. The number of people referred, tested, and treated for TB increased at the government and missionary health centers, and I was elated that the number of people healed from TB increased.

Our funder was happy with the progress, and just as I was wondering how we could keep this program going, USAID approached us, saying they wanted to support us. Funding came through African Wildlife Foundation, and we were able to continue the CBDOTS program in Mukono parish in addition to another parish, Bujengwe, bordering the park. The funding from USAID also enabled us to engage traditional healers more meaningfully. Dr. Adatu told me about an organization called THETA (Traditional and Modern Healers together against HIV/AIDS), and recommended that we work with them to engage traditional healers at Bwindi. THETA was created as an NGO in 1995. Their country director was Dorothy Balaba, who was my schoolmate at Kabale Preparatory School and who was keen to support our new initiative. Both the traditional healers and traditional birth attendants (TBAs) were taught about how to work with the local health centers in preventing and controlling TB. TBAs were also urged to refer mothers to the health centers to give birth to reduce unnecessary deaths of both mothers and children at home.

Ndhego continued to travel with me to Bwindi and became a regular member of the CTPH team, where he loved interacting with other children from the Bwindi community. I felt a great sense of achievement that not only had we implemented our first human public health program at CTPH, I had also started learning how to work while parenting, with the help of Aunty Margaret, a wonderful nanny that my mother-in-law hired for us.

To help pay the bills and enable Lawrence to focus on his career in telecommunications, he joined Ericsson Uganda as a Customer Project Manager and, because he had a good working knowledge of French, was assigned to Congo-Brazzaville for seven months. During this time, I went to visit Lawrence in 2006 with two-year-old Ndhego. When we arrived at the airport, I was astounded that hardly anyone spoke English. I had to relearn the French I had studied in secondary school. Here I was able to spend full days with Ndhego, and I reconnected with colleagues working with the Wildlife Conservation Society (WCS), including Dr. Ken Cameron, former veterinarian for the Mountain Gorilla Veterinary Project, who was particularly charmed to meet my son. One of the WCS biologists, Zorine Nkouantsi, who was Congolese and who I had met when we were invited for a gorilla health workshop in Cameroon the previous year, took me and Ndhego out for lunch at a Congolese restaurant. The only food on the menu was bushmeat or fish. When I asked what was in the bushmeat and they could not guarantee that gorilla was not included, we chose the fish.

While there, I never saw cows on the road, and our main meals were chicken or fish. I started craving red meat, and began to understand what drives people to eat bushmeat, especially if there were few other options, and where, I was told, bushmeat was easy get.

My highlight was visiting Lefini sanctuary owned by John Aspinall, whose zoo in the UK, Howletts and Port Lympne, I had visited and tested their gorillas for parasites. We drove from Brazzaville to Lefini, on a paved road, which eventually became a rough gravel road, through a beautiful savanna to a lush forest, which had a fast-flowing river. We first met the captive gorillas in a big enclosure on the main land then went on a riverboat to see other semi-captive gorillas on an island where they were being fed. We spent the night in their rustic camp, and got to meet an orphaned infant gorilla wearing a nappy and being bottle-fed. Ndhego was intrigued by the baby gorilla, which was about the same age as him, and perhaps this led to him improving on his potty training.

Congo-Brazzaville has a history of gorilla, chimpanzee, and human deaths caused by Ebola, which has a mortality rate as high as 90 percent. Over five thousand western lowland gorillas in Central Africa had died of Ebola in the past twenty years putting them on the critically endangered list because, though their numbers are over 100,000, their populations are rapidly declining due to the bush-meat trade and disease. People died who contracted Ebola not only by eating infected bushmeat but also by tending to their loved ones who were sick or had died, and carrying out traditional rituals, which exposed them to this highly contagious virus, through contact with blood and other body fluids.

Because our program of inviting traditional healers to become partners in health and conservation could prevent unnecessary deaths from Ebola, I was invited to give a talk at the National Institute of Public Health in Congo-Brazzaville. Clearly, CTPH was tapping into a great need for creating an atmosphere of cooperation that would save both animal and human life.

Chapter 16

Early Warning Systems

Historically, gorillas were only monitored when they were sick. But I wanted to be ahead of the game when it came to protecting the mountain gorillas, and I knew we would need to create an early warning system for disease outbreaks, so we could take action before a disease turned into a full-blown outbreak where many lives could be lost.

While setting up the veterinary unit of Uganda Wildlife Authority I was only able to attend to emergencies in the gorillas and other wild animals and was frustrated that I had no time to set up a system to regularly monitor their health. When Kahara the juvenile mountain gorilla developed a rectal prolapse, we were not sure whether she had picked up a parasite, bacteria, or virus from humans that caused her to strain to defecate. At the time I was only able to test for parasites, and indeed found that she had a higher than usual burden of what looked like gorilla parasite eggs. But if we had a field clinic set up that could regularly monitor the scat and health of gorillas, we would be in a better position to know whether an illness was caused by picking pathogens from humans, livestock, or other wildlife.

Back when the documentary *Gladys the African Vet* was shown on BBC1, I received a lot of letters of appreciation and offers of support, including from Dr. Charlie Ralph Garrett, a Scottish veterinary surgeon. When I let him know that we had started an NGO, he was keen to offer support and helped us design a gorilla research clinic, modeled after an award-winning ecocabin that he had designed in Scotland.

With the help of volunteers, Carole and Geoffrey Howard, from the American Jewish World Service (AJWS), we developed an action plan with three integrated programs: wildlife health monitoring, human public health and information, education and communication (IEC). Around the same time, I was encouraged to apply for an executive director position to manage the Ngamba Chimpanzee Island, a place that was very dear to me because we had taken there the first set of orphaned chimpanzees from the bushmeat trade including Kalema, the chimpanzee I had rescued. The Howards advised me to stick to establishing CTPH, though as with any early-stage endeavor, it was difficult. It was just the beginning of learning how to overcome feelings of hopelessness during my entrepreneurial journey, and I knew that I'd be more fulfilled making my unique dream a reality. The Howards helped CTPH write a three-year grant proposal for funds from the John D. and Catherine T. MacArthur Foundation based on the action plan, which included setting up an early warning system for disease outbreaks at both Bwindi and Queen Elizabeth National Parks, as well as training rangers and community volunteers to do this work. When we received the MacArthur Foundation grant, we were ecstatic to receive our first long-term funding.

The funding from MacArthur Foundation enabled CTPH to set up a base at Bwindi. We rented a house to serve as both an office and staff accommodation. We also located a plot of land two kilometers from the park boundary to build the Gorilla Research Clinic.

The clinic would be a one-room ecocabin made of soft wood. We received funding from Bayer Pharmaceuticals thanks to Joy Howell, who was also a veterinary nurse I had met as a student at the Royal Veterinary College. She arrived in Uganda from UK with her partner, Pascal Jobogo, a gentle and soft-spoken Congolese, who was an excellent chef. Joy was determined to build the clinic in ten days with the help of a builder from the Bwindi local community who found it a bit difficult taking instructions from a woman. This arrangement greatly amused the Bwindi community, because the gender roles were reversed with the woman building and the man cooking. With additional funding from the United States Fish and Wildlife Service (USFWS), we built and equipped the ecocabin, which was sixteen square meters and had a hole in the ground where we put a large 250-liter jerrycan filled with water to act as an air conditioner that circulated air to keep the ecocabin cool. Stephen applied his expertise in laboratory management and designed the layout of the shelves for the field laboratory. Joy wrote a story about building the Gorilla Research Clinic for *Veterinary Times* magazine.

During this time, the Bwindi chief warden, John Makombo, asked me to check on an adult female gorilla in Mubare gorilla group that had become lethargic. However, when I woke up that morning, six-months-old Ndhego was crying a lot, and I felt anxious as I left him with the nanny, Auntie Margaret, to go and check on the gorilla. For the first time, while walking up to the gorillas, my mind was not settled. Luckily, we found the gorillas only after forty-five minutes, and though the adult female gorilla had lost some weight, she was eating well and the rangers told me that she was improving, so I rushed back to see how Ndhego was doing. My worst fears were confirmed, he had developed a high fever. I immediately took him to the Bwindi Community Hospital not far from where we stayed. They diagnosed malaria and started treating him. That night Ndhego started passing diarrhea frequently and I feared that he would waste away, though thankfully he was eager to drink the oral rehydration fluids we were given. I decided that we needed to return to Kampala where he could get more specialized medical attention. It was the last day of construction, and we had a delicious farewell dinner cooked by Pascal. Ndhego normally really enjoyed being at the building site, but this day he was weak and unhappy when I carried him there.

The following day, we drove halfway and spent the night in a hotel in Mbarara. As soon as we reached the hotel, Ndhego started wailing so loudly and incessantly that I took him to a nearby private hospital where they discovered that he had developed a rash on top of his malaria that could be a mild form of measles. I realized that it would have been worse if he had not been vaccinated. He was put on an IV drip and given antibiotics and we were given a room for the night. Ndhego greatly improved overnight and though the hospital advised against us traveling so soon, I insisted on traveling because I wanted to be in Kampala, near his pediatrician. The terror of losing our child due to inadequate medical care in a remote location of Uganda never left me. Those with accessible adequate healthcare facilities take for granted that help will be available when they need it. Without it, diseases that could be survived can be fatal. We were frightened at how close we came.

Our CTPH funding success continued and a few months later, we began to train park staff to monitor the health of gorillas. We received funding from the Wildlife Conservation Society field veterinary program in memory of Dr. Annelisa Kilbourne, a passionate British wildlife veterinarian I greatly admired. She discovered that Ebola was killing the western lowland gorillas in Gabon. I had been devastated when she died in a plane crash in 2002 while working in Gabon and was glad to be able to continue her legacy through setting up the Gorilla Health Monitoring program at Bwindi.

The first step was for park rangers to monitor the gorillas regularly, looking for abnormalities and clinical signs of ill-health.

The second was collecting fecal samples which would be tested for parasites and other pathogens. Very soft or watery dung and blood in the fecal sample or in the night nest are a cause for concern, especially when paired with signs of sickness. In addition to collecting abnormal fecal samples, every month a fecal sample is collected from every gorilla in the habituated groups, to determine if they have a larger-than-usual parasite burden or picked up a parasite from people or their livestock. When I came across goat dung next to gorilla dung in the forest I realized how important it was to also look out for diseases in livestock. I adapted some of my experiences in North

Carolina Zoo where animals in the collection are sampled every month to check for any illnesses. We received donated microscopes and equipment from Cornell University, and Dr. Jessica Rothman, who arranged the donation, taught park rangers and my team how to identify parasites.

Another important aspect of the training was how to identify individual gorillas so that they can know which one is sick.

Our newly established early warning system for disease outbreaks was adopted in the annual operational plan of Bwindi Impenetrable National Park.

At our first workshop, we trained thirty rangers who regularly visit the gorillas and guide tourists, and over the years reached over four hundred rangers at all sectors where tourism is conducted at Bwindi and Mgahinga National Parks.

Within the first year of setting up the Gorilla Research Clinic, we discovered that the Nkuringo gorilla group in the southern sector of Bwindi that was spending a lot more time in community land had a much higher parasite burden than the gorillas in the northern and eastern sectors of Bwindi and were likely picking up parasites from the local communities that have less-than-adequate hygiene. This discovery resulted in UWA recruiting twice as many members of the Human and Gorilla Conflict Resolution (HUGO) Team, a group of community volunteers who safely herd gorillas back to the park away from people's gardens. These volunteers also received training in gorilla health monitoring. After all, they were well placed to take fecal samples and monitor those gorillas who foraged on community land. The following year, the parasite burden in Nkuringo gorilla group went back to the same levels as those of other gorilla groups.

We also conducted a study with support from Whitley Fund for Nature, which discovered that close to half of the homes in the two parishes bordering Bwindi Impenetrable National Park collect water from a source that put them at great risk of getting intestinal parasites.

One of the benefits of the Gorilla Research Clinic was that we were able to support the local Bwindi Community Hospital. They would often receive cases of diarrhea and while they offered drugs to alleviate the symptoms, they did not have time to research the cause of the infection. With our new facilities, we were able to step in and convince the hospital to allow us to analyze samples, which we would compare with the gorillas and local livestock samples. A veterinary student, Ryan Sadler from University of California, Davis, obtained a donation of fecal antigen ELISA test kits that he brought to Bwindi to conduct this research with CTPH.

We discovered that the most common cause of diarrhea in people was giardia, a protozoan parasite that causes an infection in the small intestine and is spread through contaminated water. I was not all that surprised because I myself on a few occasions had contracted giardia at Bwindi; I felt like I was going to die of dehydration, from so much vomiting and diarrhea. We found that as many as 40 percent of the samples from human infants were positive for giardia. We also found giardia in the cattle. We also looked for another intestinal protozoa, cryptosporidium, and found it in people, livestock, and the Rushegura gorilla group, though thankfully it was not causing clinical signs.[12] However, we knew the Rushegura group spent a lot of time in community gardens including Kyogo and Mukongoro villages, on the way to DRC where people had the poorest hygiene practices. This alarmed me and prompted us to recruit a second Village Health and Conservation Team member in those two villages to be able to reach a larger number of homes more frequently with critical information on hygiene, health, and conservation. As a result of our research, Bwindi Community Hospital educated families with children to collect water from protected clean sources.

With support from Primate Conservation Inc., Stephen taught the farmers how to build cattle water troughs away from human and gorilla drinking water sources, reducing the chances of picking up giardia and cryptosporidium.

Five years after implementing our One Health approach, people were becoming more hygienic, and gorillas showed markedly reduced parasite infections even when they foraged in community gardens.

Protecting wildlife involves so much more than administering healthcare, I had learned. And now I was about to learn that it also involved not only developing immediate funding sources for programs, but building and maintaining supportive lifelong relationships worldwide.

In 2007, I was featured among eight revolutionary minds in science in *Science Magazine* for linking conservation and health through regular testing of gorilla fecal samples for human parasites. As we shared what we were doing at the Gorilla Research Clinic with tourists, we caught the eye of a member of San Diego Zoo, Ruth Hayward, who talked about our work when she went back home and nominated me for my first conservation award since founding CTPH—the 2008 San Diego Zoo Conservation in Action Award, which also came with funding. Lawrence and I traveled to San Diego to receive it. There, I met my fellow award winners, Dr. Laurie Marker, who founded the Cheetah Conservation Fund in Namibia and won the lifetime achievement award, and Richard Louv, who won the conservation advocate award for his book *Last Child in the Woods*, about reconnecting children to nature and outdoor activities to reduce obesity and attention disorders.

Our hosts wanted us to make the most of the trip so that we could establish more partnerships and build a base of supporters. They took us to the San Diego Zoo, where I was able to visit the western lowland gorillas and two other species not found in Africa—koalas and giant pandas. I visited the new veterinary hospital and marveled at their state-of-the-art equipment. While visiting the zoo's Centre for Research in Endangered Species (CRES), where genetic studies by Dr. Oliver Ryder originally discovered that Bwindi gorillas are mountain gorillas, I reconnected with a Ugandan PhD researcher, Dr. Anthony Nsubuga, working in his lab. Donors to the zoo, Jerri-Ann and Gary Jacobs, started a highly innovative high school, High Tech High, where I was invited to speak. This was the beginning of a long-term relationship where one year later we hosted Jerri-Ann and her daughter Beth at Bwindi and the photos they took of the gorillas were used to make our first postcards to help with fundraising. I also gave a presentation to the Rotary Club of San Diego and was hosted by the renowned animal and environmental advocate, Joan Embrey, at her Pillsbury Ranch in Lakeside, where we enjoyed handling the snakes and sloths. All these people supported us with funding or expertise and Dr. Allison Alberts, Director of CRES, became a board member of CTPH.

The next year, I returned to California as a guest speaker at the Wildlife Conservation Network (WCN) expo, where I could share the benefits of a One Health approach to gorilla conservation to a wider audience. This time, Lawrence and I brought Ndhego, now five, and his eight-month-old baby brother, Tendo. There I was able to reconnect with Dr. Jane Goodall, the event's keynote speaker. A few years later, we hosted WCN staff and donors at Bwindi. Conservation Through Public Health was on the rise.

Chapter 17

Launching Telecentres and Hosting Royalty

During Lawrence's volunteer experiences with UNITeS in Orissa, the poorest state in India, he witnessed how telecentres enabled people to have access to critical information that was transforming their lives. After graduating with an MS in Telecommunications, Lawrence convinced me to add an Information Communication and Technology (ICT) for Development program to our One Health approach to conservation. He envisioned an internet café or community hub where people could send and receive emails and surf the internet, a model that could be adapted to improve the livelihoods of community members at Bwindi, enabling them to benefit more from the vibrant gorilla trekking tourist industry. In 2004, Lawrence served on the Jury of the first Global ICT Summit in Hong Kong, where he met and convinced the senior officer of the United Nations

Industrial Development Organization (UNIDO) to support the CTPH telecentre. Both UNIDO and Shell Solar donated solar panels; Coca-Cola provided a refrigerator; and Uganda Telecom Limited (UTL) donated a satellite dish and free internet for the first two years. UTL also put up a very big signpost on the main junction to Buhoma that we are using to this day.

Uganda Communications Commission (UCC), a government agency in charge of regulating telecommunications in Uganda, creatively raised funding through earnings from telecommunications companies that were mandated to put aside 1 percent of their revenue. From UCC funds, we were able to buy and install computers, but we still needed to figure out how to fund operational costs. Our short-term solution was to charge people to use the computers. The local community paid 100 shillings per minute (equivalent to 8 cents per minute in 2005), whereas the tourists were charged five times as much to help subsidize the costs. We converted the main reception area of the CTPH office into the telecentre. Our grand opening marked the arrival of the internet in Bwindi and it generated a lot of excitement among the local communities and tourists who were now able to send real-time photos of their gorilla trekking experience at a time when there were no cell towers or Wi-Fi hot spots. We noticed also that the tourists were interested in meeting and getting to know the local communities at the telecentre, which enabled them to form lasting relationships after they left Bwindi.

In this remote part of Uganda, most people had never seen computers and we soon realized that we needed to teach them skills. We went to Makerere University Department of Women and Gender Studies, which had a vibrant computer training program with a focus on increasing literacy levels in women. We hired two young graduates, Diana Neunje and Sarah Awino, to become our center's computer teachers. Our students included rangers, teachers, camp managers, caterers, and craftspeople who would then market and sell their crafts online. We charged 100,000 shillings for the class, the equivalent of $56 for six weeks, much less than what they would pay at Makerere University, but enough to cover the salaries of the trainers. Although only the elite in the community could pay, they became role models for others who developed an interest in furthering them-selves through learning how to use computers. This included the indigenous Batwa, who are hunter-gatherers evicted from the forest when the government declared it a national park. It was heartwarm-ing to see members of the Batwa community who had never gone to formal school taking computer classes. Having acquired computer skills, some graduates became camp managers and administrators, and one ranger went on to do a course at the Uganda Wildlife Training Institute after we nominated him for a scholarship from the Wildlife Conservation Network. We hired one of the graduates to manage the telecentre. We were excited when over fifty children from the Bwindi Orphans School came to watch educational films on the Discovery and National Geographic channels.

The Bwindi community was now able to open their minds and communicate with the outside world in ways that they had never been able to do before. Suddenly what seemed like one of the remotest corners of Uganda became much more accessible through the power of technology. Through this telecentre we trained over 150 people and were proud that 40 percent were women. An interesting revela-tion from UCC was that they provided different levels of grants for organizations in Uganda and found that those who received partial funding continued after the project funding cycle, whereas those who received full funding did not. Receiving partial funding meant that you had to charge people to use the internet to generate revenue to keep the operations going, whereas with full funding there was no need to charge the community who then got used to not paying for internet access and were not ready to pay for it after the project funding ended. It was a valuable lesson on how to set up sustainable programs that need to continue beyond donor funding. In the space of three years, over three thousand members of the local community and three hundred ecotourists paid a fee for service to access email and wireless internet.

We were so proud when the Bwindi Telecentre was a final-ist in the 2006 Stockholm Challenge Award environment category. Lawrence and I traveled with one-and-a-half-year-old Ndhego for the ceremony in the Blue Hall in Sweden. It was even more spe-cial to share this achievement with my mother-in-law and her good friend Catherine Kulubya, who joined us for the ceremony from Kosovo. We were so excited when the Telecentre won the 2007 World Summit Awards for Inclusion and Empowerment of Bwindi communities, another great honor for CTPH that won the hearts of the local communities.

★ ★ ★

We were making a name for ourselves, which didn't go unnoticed. Royal eyes were watching, and we were thrilled to engage them in our conservation work. Against all odds, CTPH had been in operation for two years. It was high time to seek a patron who could attract more people to our mission and vision, especially Ugandans and other Africans who were not in the conservation community, to become engaged in conservation. The ideal person came in the form of a cultural leader, the Queen of Buganda, with whom I had a personal connection. Her grandfather and my father had been best friends, and I had grown up knowing Queen Sylvia and her family. I was inspired by her energy and her support of many humanitarian causes. I remember staying with her in New York, before she became queen. She was working as a public information officer and research consultant at the United Nations headquarters at the time. In 1999, when she got married to the Kabaka, King of Buganda and became the Nnabagereka, Queen of Buganda, I was lucky enough to attend her wedding, which tragically was on the fateful day that my colleague, Dr. Jonathan Arusi, was killed by an elephant during the translocation.

Queen Sylvia had continued to follow my budding career with wildlife at UWA and was excited that we had founded a nonprofit and NGO to improve the health and well-being of both people and wildlife. We were impressed by her commitment to improving education opportunities for all children and in particular uplifting daughters, earning her the prestigious role as a Goodwill Ambassador for United Nations Family Planning Association (UNFPA). Both of us were involved in the Forum for African Women Educationalists (FAWE), who had made me a model of excellence in 1999 to mentor young girls while working as the first veterinarian for the Uganda Wildlife Authority. FAWE focusses on getting more girls in school to bridge the gender gap within all levels of the education system and also provides scholarships to the least advantaged children. In 2005, Lawrence and I met her in the Buganda Kingdom offices in Bulange, Mengo, and plucked up our courage to ask her to become the Patron of CTPH. We were thrilled when Queen Sylvia accepted our invitation, more so when she mentioned that she preferred to take an active role in the charities that she supported.

We now felt that it was time to officially launch CTPH field programs, which had been operating unofficially for a year.

The launch was a momentous occasion with literally over one thousand people attending, including local leaders, Uganda Wildlife Authority, members of the local community, the media, and visitors from Kampala including my mother and Lawrence's father, Retired Lieutenant Colonel Kenneth Dako.

Queen Sylvia started off by having lunch in the Telecentre before she sent an email, then cut a ribbon. This was followed by songs and dances from Bwindi Orphans School, who performed "the gorilla dance"; Bwindi Conservation Actors and Rutendere Health Promoters, who we were working with in our community health and conservation programs; and the Batwa drama groups. Numerous speeches were made, donations pledged, and the Uganda Telecom Limited Company announced they were donating a satellite dish and two years of free internet. As CTPH Founders, Lawrence and I gave a speech about why and how we started CTPH and thanked everyone for supporting us and the important cause of gorilla conservation. The Queen presented certificates to students who had recently completed the certificate in basic computer skills at the CTPH Telecentre. They were the lucky cohort that graduated in the presence of royalty. The Batwa people immediately related to this cultural leader from Buganda and requested a special audience with Queen Sylvia, which she granted.

While in Bwindi we took this opportunity to take the Queen to see the gorillas—the first queen in the world to do so. Habinyanja gorilla group, whom we were to track, were the largest habituated gorilla group in Bwindi. It was a special moment when I introduced the eldest adult female, Mukeikuru, which means "old lady." Queen Sylvia named her infant Ntuuse, which in Luganda means "I have arrived." This was very appropriate after the long journey of ten hours' drive from Kampala and five hours on foot to find these charismatic and vulnerable gentle giants in the famous impenetrable forest. We ended the day with a visit to our Gorilla Research Clinic, where the Queen, though tired, was eager to see how we analyzed fecal samples from the gorillas she had just seen. Having successfully hosted a royal visitor at Bwindi, we were ecstatic, and unaware that soon, we'd be hosting another royal visitor.

★ ★ ★

Meanwhile, the Bwindi telecentre continued to open doors for local people and caught the attention of Bill Farmer, the technical adviser for business development at UWA. He was so impressed with the center that he contacted Lawrence about setting up a similar project at one of the oldest protected areas in Uganda, Queen Elizabeth National Park (QENP) and encouraged us to apply to the British High Commission for funding. Unlike Bwindi which was created in the 1990s when community conservation had just started to be implemented, Queen Elizabeth National Park was created in the 1950s deep in an era of fences and fines. At Bwindi, about 90 percent of the staff at the national park were from the local community in contrast to QENP, where close to 90 percent of the staff were recruited from far away in northern Uganda because they were better at fighting poachers. This immediately excluded the local communities from getting jobs in the national park. Instead, they were arrested for entering the park, and the most resentful were the Basongora pastoralists who had cultural sites inside the park that they could no longer access. It so happened that at around the same time in November 2007, Uganda was selected to host the Commonwealth Heads of Government Meeting (CHOGM), and this new telecentre was going to be selected as one of the projects that they visited. Royal visitors from the UK were scheduled to visit the national park named after

Queen Elizabeth, when she'd visited with her new husband, Prince Philip in 1954.

With a grant from the British High Commission, we began to build the QENP telecentre. Barclays Bank donated solar panels, and I-Way Africa donated a dish for satellite communication. The building was to serve the dual purpose of a CTPH Telecentre and UWA Visitor Information Center at the park, with a gateway enabling visitors to register as they entered to take the scenic drive along the top of the crater to the park headquarters at Mweya. When the local community got wind that someone from the royal family was coming, they requested to speak to the Duke of Edinburgh and tell him all their problems that the establishment of the park had created. We managed to calm them down and promised to pass their request on to the Royal family and the British High Commission.

The member of the royal family who arrived to launch the telecentre was Prince Philip himself. There was a flurry of excitement and a lot of preparations for his visit. This included adhering to the dress code fit to receive British royalty, where women were to put on traditional dress or uniform or smart dresses with hats or business suits, and men were to put on suit and tie or uniform. It was very unusual for people in Uganda to put on formal hats, so I turned to my mother to help me look for one. We eventually landed on a woman from Madagascar who was selling beautiful straw hats in a boutique in Kampala, and once I found the hat, I selected the outfit to go with it, a brown and orange floral skirt and beige top for the occasion.

A few days before Prince Philip's visit, we did some work in the park taking samples from buffalo. We almost got trampled on by an angry lone bull; however, this was nowhere near as nerve-racking as hosting royalty.

On the big day we put up a huge sign welcoming Prince Philip and all stood impatiently and nervously waiting for the Duke to arrive while sipping fresh lemonade juice. We finally saw a flight land at the Kasese airstrip and then twenty minutes later, a car driving very fast toward Kikorongo. Finally, he exited the car dressed more casually than all of us. He wore well-worn shoes, much to the amazement of his hosts, and appeared to be very relaxed and happy to be back in the bush. I was honored to sit between Prince Philip and the Minister of State for Tourism, Hon. Serapio Rukundo. Also seated at the table were other key officials from the Uganda government, UWA Executive Director Moses Mapesa, UWA Board Chair Andrew Kasirye, and Lily Ajarova, heading the Ngamba Chimpanzee Sanctuary. Sitting on the other side of the Duke was the British High Commissioner's wife, Elaine Gordon, who took a lead in planning the whole visit. When the Duke pulled the chair for me to sit, it was a great honor that I almost declined because it is unheard of in my Buganda culture where women are supposed to kneel to the king.

Prince Philip talked to me about how when he was the President of World Wide Fund for Nature (WWF) for many years, they introduced sport hunting to benefit the local communities who would receive a revenue share from every animal that was hunted and asked me if we allowed sport hunting in Uganda. I told him that it was being tested in wildlife reserves that had little or no tourism. He also asked me how the local communities of Queen Elizabeth National Park would benefit from our telecommunications project. I explained how we had hired two young women from the local community to work at the telecentre, which we hoped would improve the relationship between the community and the park. I spent so much time talking to him during the one hour that I hardly had a moment to enjoy the delicious lunch, which, to his credit, he observed and apologized for making me talk too much to eat.

After lunch, the next stop was the telecentre itself, where Lawrence presented the project to the Duke before he sent the first symbolic email, which he simply signed as "Philip." He walked past a line of awed people. These included the staff from UWA and CTPH, three-year-old Ndhego, leaders from Kasese District, and Mzee Eliphaz, the local opinion leader who first stopped me from taking samples from cattle in his community. A representative from Microsoft attended. This led them to donate a motorcycle to promote the roving telecentre concept of taking laptops on a bike to the local communities to surf the internet as an innovative way to bridge the digital divide in the hardest-to-reach areas. The Duke cut a ribbon and officially launched the telecentre before being whisked off to his next event. He was driven on the legendary crater drive, a route he had taken over fifty years earlier with his wife, the newly anointed Queen Elizabeth.

The Duke had seen the park in its infancy and now could see the positive additions that were taking place to uplift the lives of the community.

Two years later, in November 2009, Lawrence was particularly excited to host the inventor of the World Wide Web, Sir Tim Berners-Lee, whom he took to visit the Queen Elizabeth telecentre and track the mountain gorillas in Bwindi Impenetrable National Park.

The two telecentres at Bwindi and Queen Elizabeth National Park were able to train over 300 people from the local communities in basic computer skills and the QENP center was managed by Stella Mboneko from the Basongora pastoralist community.[13] On top of enabling the local communities to earn a living through the internet and learn about other initiatives in the outside world that they could apply to their lives, the telecentres greatly improved the relationship between the communities and the national parks.

Chapter 18

Embracing Family Planning

So much work had been done to establish Conservation Through Public Health, but I knew it was only just the beginning of the journey to build a model that could change the world. On a flight, I met a woman who told me about an organization called Ashoka, which focuses on supporting individuals and not organizations, and nurtures leading social entrepreneurs with systems-changing ideas. To become an Ashoka fellow you must show creativity and an entrepreneurial spirit, and your new idea should have potential for great social impact. Another important criterion is having a strong ethical fiber. The woman, Irene Mutumba, had become an Ashoka fellow for her idea called the Private Education Development Network, that was transforming the Ugandan education system by teaching kids entrepreneurial skills at an early stage of their lives. Irene nominated me to become an Ashoka fellow for our One Health approach that she felt was transforming conservation practice in Uganda. Up to this point I had not considered myself an entrepreneur.

Though we were benefiting public health by bring health services to the last mile users around protected areas, the really big idea was a new approach to conservation by improving the health of people, animals, and the environment together. Several months after the Ashoka country director Debbie Serwadda and her program manager Abu Musuuza visited Bwindi to see for themselves, I became a fellow for merging Uganda's wildlife management and rural public health programs to create common resources for both people and animals. The fellowship came with a three-year stipend for me to focus on developing this new idea, and connections to additional funding and recognition. One such connection was with the PBS show *Frontline World* where Singeli Agnew filmed our One Health work to prevent and control Tuberculosis.

I was pleased with how the CBDOTS program was going. Not only were we achieving recognition, but the number of people being referred and treated for tuberculosis was increasing every day, and the community was embracing our new approach to conservation. Having seen the success of this project, in 2006, the new USAID Population Officer, Heather d'Agnes, asked us to add family planning to the CBDOTS model and perhaps get the same volunteers who were watching people take medication to be the same ones who we trained to encourage their community to adopt family planning as well as distribute contraceptives to those who wanted them.

To incorporate family planning into the CBDOTS model, Heather asked us to focus on one target group, either women, men, teenagers or couples. I looked around me and with Vaster as my main frame of reference, saw that most teenage girls were unfortunately married off by the age of fifteen after getting pregnant. I also soon realized that men and women were not openly talking to each other about family planning and the use of contraceptives. My gut feeling was to focus on couples.

USAID could not directly give CTPH funding because the administrative requirements were too arduous for a small start-up nonprofit. So, they provided funding to us through an organization based in

Washington, DC: Camp, Dresser and McKee International. This organization also provided valuable advice on managing the project and more importantly allowed us to be creative and develop an impactful program to improve access to family planning and healthcare.

I did not have much information about how the community felt about family planning and requested Mbarara University to send us some students to conduct a needs assessment for family planning around Bwindi. They camped at the Kayonza government health center for two weeks and had separate focus group discussions with men and women, and also went to churches to talk about family planning. Though we wanted an independent assessment, I had the privilege to attend one of the sessions, and was extremely impressed with how these young medical and nursing students were engaging the local communities and getting them to express their feelings about what turned out to be a highly controversial subject not only in Uganda, but also in the United States, where the funding had come from.

The lack of family planning meant that women did not have control over their bodies. Many of them did not want to have a baby every year but were resigned to their fate. The majority of the women did not have the support from their husbands and when it was time to get a new supply of contraceptives, they would lie to their husbands that they are going to the market and then would secretly go to the health center to either get an injection or pills. Whenever their husbands found out that they were taking the pill, they would throw the pills in the pit latrines. Worse still, if they managed to successfully hide the fact that they were taking birth control, their husbands would beat them up for not getting pregnant.

To avoid this cycle of domestic violence, we decided that it was best to engage couples through peer education and get both husband and wife to see the benefits of jointly planning for the number of children that they were able to manage. What resonated most with the men was being able to reduce poverty in their homes through balancing the family budget. Women embraced birth control because it gave them more control over their bodies, freeing them up to do something else with their lives in between having babies, such as starting a business.

Some churches still preached the message in the Bible that God said "go forth and multiply the earth." However, I strongly believed that the earth's resources could not sustain this type of population growth. There was simply not enough to meet the needs of all the children who women did not plan to have, and God did not intend for people to suffer and starve. This is how we got the religious leaders to modify the message to their congregation, over whom they exerted great influence. The students discovered that the Bwindi community had many myths and misconceptions about birth control. Some of them thought that if you took it, you would never have a baby again, while others firmly believed that your womb would rot.

We called for meetings with the local community leaders to introduce this new program. Just like the CBDOTS program, we talked about what we would like to do and asked them what they thought about the same volunteers looking after TB patients to be the ones who distribute contraceptives. They were excited about this new program, but preferred that the benefits should be spread more evenly by selecting one person from each village to be the volunteer reaching everyone in their village. I was once again humbled by their wisdom to identify what worked best for their community. We asked them to select that person from each village who should be trustworthy and could read and write because they needed to be able to collect data to determine if the program was making a difference. At that meeting they jointly selected the volunteers, enabling us to begin with twenty-two community conservation health workers from twenty-two villages in two parishes with intense conflict between people and gorillas. We selected two more people from each parish to supervise them, making a total of twenty-six. I did not think much about it at the time, that having women as half of our volunteers was enabling us to achieve something bigger, reducing gender disparities. Over time an unintended benefit of this PHE program was that among our volunteers, men became more engaged in healthcare and family planning, and women became leaders in their community promoting conservation and better management of natural resources, breaking societal norms, and having a longer-lasting impact.

It was a delight to work with captive chimpanzees at the Entebbe Zoo as part of my working holidays from university. These orphaned chimpanzees were victims of the bushmeat trade and enjoyed being cuddled because they were still missing their mothers. *Photo courtesy of Gladys Kalema-Zikusoka*

Four years later I was overjoyed to begin my journey as a wildlife veterinarian after graduating from the Royal Veterinary College, University of London. *Photo courtesy of Gladys Kalema-Zikusoka*

Lawrence hid this surprise from me on our wedding day. He played "Malaika," a popular love ballad meaning "My Angel" in Swahili, on his saxophone as a duet with the leader of Uganda's legendary Afrigo Band, Moses Matovu. *Photo courtesy of the Kalema family*

A few days later I prepared my first official meal as a married woman to over fifty guests at his grandparents' home in Kampala. It was a lighthearted moment when I followed my tradition and knelt down to greet him with our host, grandmother Anita Katiti Zikusoka. *Photo courtesy of the Zikusoka family*

I was too young to remember this photo taken with all my family at our home in Kampala. I was being carried by our eldest sibling, my sister Betty Nakalema. Peter Martin was on the right of my father, Apollo Katerega in front of him, and Betty was next to him. William Kalema Jr. was to the left of my mother, at forty-one, and Veronica Nakibule in front of her. *Photo courtesy of the Kalema family*

Thirty years later, my sister Veronica Nakibule was my matron of honor when we had my traditional wedding ceremony at our ancestral home in Kiboga, putting on gomesi, a Buganda ceremonial dress. *Photo courtesy of the Kalema family*

The mud hut in which I lived my first time in Bwindi, studying parasites and bacteria in the mountain gorillas. I was too sick in this photo to risk approaching and infecting the gorillas. I had no idea then, that three years later, I'd be in a TV documentary called *Gladys, the African Vet,* shown below with producer Jane-Marie Franklyn. *Photos courtesy of Gladys Kalema-Zikusoka*

Initiating the translocation of endangered species was a major highlight of my career as Uganda's first wildlife vet. We moved elephants, assisted by the local community, from Mubende to the safety of Queen Elizabeth National Park. Supported by the team from Kenya Wildlife Service, we moved giraffes from Lake Nakuru National Park in Kenya to restock Kidepo Valley National Park in Uganda. The giraffes were driven to Eldoret airport before being flown to Kidepo airstrip in a military Hercules cargo aircraft. *Photos courtesy of Gladys Kalema-Zikusoka*

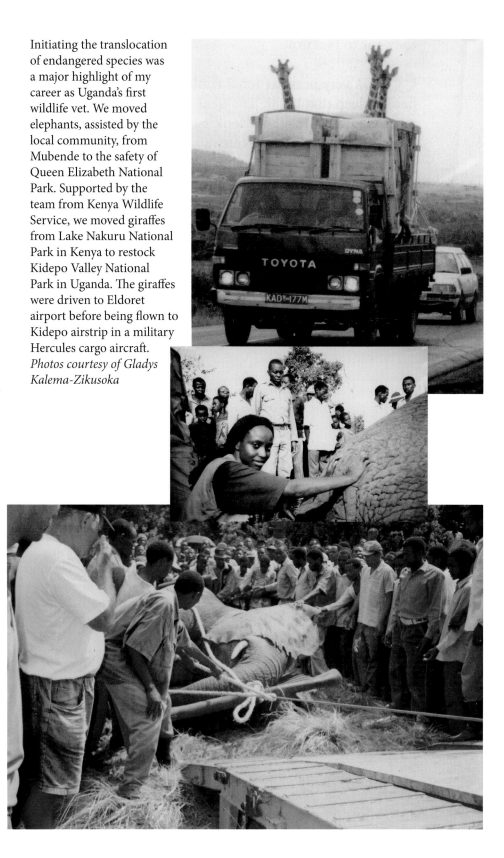

This newspaper clipping features the headline "Akamegga Enjovu Kenkanawa," meaning "How small is the one who brings an elephant down," a Luganda proverb about a rat that brought an elephant down by going up its trunk, and thus compared it to our elephant translocation. *Photo courtesy of Gladys Kalema-Zikusoka*

We tested buffalo for diseases they could be sharing with cattle grazing in and around Queen Elizabeth National Park, some of which could be passed on to people. After I darted the buffalo, we monitored him with UWA warden and veterinarian Dr. Margaret Driciru and veterinary intern Dr. Keren Kyabagye. Kityo held the buffalo's head with UWA research assistant Peter Achoroi, who tagged each buffalo. CTPH chief vet technician Stephen Rubanga collected ticks and blood from the buffalo. *Photo by Conservation Through Public Health*

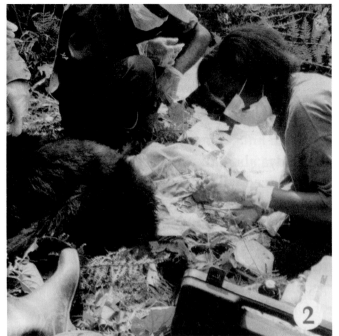

I successfully performed surgery on Kahara, a six-year-old mountain gorilla with a life-threatening rectal prolapse, assisted by the rangers we had trained who ably monitored her breathing during the operation. *Photo courtesy of Gladys Kalema-Zikusoka*

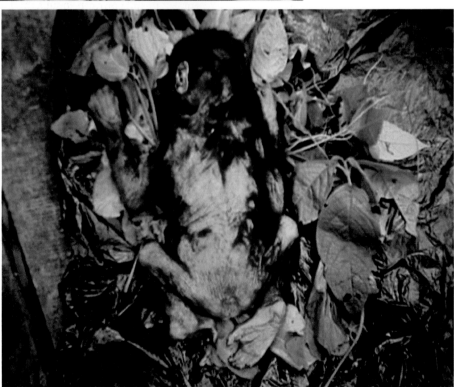

Sadly, we were not able to save the life of Ruhara, an eight-month-old infant gorilla. His body was still crawling with scabies mites when we conducted the necropsy. Luckily, we were able to save the rest of his family with one dose of Ivermectin, which cleared all the parasites in their bodies. *Photo courtesy of Gladys Kalema-Zikusoka*

I found that engaging children in theater got them to appreciate gorillas and understand why they need to be protected. We got Rutendere Health Promoters to perform a play at Kyeshero Primary School. *Photo by Conservation Through Public Health*

When we launched CTPH programs at Bwindi, children from the Bwindi Orphans School performed the "Gorilla Dance" in front of HRH Queen Sylvia of Buganda and one thousand guests, who were greatly amused and impressed. *Photo by Conservation Through Public Health*

An adult female gorilla in Binyindo gorilla group bonding while breastfeeding her two-year-old baby. Mountain gorillas start to wean their infants at the age of three and then conceive. This natural birth spacing of four and a half years is ideal because the new baby is born when the elder sibling can make their own night nest and help mum to babysit. *Photo by Taylor Steinberg*

Nyampazi's baby is riding on his mother's back. Nyampazi is from the Mubare gorilla group and was given this name because she loves eating ants. *Photo by Ryoma Otsuka*

Binyindo, the lead silverback of Binyindo gorilla group that broke off from Habinyanja gorilla group, was given this name because of the cut in his nose. He now has a cataract in his right eye. But it is not preventing him from leading a normal life and heading a family. *Photo by Taylor Steinberg*

We visited Village Health and Conservation team member Flora Kyomukama with our boys. Ndhego wore a mask that had been made by her Batwa community. The Batwa were evicted from the forest in 1991 when Bwindi became a national park and gorilla tourism began. *Photo by Jo-Anne McArthur/We Animals Media*

Kavuyo from Habinyanja gorilla group when he was a young adult male blackback. Kavuyo means "chaotic and daring." This photo was taken during heavy rain in Bwindi Impenetrable National Park and he just sat still and stared at us. *Photo by Jo-Anne McArthur/We Animals Media*

Mother Kanyindo with a dent in her nose bonding with her infant, Rushokye, from the Rushegura gorilla group. *Photo by Ryoma Otsuka*

We translocated two seven-week-old orphan cheetahs from Pian Upe Wildlife Reserve to the Uganda Wildlife Education Centre, formerly Entebbe Zoo. My sons Tendo and Ndhego joined us. Within a few weeks the cheetahs had changed from skinny cubs to round balls of fur. *Photos by Conservation Through Public Health*

After one year, they had almost grown to adult size and it was a delight to check on Pian and his sister, Upe. *Photo by Jo-Anne McArthur/We Animals Media*

After winning the Whitley Gold Award in 2009, I was elated to introduce my mother, sister and two-month-old Tendo to HRH Princess Anne, who handed me the award. *Photo by Whitley Fund for Nature*

It was a proud moment to receive the Golden Jubilee Award from His Excellency President Museveni of Uganda on International Women's Day in 2017 for my work as a veterinarian and conservationist. *Photo by Abu Mwesigwa*

A habituated mountain gorilla foraging on banana stems and fruit in community land outside Bwindi Impenetrable National Park. When gorillas lose their fear of humans, they are more likely to leave the safety of the national park, putting them at greater risk of acquiring diseases from people and getting injured. *Photo by Emmy Gongo*

Rafiki, the former lead silverback of Nkuringo gorilla group. Rafiki means "friendly" in Swahili. His group was the first to be habituated for tourism in the southern sector of Bwindi. He was tragically killed by a hungry bushmeat poacher who speared Rafiki while hunting bush pigs in the forest during the COVID-19 pandemic. *Photo by Uganda Wildlife Authority*

We hiked up a steep hill through Nyamishamba village adjacent to Bwindi Impenetrable National Park to check on Habinyanja gorilla group. I was happy that they were all looking healthy. However, during the visit it started raining heavily and when the rain subsided, I collected fecal samples from their night nests, which thankfully all looked normal. *Photos by Jo-Anne McArthur/We Animals Media*

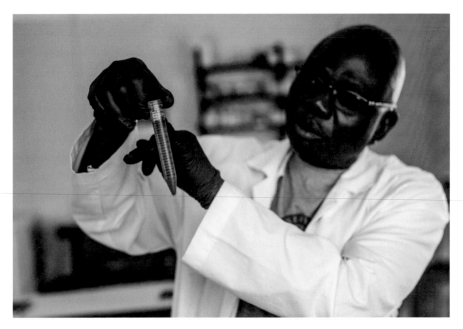

CTPH co-founder Stephen Rubanga checked the fecal samples we collected from the gorillas for parasites, and also preserved them in RNA later to test for viruses such as SARS-COV-2 which causes COVID-19. *Photo by Jo-Anne McArthur/We Animals Media*

During the COVID-19 pandemic, CTPH led a team of conservation NGOs to successfully advocate to Uganda Wildlife Authority for mask-wearing to become mandatory for anyone coming within ten meters of the endangered mountain gorillas. We trained the park rangers to enforce these rules. In this photo we were checking on Rushegura gorilla group in Bwindi Impenetrable National Park a few weeks before primate tourism reopened. *Photo courtesy of Conservation Through Public Health*

These are the lucky students who graduated in front of Royalty. HRH Queen Sylvia of Buganda handed them certificates in basic computer skills from Makerere University, Department of Women and Gender Studies. Lawrence and I joined the photo. *Photo courtesy of Conservation Through Public Health*

While launching the telecentre at Queen Elizabeth National Park, Lawrence explained to HRH the Duke of Edinburgh how bringing technology to the local communities was going to change their attitudes to conservation, and asked him to send the first email. *Photo by Conservation Through Public Health*

Alfonse, the senior traditional healer and his wife, Village Health and Conservation team member Miriam Bufumbo (below), live in Mukono village adjacent to Bwindi Impenetrable National Park where Mubare and Rushegura gorilla groups often range. Miriam is presenting a flip chart that she uses when she visits homes in her village to encourage families to have the number of children they can afford to keep healthy and send to school. This makes families less dependent on the forest for food and fuel wood. *Photos by Jo-Anne McArthur/We Animals Media*

Hope Karire from Mpungu subcounty in her "Ready to Grow" garden tending cabbages that we provided to reduce hunger and poaching in the vulnerable Bwindi local communities during the pandemic. *Photo courtesy of Conservation Through Public Health*

The first time we wore masks to visit the mountain gorillas in Bwindi when the COVID-19 pandemic began. I held a practical training session with ranger guide Goreth Nyibiza and her team who took us to Mubare gorilla group that day. *Photo courtesy of Conservation Through Public Health*

I visited Village Health and Conservation Team (VHCT) member Rehema Asiimwe at her home and found three other VHCTs, Oliva Kesande, Jane Orikiriza and Jeninah Tugabirwe who we had a meeting with. We talked about the progress they are making and challenges they are facing in providing contraceptive injections and getting people to adopt good health and conservation practices and protect the mountain gorillas. *Photo courtesy of Conservation Through Public Health*

VHCT Hope Matsiko administers contraceptive injections to women in the comfort of her home. Injectable contraceptives like Depo-Provera and Sayana Press are the most popular among the Bwindi local community. I was excited when this FHI360 research project CTPH participated in led to a national policy allowing community health workers to give contraceptive injections. This accelerated voluntary adoption of family planning in the women at Bwindi. *Photo courtesy of Conservation Through Public Health*

I took my mother to visit the mountain gorillas for the first time in 2000. She wore a skirt and the local women warmed up to her. My mother was thrilled to meet the gentle vegetarian giants and so was Auntie Rita Kiwana (not pictured) who joined us for this historical trek. *Photo courtesy of Gladys Kalema-Zikusoka*

Nurturing the next generation, with our boys Ndhego and Tendo, outside our Gorilla Health and Community Conservation Centre with a panoramic view of the top of Bwindi Impenetrable National Park, spanning 321 square kilometers (124 square miles). *Photo by Jo-Anne McArthur/We Animals Media*

It was a joyous day and momentous occasion when we celebrated ten years of Conservation Through Public Health. The guest of honor was CTPH patron HRH Queen Sylvia of Buganda. We cut the cake with her daughter Princess Sanga, and CTPH board chairperson, Irene Mutumba. The cake was generously provided by Sheraton Hotel. *Photo courtesy of Conservation Through Public Health*

The UK ten-year anniversary celebration resulted in the building of the Gorilla Health and Community Conservation Centre with generous support from Tusk Trust. In this photo, we are holding a training workshop with the Gorilla Guardians on gorilla health monitoring and preventing COVID among people and between people and gorillas. *Photo by UNEP/Kibuuka Mukisa*

I joined our lead farmers to sort coffee at one of their beautiful farms in Mpungu village bordering Bwindi Impenetrable National Park. After having harvested the coffee, we watched them floating it; the coffee that sank was pulped to remove the outer coat, and then sorted on the drying rack to create parchment. *Photo by Jo-Anne McArthur/We Animals Media*

(Above) I helped the farmers to selectively harvest ripe red coffee berries to produce premium and specialty coffee that we bought from them at an above-market price. *Photo by Sarah Marshall*

(Below) I named our first coffee (100% Arabica) brand after one of my favorite gorillas, Kanyonyi, the former lead silverback of Mubare gorilla group, who I knew since he was a baby. *Photo by Conservation Through Public Health*

(Right) We started the Gorilla Conservation Café in Entebbe, Uganda's first conservation café to build a brand community around saving gorillas one sip at a time. *Photo by Gorilla Conservation Coffee*

We hired an experienced nurse who was also a midwife, Sylvia Nandago, to head the program. We designed forms for community conservation health workers to record the number of homes they visited and women and men they referred to local health centers to obtain a method of family planning, as well as recording what contraceptive method they took up. In the first year the number of new users of contraceptives increased from 35 to 145, and in the second year another 147 new users signed on. However, we found out that though women preferred the injection because they only needed to excuse themselves from home once every three months and sneak to the local health centers to receive it on market day, they would find overworked nurses and midwives dealing with very sick children and would often go home without getting the contraceptive and then conceive. This prompted us to approach Family Health International (FHI360), an organization piloting a program where voluntary health workers delivered the injections every three months, and CTPH became their fifth partner, to train the community conservation health volunteers to give community-based Depo-Provera injections in the comfort of the volunteer's home. This led to the number of family planning users doubling to 350 in the third year. It was a major breakthrough and became a national policy in Uganda, which was expanded to other countries in Africa.

One of my most heartwarming testimonies was a woman who owned a shop and had three girls and once our program was introduced to her she decided to stop looking for a boy to be an heir, and concentrate on educating the girls instead. This was helping to ensure a bright future for her children, and she went on to teach others in her community about family planning as a means of breaking the cycle of poverty.

Convincing communities to change their behavior around the sensitive issue of family planning and conservation wasn't easy, but by developing innovative approaches, we were able to get the message through. One approach we took was by working with Ashoka Fellow Craig Esbeck, Founder of Mango Tree Enterprise, who developed affordable and easily obtainable teaching aids—flip charts made out of sisal, a local material. We collaborated on creating a set of visual aids to educate communities with an integrated health and conservation message that started off with two families—one with positive impact on the gorillas and their habitat and one with negative impacts—based on the number of children they had, which also had an impact on the health of their families. This type of communication tool has proved really effective in changing behavior not only in Uganda but also in other developing countries. What became clear in all of this is that through our knowledge of the culture and the help of the local community, we were able to develop an effective tool that worked. So often, conservation planning does not involve local community members who are aware of what will work and what will not.

We collected data measuring how many people were changing behaviors and attitudes as a result of the flip chart. We also measured the number of people identified and referred for scabies, which had affected the gorillas, as well as other common and potentially zoonotic health conditions including tuberculosis and HIV/AIDS.

One day at a meeting in the Kanungu district health office, we told them how impressed we were that the volunteers were visiting homes including those that were hard to reach at the edge of the park boundary. Dr. Ssebudde and the senior public health nurse, Florence Rwabihunga, asked us if the communities' homes were becoming more hygienic as a result of these visits, and I didn't know the answer. I realized we needed to find a way to measure those changes as well.

With a grant from the Whitley Fund for Nature (WFN) we designed and implemented a plan to improve community hygiene and raise awareness of contamination by educating people about building latrines at their homes and keeping them clean with installed hand washing stations. When my WFN grant application was in its finalist stage, I was invited to London with my family to meet the jury. I could not believe it when I won the Whitley Gold Award, the green Oscars for outstanding leadership in nature conservation, which was given to me by Her Royal Highness Princess Anne, in the presence of over three hundred conservationists and my family. Sir Edward Whitley mentioned that I had brought the oldest and youngest people to the ceremony including my mother of eighty years old, and my second son, Tendo, who was just two months old, along with his playful four-year-old brother Ndhego. Winning the Whitley Gold Award for our new approach to conservation keeping gorillas healthy by improving the health of people was a huge validation for CTPH. Healthy gorillas enabled tourism to thrive, and the benefits were shared with the local communities giving them an economic incentive to protect the gorillas. We received a lot of media attention including the BBC's *Excess Baggage* and the *Guardian* in the UK, and the *New Vision*, as well as endorsements back home, where I received a congratulations letter from the minister of foreign affairs, Hon. Tugume, and a congratulations message from the Uganda Wildlife Authority executive director, Moses Mapesa.

The Whitley Gold Award provided two years' funding of £60,000 to improve the health of the people, gorillas, and their environment so that when gorillas forage in their gardens, they found cleaner homes with no dirty clothing on scarecrows, no open defecation, and no uncovered rubbish heaps.

Within one year the proportion of pit latrines with handwashing facilities had tripled from 10 percent to 30 percent. I was also excited that the number of people referred for tuberculosis testing had increased eleven-fold. The same program was initiated in the second year of funding from the Whitley Gold Award to neighboring DRC to improve homes around Virunga National Park, where mountain gorillas are found in the Mikeno sector and eastern lowland gorillas are found in the Mount Tshiabirimu sector.

When we introduced the village health and conservation volunteer model to the minority Batwa hunter-gatherers, they also embraced the family planning program. We called them VHCTs (Village Health and Conservation Teams). When the Bwindi chief warden, Pontious Ezuma, expressed his doubts as to whether the Batwa also needed to adopt family planning because their ethnic group is so few in number, Flora Kyomukama, the first Batwa VHCT, said "family planning is important to me because I only want to have the number of children that I can manage to provide for." Flora continued to become a role model in her community when she successfully encouraged them to acquire handwashing stations, particularly important because the Batwa had the poorest hygiene, leading to a higher rate of infectious diseases. When CTPH Community Health and Conservation Field Officer Alex Ngabirano conducted a survey in one hundred homes of the Batwa, he found a handwashing station at only one of them. In one of the Batwa settlements Alex was shocked to find children who had been sent home from school because they had scabies. This settlement was bordering the park and sometimes visited by the mountain gorillas. We recruited fourteen Batwa VHCTs to improve the hygiene, health, and well-being of people in their settlements.

Within the first year, the newly recruited community conservation health volunteers requested livestock so that they could earn an income to sustain their volunteer efforts. Camp Dresser and McKee International agreed for us to reallocate some of the funding for workshops into buying livestock for sustainability. Stephen, having worked for the Ministry of Agriculture, Animal Industry and Fisheries (MAAIF) for over twenty years before joining CTPH, had experience in distributing livestock to rural populations and strongly advised against giving individual animals to each person because depending on how good they were at rearing animals the benefits would not last long. It was better to give them to the communities as a group activity that brought them all together. Mukono parish volunteers requested goats, and Bujengwe parish volunteers requested cows. Among them, two people in each parish volunteered to keep animals in their land, and then when they gave birth, they would give the offspring to another volunteer until they all received an animal. Running alongside our program were also Village Saving and Loan Associations (VSLAs) introduced by CARE (Cooperative for American Relief Everywhere) through the Bwindi Mgahinga Conservation Trust (BMCT). The initiative encouraged villages to save money, and as a result of the livestock program CTPH had introduced, the volunteers found that they were now in a position to put money aside. We were very excited that the community volunteers had built upon what we had started with them. This has been such a huge success and for the next decade no volunteers dropped out because the money they earned from the livestock supported them when our funding ran out.

The finance system devised to keep records and share funds propelled us to receive more awards and funding. When invited to show a potential donor the system, Sam Rugaba, a VHCT leader, proudly pointed to a small black metal box with three locks that had the money. It was designed so that three people had to be present to access the funds and records. When the two other VSLA members came with their keys, they opened the box and explained how it all worked, while Sam showed us the records. This really warmed my heart.

This innovation led CTPH to win the 2012 Global Development Network Japanese Award for Most Innovative Development Project. It was the first time a Ugandan organization had ever won this award. The award came with funding of $30,000, which enabled us to expand the Village Health and Conservation Team and Village Saving and Loans Association model to other parishes around Bwindi— Nteko and Rubuguri—with high human and gorilla conflict, where we worked with their most active village health teams volunteer from each village. Winning the award also meant that we could apply for additional funding of $200,000 from the Japanese Social Development Fund to expand our model.

While attending a thirty-year celebration for Ashoka in France, I received the tragic news that Mizano, a playful blackback in the Habinyanja gorilla group was missing and suspected to be dead. I called Stephen to go and investigate and together with a CTPH veterinarian, Dr. Hameed Katerega, they walked seventeen kilometers inside the forest and found the lifeless body of the ten-year-old adult male gorilla. They conducted a postmortem that revealed that a spear went through the right side of his shoulder and punctured his lungs, leading to hemorrhage and a painful death. It was shocking news and a sad day for conservation, because I had assumed that all the communities around Bwindi had received so many benefits from conservation that they would not think of harming the gorillas, but I was wrong. A poacher had entered the park to hunt duikers and Mizano got into a fight with the man's hunting dog, which led him to spear the gorilla several times until he died. The Bwindi park management worked with the police, whose dogs traced the blood of the bleeding dog from the scene of the crime to the home of the poacher. He was arrested and put into a local jail and released after two weeks with a fine of just $20. This outraged everyone, including our VHCTs who first told me about the verdict, questioning why he was given such a small sentence after committing such a severe crime. I was so upset I found myself writing to the UWA executive director, Dr. Andrew Seguya, complaining about this outcome.

What stunned me was that this poacher had received a goat from UWA a few years ago, but when the gorilla got into a fight with his hunting dog, his gratitude for the goat didn't stop him from killing Mizano. This took me back to Stephen's valuable advice not to give individual livestock to community members, but instead develop a project around them so that they had a viable livestock enterprise that brought them together with others and reminded them why they had received the livestock and helped to improve their attitudes to conservation. In spite of this great tragedy, I was particularly encouraged that it was the VHCTs who told me about Mizano, which meant that our One Health approach was making communities care more about the gorillas, and ultimately changing their attitudes to conservation. A few years later, with support from National Geographic Society, we set up a VHCT network in Mpungu parish, where this poacher came from.

One of the results of the broad outrage is that UWA began to intensively engage the local magistrates, including bringing them to visit the gorillas at Bwindi, which helped them to understand the value of wildlife, in time for another similar tragedy that happened nine years later.

Meanwhile, our PHE program contributed to the number of women using modern contraceptives increasing from 22 percent to 67 percent within ten years, higher than the national average for rural areas, which increased from 30 percent to 45 percent. Twelve years later, the community-based Depo-Provera program is still going strong. I became emotional when a former staff member with Family Health International, Leonard Bufumbo, told me that he often talks about this pilot project as an example of a sustainable project with long-lasting impact. I am also particularly pleased that gorillas are falling sick less often and have not had another scabies outbreak, possibly because there was an improvement in the hygiene of their human neighbors, which we are measuring by the increase in homes acquiring handwashing facilities, that started at 10 percent and went up as high as 75 percent in the most frequently visited households. There has been a reduction in human and gorilla conflict because VHCTs report homes visited by gorillas and other wildlife, leading to a faster response from the Human and Gorilla Conflict Resolution (HUGO) teams of Gorilla Guardians.

Chapter 19

Farewell to Mubare's Legendary Silverback

For me as a scientist and a conservationist, numbers and statistics had been crucial in monitoring the mountain gorillas and their neighboring human community. However, there are times when stories about individual gorillas are more impactful than data. When I first started working with mountain gorillas in 1994, one year after tourism began at Bwindi, there were only two gorilla groups habituated for tourism, Mubare and Katendegyere. The Mubare gorilla group was headed by Ruhondeza, a middle-aged silverback, who stopped charging or running away from people at a distance of five meters. Ruhondeza, named because he liked "sleeping a lot," soon became one of the most well-known gorillas in Bwindi Impenetrable Forest. His accommodating nature enabled gorilla tourism to begin in Uganda, which helped to lift people out of poverty. Though Ruhondeza was smaller than the other silverbacks, he had the largest number of adult female gorillas, as many as six, to himself and was calmer and therefore easier to habituate than the Katendegyere gorilla group that had only one female and many big males. Because Ruhondeza managed to attract several females from other groups, along with their infants and juveniles and a few adult males, his group was calm and stayed together. Twenty years later, the number of gorilla groups habituated for tourism grew from two to seventeen, and Ruhondeza's group began reducing in size as he got older and weaker. The younger and bigger silverback gorillas fought with him and female gorillas transferred to their groups because females gravitate to a stronger silverback for protection even at the risk of losing their infants.[14]

In 2012, I received a call that Ruhondeza was no longer keeping up with his group, which was down to five individuals, and he was spending more time in community gardens. Knowing how old he was, and having seen the same thing happening to Mugurusi the former silverback of Katendegyere, who also became too old, and eventually could not keep up with the rest of his group, I suspected the worst for our legend. The chief warden asked me to check on him and advise them. They were uncomfortable with him staying in community land and were prepared to have him translocated back to the park. The park ranger took us to check on him, and we moved with darting equipment just in case we had to take him back to the park. That day I set off at 8 a.m. with Lawrence and Stephen and CTPH community health coordinator Joseph Byonanebye.

We drove five kilometers from the park office to Kyumbugushu village and then got out of the car and walked for thirty minutes until we came across women and children digging in the fields. We asked them if they had seen a silverback gorilla and they pointed in the direction where they had spotted him. Ten minutes later we asked another community member until finally like magic, we got to Ruhondeza. It is easier to track a group of gorillas because they leave a huge trail of damaged vegetation, so I was relieved when we found him with help from the community.

He was hiding away from the sun behind a shrub and eating leaves. Though he was lethargic and weak, he appeared to be very calm and settled. He seemed to blend in with the people around him, the kids who were running around and looking curiously at us, and the owners of the land who were digging nearby. I thought of what it takes to translocate a gorilla, and wondered how Ruhondeza would cope in his weakened state. I also feared that if we finally successfully got him back in the park, he would only return to the community a few days later, where he would not be competing with other stronger younger males for territory. It dawned on me that he felt safer being in the community of humans than with other gorillas in his forest home. I asked the community if they had seen Ruhondeza eating banana plants, and they confessed that he sometimes ate bananas and the stem of a plant, and even a few coffee berries. I asked them if they minded him being there and they said that he was not threatening and the damage to their crops was very small. I turned to my team and asked them what they thought, and they all expressed surprise at how comfortable the gorilla was in the Bwindi local community. I sadly accepted that Ruhondeza did not have long to live and it was probably best not to attempt to translocate him back to the park.

We had a meeting with our Village Health and Conservation Team of local volunteers. Their task was to encourage their communities to tolerate Ruhondeza in the village—particularly since his calm and accommodating nature had enabled gorilla tourism to begin in 1993, changing the lives and future for many people in the Bwindi community forever. In the meeting Sam Rugaba assured us that when their own elders become very weak, they look after them, so why should this not apply to Ruhondeza as well? All the other VHCTs nodded in agreement, and I felt assured that he would be safe. I passed this information on to the chief warden, who took my advice.

Ruhondeza was accepted in the Bwindi community, where they tolerated him eating banana plants or the occasional coffee berry. When the fateful day came and his lifeless body was found in the community land, they called the park warden, who got his staff to carry the body to the park office. He was laid to rest in a grave near the office, and the Bwindi community members came to pay their last respects to a legend. Though I was very sad to lose Ruhondeza, estimated to be fifty years old when he died, I was glad that he spent his last days in a dignified manner being cared for by the local communities whose lives he had changed. Ruhondeza saw as many as fifty thousand human visitors in his lifetime. This act of kindness from the local communities and willingness to tolerate Ruhondeza signified how far conservation efforts have come in Bwindi, and that true friendship between people and wild animals is, indeed, possible.

To this day the Bwindi legend is remembered through the "Gorilla Our Friends for Ever" campaign, Ruhondeza village walk, and other community experiences and also through his son, Kanyonyi, who took over the Mubare Gorilla Group after he died. When we started to engage smallholder farmers around Bwindi Impenetrable National Park to market their coffee, I named the first brand of our Gorilla Conservation Coffee after Kanyonyi.

Chapter 20

Taking Our Message to the Children

Having made great progress with changing the behavior of adults, we turned to the youth and decided to focus on schools. After all, this is also how I first got engaged in conservation while reviving the wildlife club at Kibuli Secondary School, my high school in Uganda.

Lawrence connected with colleagues in upstate New York to develop a partnership between Bwindi Community Primary School and the Board of Cooperative Educational Services (BOCES) program to enrich the understanding of natural and social sciences through cross-cultural distance learning between primary school children at Bwindi and junior high school children in Rochester, New York.

Though these children lived in completely different worlds, they connected over the internet to learn about a different culture. The kids in New York got up early to join the virtual meetings at 8 a.m. while the kids in Bwindi stayed an hour later at school to connect at 4 p.m. I was amazed to hear the kids in Bwindi asking, "Do you work in the garden to maintain your crops before you go to school?" while the kids in America asked, "What is your favorite toy?" Although I understood both cultures, I was astonished at how different their realities were, and how bringing them together through the internet was helping to increase their understanding of conserving gorillas and other wildlife as well as helping them to develop empathy for one another.

The discussions were led by Tadge O'Brien, who Lawrence and I eventually met when I traveled to the United States to give a talk at Colgate University. He arranged for me to speak at all the schools taking part in the cross-cultural distance learning program.

In addition, I got to speak with children in the UK, who were just as excited, and several years later to children all over the world through an amazing virtual educational program called Exploring by the Seat of Your Pants, founded by National Geographic Explorer Joe Grabowski.

Teaching young people is where it all begins and my affiliation with Ashoka turned out to be a great opportunity for someone near and dear to the heart of CTPH. The Dalai Lama had partnered with Ashoka to launch a program to nurture qualities of compassion and empathy among emerging leaders between the ages of twenty and thirty-five. They would act as important changemakers to make the world a better place. Ashoka asked me to nominate someone on our staff who would best fit their criteria. I selected Joseph Byonanebye, who was passionate and fully committed to our CTPH mission. Often, on his own volition, he gave the staff motivational talks and really enjoyed working with the local community. Joseph was so happy to be given that opportunity, and came up with a project to adapt the Population Health and Environment (PHE) flip charts we had developed for adults for students in secondary school. This was a sensitive age for teenagers and the right time to start talking about sexual and reproductive health before it was too late, particularly in a community where girls commonly got pregnant and were married off at fifteen years old.

Joseph and David Matsiko, the Bwindi field office manager, targeted secondary schools, including Namiyaga Secondary School where David had studied and become a teacher before doing the telecentre course and joining CTPH. The integrated population, health, and environment (PHE) flip chart was adapted to include a story about the father being caught and arrested by the park rangers while poaching duikers in the national park. Some of these children's fathers and grandfathers were poachers and still entering the forest to hunt wild animals sharing a habitat with the mountain gorillas. When the Bwindi Impenetrable Forest was delineated as a national park in 1991, this traditional way of life was forbidden. Engaging children meant that they could influence their parents not to poach. I know I influenced my mother to become a conservationist when I revived the wildlife club at Kibuli Secondary School at the age of eighteen, and inspired her to fund the stickers I made. She has taken an interest in my work ever since.

Joseph eventually went to the United States to pursue a master's degree and later a PhD in public health with a focus on One Health at the University of Wisconsin–Madison, and still gives presentations on behalf of CTPH, as well as helping us to fundraise.

Through the Ashoka network, I also got to meet Trevor Dudley, an Ashoka Fellow who founded the Kampala Kids League, which teaches kids through sports. In order for a team to win, they also have to get the highest marks in the quiz. This highly innovative model was enabling many children in Uganda to grow holistically and relate to each other through the universal language of sports. Ashoka encourages their fellows to jointly implement projects. Trevor and his wife Anne, a dynamic couple from the UK, managed to get corporate sponsors for soccer tournaments, and some of the boys, who were often from disadvantaged families in Uganda, were spotted by scouts and got to play in the league clubs in the UK. It was their way out of poverty and inspired many children in Uganda to use their passion for sports to further themselves.

Soon, we connected with two young British men, Mark and Guy. Mark was Trevor and Anne's son. And Guy Hodgkinson was a nineteen-year-old interested in taking a gap year in Africa volunteering with an organization working with wildlife. We hosted Guy in Uganda the following year. He was a talented cricket player, and being highly self-motivated he jumped on the idea of helping us set up a kids' sports league at Bwindi. Together, Guy and Mark planned the project, and Guy got his parents to donate some money toward the league.

Working closely with our field office manager, David Matsiko, they launched the Impenetrable Kids League starting with Mukono Parish, an area with high human and gorilla conflict. One hundred and eighty pupils were selected from six schools in Mukono Parish. Each of the school teams was named after a primate that could be found in Bwindi Impenetrable Forest: Gorilla, Chimpanzee, Galago (bush baby), Baboon, Red-Tailed Monkey, and Black-and-White Colobus Monkey.

CTPH developed a conservation education curriculum and provided lessons to the participants, while the Kampala Kids League trained coaches, provided training materials and soccer balls, and oversaw the tournaments. Winning the game was dependent on winning the quiz and the game. Three teachers from each school were trained to support the kids. The boys played soccer, and the girls played netball. I remember smiling one day when David told me that the girls had changed from netball to soccer. I was pleased that their confidence was growing to feel that they could do anything that the boys did. With funding from Disney Conservation Fund, we continued supporting the Impenetrable Kids League.

Our two sons, Ndhego and Tendo, grew up kicking a ball from the age of two because Lawrence loved soccer. He'd always wanted to be a professional soccer player, but his mother talked him out of it to take a more predictable career path. Lawrence taught the boys how to dribble, score, and control the ball, and Kizito, our housekeeper, taught them how to catch goals, having been the best goalie in his home village. The boys ended up being among the best in their class and excelled in tournaments. Their passion for soccer enabled them to bond with the children at Bwindi, who were naturally talented players, and they developed lifelong friendships. This opportunity to connect through sports helped Ndhego and Tendo to develop empathy for children who were less fortunate than them, which really warmed my heart. Knowing that empathy is one of the traits that Ashoka recognizes in changemakers, I am hopeful that they will change the world as they achieve their dreams.

Chapter 21

Celebrating Ten Years of Success

I couldn't quite believe that we had made it to a decade, having faced hardships and obstacles along the way. 2013 started off as a particularly difficult year, because in 2012 we were involved in activities that took us away from our core programs at Bwindi and resulted in CTPH doing less fundraising than in previous years, and we had run out of money.

But our ten-year anniversary was an opportunity to get back on track. Three separate celebrations were planned in Uganda, the US, and the UK. Marking a decade was a golden opportunity to shout out our achievements and attract urgently needed funding. I also felt that it was important to thank our friends, donors, partners, and stakeholders who had been with us during the first decade. We held the main event on August 7, 2013, at the CTPH offices in Entebbe with our patron, Her Royal Highness the Nnabagereka of Buganda, Queen Sylvia Nagginda, as the guest of honor. We'd had to sometimes use my husband's salary to fund CTPH work and, this time, Lawrence vehemently refused to use it for the ten-year celebration, and insisted we go back to the corporations we had approached when launching CTPH field programs and get them to support us, which they did!

I also saw this as an opportunity to educate the Ugandan public about the importance of using culture to promote conservation. Consequently, I decided to host the first part of the event at the Uganda Wildlife Education Centre (UWEC) which was also a zoo, housing animals that represented the symbolic clan animals, or totems, of Uganda, including elephants, lions, leopards, buffaloes, giraffes, otters, birds, black-and-white colobus and vervet monkeys.

Queen Sylvia (of the cane rat clan) and her daughter Princess Sanga petted the southern white rhinos, met Hamukungu the elephant, and opened a new Omusu or cane rat exhibit. Though the cane rat is a delicacy in most parts of Uganda, belonging to a clan prohibits you from killing or eating that species.

This was followed by a reception at the CTPH office. Over three hundred guests attended—friends and supporters of CTPH along with media who were attracted by the Queen's engagement in wildlife conservation. Sheraton Hotel Uganda catered the event, the Coca-Cola Company offered tents, and Ripples donated drinking water. I was particularly touched when our Ugandan landlady, Veronica Kayihura, donated $200 by discounting our rent.

It was a momentous and joyful occasion; people dressed in chimpanzee and gorilla outfits entertained the guests. The date coincided with our wedding anniversary, which resulted in a light-hearted moment when I scribbled something for Lawrence to refer to in his speech and he stated that after twelve years of marriage, he still couldn't read my writing. Looking around the room, I thanked all those who had climbed on board with us as we set off on this untrodden path: Stephen Rubanga, our third founder, our staff, volunteers, donors, partners, and our parents. The chart we created to commemorate our ten years had as many as one hundred organizations.

The Queen spoke passionately about the importance of culture when it came to conservation. She amused everyone when she said that she heard that the Omusu cane rat is very delicious, but of course being of the clan, she wasn't allowed to eat it. This was such an important message that emphasized that there would always be a group of people who would protect wildlife in the Buganda Kingdom.

Our second ten-year event was generously hosted in the United States by the Woodrow Wilson Center in Washington, DC, as a seminar held at the invitation of Meaghan Parker, who encouraged me to be open about the challenges, as well as our successes during the first decade.

The UK celebration included presentations at primary schools in Cookham and a BBC radio interview, and was crowned by an intimate reception for our donors and supporters held at the London residence of the Ambassador of Belgium.

During my speech I talked about the great need to build a permanent home for CTPH after ten years of testing our approach to conservation. Following the event, Charlie Mayhew contacted me to see if Tusk Trust could fund this new building.

We situated the new building on one of the highest points, with panoramic views of the top of Bwindi Impenetrable Forest, and named it the "Gorilla Health and Community Conservation Centre." We built the center with the same lightweight volcanic rock that derives from Kisoro, giving it a rich character and amplifying the ecofriendly design concept.

As the building took shape, I thought about how lucky I was to have the best office view in the whole world, where on a clear day you could see the Nkuringo sector of Bwindi at the end of the 321-square-kilometer impenetrable forest in the southern part of the national park. Sometimes you would hear chimpanzees and black-and-white colobus monkeys. However, the most common wild visitors were the baboons, who unashamedly fought loudly among themselves in the garden. One was even caught smashing the glass door of our center, which we had to replace with a wooden door.

The center enabled us to develop research partnerships hosting university students from around the world. It was also a platform to educate local communities and tourists about our innovative approach to gorilla conservation and get a behind-the-scenes tour of how gorillas are protected.

And, it gave us renewed energy to host volunteers from around the world. High-end tour operators often brought their guests to learn about how we were protecting the mountain gorillas and engaging local communities in conservation, and some of them became individual donors to CTPH.

Because the new building only had one room, we could not conduct bacterial analysis that needed more sterile conditions and could easily get contaminated from the regular parasite analysis that we showed visitors when they came to visit. So Tusk Trust stepped up again, giving us follow-up funding to build an addition, which enabled us to start conducting bacterial analysis. Stephen convinced the Rare Species Fund to help equip the new center with essential laboratory equipment. We now had enough space to conduct comparative investigations of several types of infections. One veterinary student we hosted, William Fugina from Cornell University, found salmonella and shigella, which can cause potentially very severe diarrhea in gorillas, people, and livestock. We also trained our wildlife health technician, Enos Nahabwe, to be able to continue the investigations and build upon William's studies after he had returned to the United States. It was exciting for our team of Ugandan staff to be able to work with students from other countries and build each other's skills.

I continued collaborating with other universities and in particular the Royal Veterinary College, where I had trained. We hosted Melisa Unger from my alma mater, who studied another harmful protozoa, entamoeba, in gorillas and livestock, and we published a paper on the study.[15]

Another RVC student found an alarmingly large quantity of parasite eggs in gorilla intestines. A visiting student from St. George's University in Grenada was able to culture the eggs, revealing that half of the most common species of roundworm, *Strongyloides*, found in the gorillas were from people and the rest from gorillas, which was alarming and enabled us to better manage gorillas that had a large

worm burden and showing clinical signs. We noticed that deworm-
ing some of the gorillas helped their coat improve, an indication that
they had been either carrying too high a burden of their normal
parasites or picking up parasites from people. The study was taken a
step further by a visiting Mississippi State University veterinary student who not only conducted studies on parasites of the gorillas, but
also donated equipment for our center. We built partnerships with
Makerere and Mbarara Universities to host more local veterinary,
public health, and science-focused students from Uganda. We were
helping university students from around the world collaborate and
build upon one another's findings.

One of the rooms was made into a hall where we held meetings
and training workshops with local stakeholders including the park
staff, local government officials, students, NGOs from the conservation and health sector, local volunteers like the Gorilla Guardians
from the human and gorilla conflict resolution teams and the VHCTs.
This center became a safe and energizing space for building strong
relationships with external partners and stakeholders where we could
openly talk about successes, challenges, and opportunities. It also
became a center of learning for people from other regions in Uganda
and neighboring countries, such as DRC and Kenya.

Chapter 22

Expanding Our Brief beyond Bwindi

Virunga National Park

My dream for CTPH had always been to share our model with others who were open to exploring a One Health approach, and I soon had my chance. I first met Jean Claude Kyungu in the 1990s when The Gorilla Organization (TGO) invited me to a workshop in Rwanda. I reconnected with him again in 2004 at a gorilla conservation workshop in Goma in the Democratic Republic of Congo and told him that we had started an NGO to improve the health of gorillas and people together. He invited me to give a presentation about CTPH at a workshop on gorilla conservation in Butembo.

Following the event, I got the chance to visit the gorillas in Mount Tshiabirimu. After spending the night in Buruci, it was a steep two-hour climb before we finally reached the forest and were able to check on the nearest gorilla group. It was fascinating to walk in a forest at a higher altitude than Bwindi where the main vegetation was bamboo. I noticed that the gorillas looked the same as those at Bwindi, and were also well habituated. The numbers had shrunk to a tiny population here. We decided that North Virunga National Park, home to the eastern lowland gorillas and the only other population of mountain gorillas, was a perfect place to scale up the One Health model we had developed at Bwindi. A few months later, we recruited a locally based large-animal veterinarian from Butembo, Dr. Joseph Mavisi, on the recommendation of Kyungu. The following year we invited Dr. Mavisi and the vet from L'institut Congolais pour la Conservation de la Nature, Dr. Arthur Kalonji, who was based farther south in Goma, to Bwindi for training in gorilla health monitoring. They traveled with the Mount Tshiabirimu head ranger, named Safari. It was wonderful to be able to help gorillas in DRC by training their guardians and to compare experiences with Uganda.

A few months later, Kyungu reported to me that a female gorilla, Muhokya, was losing weight. I traveled there with Lawrence and Stephen. We crossed the border in the morning and were met with a warm welcome in the true Congolese tradition that included a mid-morning Primus, the local beer. We eventually drove to Buruci and having got there in the afternoon, hiked up the mountain to the base camp at Kalibina. Lawrence carried with him Uganda waragi, a spirit that tastes like gin, which was greatly appreciated because everyone was so cold that afternoon. We went to visit the nearby gorilla group in an area of the forest with no trails and it was tough going. That night we sat by the fire telling stories while trying to keep warm, and got up early to check on the sick female gorilla. Before we set off, we were offered a very big breakfast that consisted of a buffet of potatoes, fish, vegetables, fruit, and bread. Naively, Lawrence and I felt that it was too early to eat that much and opted for a light breakfast of fruit and bread, unlike our Congolese colleagues, who knew better.

We left at around 8 a.m. to check on the gorillas and after crossing a swampy patch of the forest with bamboo, we began a four-hour climb up a steep hill. As we were approaching the team that had gone ahead of us, with only a thirty-minute walk left to go, we received an alarming radio message that the lead silverback gorilla had started fighting with a lone silverback gorilla. The advance team was worried that the gorillas would start moving very fast away from the conflict and we would not be able to catch up with them.

By that time, I was slowing down considerably. Safari offered to carry me after I openly admitted that I was exhausted and depleted, but my husband was reluctant for me to take up this offer. We walked for another hour, but the group kept on moving until Safari advised that we were unlikely to see the gorillas that day.

When I asked the advance team of trackers about the gorilla, Muhokya, they told me that she looked stronger today and had started eating more. Though we were very disappointed not to have seen her or her group members, we realized that we needed to get out of the forest before dark. We walked back down the hill with aching muscles and low blood sugar levels, and then packed our bags at Kalibina and continued down the next steep hill to the vehicle. Though I was the only one who expressed that I was very tired, I later discovered that all the men on the trek including the Congolese rangers were as well, but too proud to admit it. In true Congolese tradition we even stopped at a nightclub, but were all too exhausted to enjoy it. Stephen was feeling ill. We finally drove back to Uganda the next day, where Stephen was diagnosed with pneumonia.

Eventually the female gorilla got better without any treatment, which was a huge relief. Jillian Miller, the Gorilla Organization Director, managed to obtain funding from Zoological Society of London (ZSL) for us to train the rest of the park rangers in gorilla health monitoring at Mount Tshiabirimu. I returned a few months later to hold the ranger training workshop with Stephen together with a dart gun, to demonstrate to Dr. Mavisi so that he could attend to sick gorillas in a timely manner.

But the DRC is in precarious upheaval. A few weeks after the ranger training workshop, Mai-Mai rebels attacked the camp and captured and killed Safari and other rangers. We had narrowly missed the massacre. I was devastated by the injustice of it all.

A similar incident occurred at Mount Tshiabirimu when we were called to conduct a postmortem on a gorilla. When Dr. Mavisi collected Stephen, they decided to take a shortcut to Kyondo and fell into an ambush of Mai-Mai rebels. The only reason why I hadn't joined them was because I was with my sons, so I had dropped Stephen at the DRC–Uganda border. Stephen and Dr. Mavisi somehow managed to still conduct the postmortem and left the DRC unharmed by the rebels.

Despite the upheavals, the gorilla health monitoring program continued to be funded by United States Fish and Wildlife Service (USFWS), which enabled us to intensively monitor all the few remaining eastern lowland gorillas at Mount Tshiabirimu through monthly collection of fecal samples from each individual gorilla and analysis for harmful parasites.

One year later we received funding to expand the Village Health and Conservation Team (VHCT) approach to DRC. We discovered that they already had community health workers who were attached to the center and were able to provide health services to many homes around the park. So, we decided to engage all of them as community conservation health volunteers. We worked with the community volunteers to conduct surveys in over four thousand homes to get a baseline that revealed very poor hygiene and sanitation, as well as extreme poverty with most people living in temporary houses. With more funding from United States Fish and Wildlife Service we continued to support these community volunteers, but after the funding ended and civil war disrupted them, the program stopped functioning.

A few years later, with funding from the Japanese Social Development Fund, we reengaged the volunteers, some of whom we had to find in refugee camps. We adapted our model by not having full-time paid staff on the ground and instead contributed to the salaries of two staff, Jean Marie Kambale at Mount Tshiabirimu sector and Gato Diouf at Mikeno sector, from the local health centers to supervise seventy-six VHCTs, reaching over four thousand homes. This time round we were able to give the VHCTs incentives of group livestock projects and Village Saving and Loan Associations (VSLAs), which has kept them going to this day. They were trained by our Bwindi Community Health and Conservation Field Officer,

Alex and cofounder Stephen, and continue to work hard bringing much needed services and hope to one of the poorest areas of DRC, checking on communities who share their habitat with gorillas as well as reducing deforestation from local communities at Kyavinonge who were cutting trees in Virunga National Park to make charcoal. This also reduced the threat to the critically endangered eastern lowland gorillas of disease spread by uncontrolled movements of people entering the park.

Though DRC is a largely Catholic country, the communities were very keen on family planning because they wanted to reduce poverty in their homes. However, the contraceptives in Mount Tshiabirimu sector were not free, and for people living below the poverty line, it was going to be difficult to buy them. Sadly, this limited their adoption of modern family planning methods.

In spite of all the obstacles of volcanic eruptions and periodic rebel attacks on the community members, thus far the mountain gorilla population has been spared. Not so, the eastern lowland gorillas, which have continued to drop in number.

Queen Elizabeth National Park

Building upon the research we had conducted on tuberculosis, I also wanted to adapt the One Health model from a forest habitat to a savanna ecosystem that may not necessarily have great apes, but also has other important endangered and threatened wild animals.

Queen Elizabeth National Park allows some level of human settlements within the park. Historically this park had pastoralist, cattle-keeping nomads who lived among the wildlife until it was declared a national park in 1952, after which they were pushed to the edge of the park to live within eleven fishing enclaves. Realizing that the pastoralists were both an imminent threat and a long-lasting solution to conserving Queen Elizabeth National Park, we had to listen to them. After my first trip to give a presentation about CTPH in DRC, this was my next stop. Our meeting with the seminomadic cattle-keeping community living in and around the park showed us that they resented Uganda Wildlife Authority (UWA) for not allowing them to graze in the park. They were aware that diseases can spread between wildlife and livestock, but insisted that the wildlife was the culprit.

We talked to them about the idea of recruiting community animal health workers who could reduce this disease risk to their cattle and also teach them to promote conservation. They liked the idea because we were showing them that we also cared about their needs especially because they valued their cows as much as they valued their children and themselves. We engaged them in conducting comparative disease surveys looking for the same diseases in cattle and buffalo that could also spread to people, focusing on buffalo that grazed outside the park in the eleven community enclaves. We found brucellosis, which causes cattle to abort their fetuses and causes recurring fevers in people, and Rift Valley Fever, which causes similar symptoms in people and cattle. We also found foot-and-mouth disease, which does not spread to people, but impacts the health and well-being of their cattle, giving them painful sores in their mouths and on their feet, causing them to lose weight and produce less milk. This time around we did not find tuberculosis (TB) in the buffalo and cattle, showing that this disease was disappearing from the ecosystem, which was incredible. However, a few years later another disease, peste de petits ruminants (PPR), which in goats and sheep causes respiratory signs coupled with foul smelling diarrhea, started to appear in the buffalo and cattle.[16]

We started to engage the pastoralists at a time when their relatives in DRC were illegally bringing their cattle over to settle inside the park and build temporary shelters. Their cattle had obvious symptoms of foot-and-mouth disease. The law enforcement rangers sprang into action to prevent encroachment on the park, which met with resistance. At one point there was so much tension between the community and the park that community members put nails in the road to puncture the tires of the UWA vehicles, slowing them down enough to be attacked. When the UWA wardens told us not to go to the villages because it was dangerous, Stephen and I discussed this extensively and both agreed that this was exactly the time to go in and show that a One Health approach could help to improve relations between the community and the park management.

We developed brochures about the diseases shared between buffalo and cattle in the local languages, including the local names for these diseases. We created a new team of thirty community volunteers dedicated to the health of livestock in the Kasese district portion of the park and called them community conservation animal health workers. Stephen and I took blood samples from their cattle and attended to their illnesses, and used this opportunity to train the new volunteers. We also trained rangers and the volunteers to report animals found dead inside and outside the park, and gave them a simple kit of microscope slides, scalpel blades, gloves, masks, and equipment to enable them to take skin tissue samples from the animals' ears, which is enough to diagnose most diseases, including anthrax. However, mistrust between communities and UWA had to be addressed, so we set about convincing the UWA wardens to work more closely with the local communities. The community volunteers turned out to have impressive skill and passion for collecting samples and giving the buffalo injections of antibiotics.

One day I received a message from the chief warden, Nelson Guma, excitedly informing me that "your volunteers are very brave, they rescued a baby elephant that was drowning and managed to tie her in a crude fashion to a rope and got her to the mainland." I felt so proud of them. The wardens and rangers could not trace the mother, and the baby was brought to the Uganda Wildlife Education Centre for intensive nursery care, becoming their first elephant at the zoo. She was eventually joined by another elephant that was abandoned by its mother in the same area. We decided to name the baby "Charles Hamukungu" in honor of the person who rescued her and the village whence she came, and the rescuers were made honorary wardens for this heroic act. We have excitedly watched Hamukungu grow from a two-month-old baby elephant when she played with our two boys to a healthy and friendly 4.4-ton adult female. She has taught many Ugandan children to appreciate wildlife and is a favorite at the Entebbe Zoo, especially among those who are from the elephant "Njovu" clan.

These experiences drew our older son Ndhego to volunteer as a junior zookeeper when he was thirteen years old. He wrote about this in the local *New Vision* newspaper's *Toto* children's magazine, and from there wrote a children's book, *Zoo Keeper for a Week*. Ndhego's favorite was the giraffes because he found it so much fun climbing on a truck to feed them carrots. However, he wasn't allowed to work with the chimpanzees because being even more closely related to us than gorillas the risk of disease spread is too high. He got a lesson not only in genetics but also in epidemiology. He learned about how easily close relatives can make each other sick and that children under fifteen are more likely to carry childhood diseases that could spread to the endangered chimpanzees.

Budongo Central Forest Reserve

With funding from the Darwin Initiative, we expanded our award-winning village health and conservation team model to another great ape habitat: the community surrounding the chimpanzees of Budongo Central Forest Reserve.

Ten years later, we had found that the families at Bwindi Impenetrable National Park who were visited most had much better health practices, hygiene habits, and adoption of family planning and conservation practices. This motivated us to train all village health team members supported by the Ministry of Health in the six parishes where gorillas forage in community land to become village health and conservation teams, so that they had fewer homes to follow and could reach all of them more frequently. This change in policy at CTPH increased the number of VHCTs from eighty-four to 270 who regularly reach thirty thousand people in six thousand homes. Thus at Budongo we engaged all VHTs as VHCTs.

But it was a steep climb to get there. Budongo presented new challenges. Here, bushmeat hunting was much more prevalent than in Bwindi. People in Budongo even ate primates, mainly baboons and more rarely chimpanzees that raided sugarcane and other crops in their gardens. In turn chimpanzees sometimes grabbed and killed human infants who were crying while their mothers were digging in the gardens next to the forest. Baboons were equally hostile. This also predisposed the local community to zoonotic diseases such as Ebola and other deadly viruses that were more likely to spread from fellow primates than other wildlife. The local community went as far as believing that if you ate a baboon you would be cured of a headache. Budongo was also surrounded by many people who had set aside land to grow sugarcane for the nearby Kinyara sugar factory. Chimpanzees had more opportunity to interact with people who entered the forest reserve or when they raided sugarcane in growers' gardens, putting them at great risk from human respiratory infections as well as intestinal diseases through open defecation. I also realized that it was going to be much more difficult to get the Budongo community to protect chimpanzees because they did not receive a share of tourism revenue from the National Forest Authority (NFA). Unlike the Bwindi local community, the Budongo community had no incentive.

As a small and nimble grassroots NGO and nonprofit, I realized that it was not realistic to have a CTPH office at Budongo; we needed to work closely with partners on the ground to implement the One Health model. Though the funding was only for one year, we were able to make inroads to improve the communities' health and conservation attitudes through partnerships with locally based NGOs, Jane Goodall Institute, and Budongo Conservation Field Station.

Lake Victoria Basin

Not all expansion went smoothly. We were invited by the John D. and Catherine T. MacArthur Foundation to bring our One Health approach to Lake Victoria Basin to prevent over fishing and pollution in the largest lake in Africa. However, because the focus was aquatic species, I was drawn by the idea of partnering with other organizations such as Pathfinder International, to help them develop their own village health and conservation teams. This time, we would support while they took the lead. Ecological Christian Organization (ECO) in Uganda and OSIENALA (Friends of Lake Victoria) in Kenya also came on board, and together we formed a consortium to apply for funds for the project. But soon we found that unlike our previous donor-funded projects where I was in charge, we had to wait for Pathfinder to approve every activity and report before we could obtain funding to continue, which ended up limiting my creativity to make our model work in a marine ecosystem.

Though I enjoyed learning about conservation issues in a different habitat and developed long and meaningful partnerships with ECO and OSIENALA, I did not feel that our strengths were being harnessed in such a consortium. The additional energy it required for me to get our reports approved and funding more quickly disbursed to implement activities on time resulted in me not focusing on applying for funding to keep the Bwindi programs going. I realized that we needed to be more discerning about the groups we partner with to achieve our goals. When the endeavor with Pathfinder ended, I found that CTPH had run out of money because I had neglected the heart of our core mission. We had to lay off beloved staff and go without salaries for a few months. This happened right before our tenth anniversary, which resulted in restarting our programs at Bwindi. But it was a difficult lesson for me to learn that no matter how attractive a consortium looks, as a leader it's important to always prioritize the core activities of the organization. I vowed never to get distracted from looking for resources to keep the gorillas healthy and their habitats secure.

In the end, some elements of the CTPH approach were adapted in the Lake Victoria Basin, and I learned about other ways of promoting conservation and health together such as getting communities to improve health and ecofriendly practices through having "model" homes to inspire the community. It also opened my eyes to the potential of clean energy-saving cook stoves in achieving benefits for both conservation and health through reducing smoke-induced acute respiratory distress from the traditional three-stone stoves, and potentially the number of trees that are cut down from the forest for firewood.

Chapter 23

From Practitioner to Policy Maker

Never in my wildest imagination had I thought I would come so far in effecting positive change for wildlife and people. I was busy running an NGO and serving on boards of wildlife organizations, but I always kept a hand in my true passion for veterinary medicine. I often would advise on veterinary issues and help recruit vets, but it was always a highlight when I could roll up my sleeves and be a practical vet. When I was asked to translocate a pet zebra from a farm near Kayonza Wildlife Reserve in western Uganda to the Uganda Wildlife Education Centre (UWEC), I was delighted to help both as a veterinarian and board member. As an orphan, the zebra had been looked after by well-meaning people after straying from the reserve to their cattle farm, until he grew into an adult and became too difficult to manage when he started biting people. Leading this translocation with a team from CTPH and UWEC was a lot simpler than the elephant translocation from Mubende, and it was good to see the zebra settled safely where he could teach visitors about his species.

Then one day, I received an email from the government with a very different request. This time, the minister of tourism, wildlife, and antiquities, Hon. Ephraim Kamuntu, invited me to become a board member of the Uganda Wildlife Authority (UWA). I was excited to serve on the board of an organization that had given me my first job.

I was among the youngest board members at forty-two. The board chair, Mr. Ben Otto, who was in his seventies, was an excellent leader with decades of experience including before the Idi Amin era, and respected everyone's decision no matter the age or gender. He also told me that he had met and greatly admired my father. He said my father was one of the most upright and highly respected civil servants at the time, which made me feel so proud. His words echoed what other colleagues had told me about my father and made serving on this government board even more special.

Also newly serving on the board was Captain John Otekat, my first immediate boss after graduation from vet school. We were both elated to receive a congratulations message from our mentor, Professor Eric Edroma, who was the UWA executive director at the time. This was a lovely reminder about how they empowered me to fulfill my potential so early in my career. It felt like everything was coming full circle.

The board was facing the task of solving the problems at Mount Elgon National Park. Created in the 1990s, at the same time as Bwindi Impenetrable National Park, Mount Elgon had been designated a UNESCO Man and Biosphere Reserve for its exceptional biodiversity including hardwood trees, unique vegetation, and caves that elephants mined for salt. However, the indigenous communities that lived in the forest when it used to be a forest reserve, the Benet and Sabiny, had been evicted for it to become a national park. They had been reluctant to leave the mountain because it was also a sacred cultural site. Unlike the Batwa in Bwindi, who had moved to settlements, some of the Benet refused to leave. The Sabiny, who used to enter the park when it was a forest reserve to cut timber or firewood for cooking, continued to enter the park to also graze their cattle and plant maize and other crops. During election time the level of these illegal activities intensified as prospective members of parliament promised the local communities that if they voted for them, they would be allowed free access to the forest. As a result, human activity led to landslides that periodically buried and killed hundreds of people. It was the perfect shocking example of how destroying the environment could lead to the loss of lives.

Further, the mountain was also a source of clean fresh water for the surrounding communities and other populations several miles away in the Lake Victoria Basin, in eastern and central Uganda and western Kenya. Tourism at Mount Elgon was not as vibrant as at Bwindi, where gorilla tourism was rapidly transforming the lives of the local population. So NGOs started innovative projects to enable the communities and other stakeholders to benefit from the national park by sustainably tapping the water sources through "payment for ecosystem" services. Corporations that were depending on clean water for their business would pay community members not to destroy the water source in return for much-needed benefits. However, family planning was one thing missing from this model.

Tensions were high in Mount Elgon. Riots took place around the area after a soldier who had been working with UWA rangers had accidentally killed a community member. It was clear the board had to act. As head of the planning and research committee, I was asked to lead a delegation to address this issue. When we arrived at the park headquarters, we met the chief warden, Dr. Adonia Bintoora, and the community conservation warden, Godfrey Matanda. We learned that the community member had defied the soldier's orders not to enter the park to poach duikers and had also attempted to cut him with a panga, so the soldier shot the panga and when that did not work, he shot him in the leg. Unfortunately, as he was taken to hospital he bled to death, sparking the intense riots.

We met the bereaved family and the local leadership and other community members to console them and talk about how we could prevent such incidents happening in the future.

One answer was to bring the work of CTPH to this community to offer our One Health approach to conservation. The very high human population growth both inside and outside the park and very large family sizes were causing immense pressure. At Mount Elgon there was also a high rate of teenage pregnancies because they were untruthfully told by some members of their community that if you had a baby early you could be given free land, which further exacerbated the poverty and pressure on this fragile landscape.

With funding from the Japanese Social Development Fund and Darwin Initiative we expanded to the Mount Elgon area districts of Bukwo, Kween, and Bulambuli training community health workers to become village health and conservation teams. People started planting trees, acquiring handwashing facilities, and adopting family planning methods, which served to improve their health and well-being and mitigate the conflict between community members and the park rangers.

But I had not realized how much work was needed for this national park to coexist with the communities. To deal with the human and wildlife conflicts that kept cropping up all over the country, community-based conservation efforts needed more staff and a bigger budget.

Another thing that became clear was the board needed to actually visit the protected areas before approving any plan, to become aware of the stakeholders' day-to-day challenges. It was clear that traditional ways of protecting wildlife through law enforcement wasn't working well enough.

The idea for more intimate plan management became the norm. When approving the general management plan for Queen Elizabeth National Park to guide management of the park for the next decade, I recommended that each enclave needed its own community conservation rangers, because if there were enough people educating the community and directly addressing their concerns there would be less need for them to fight the park management and enter the park to poach. When this number of community rangers doubled, law enforcement could be reduced by the same amount.

In recognition of the essential role the rangers played in protecting wildlife, engaging local communities, and guiding tourists—they really were our frontline staff—we gave them smarter uniforms and better housing and doubled their salaries.

I visited many protected areas, one of which was Pian Upe Wildlife Reserve to approve general management plans. I had been at Pian Upe thirteen years earlier to conduct surveys in buffalo and the endangered roan antelope to investigate rinderpest, a viral disease also known as cattle plague that primarily affects the intestines and upper respiratory tract of cattle and buffalo.

It was a remote wildlife reserve that was rarely visited by tourists, but had the most interesting species including cheetahs, caracals, lions, eland, sitatunga, oribi and ostriches, and at 2,275 square kilometers was the second-largest protected area in Uganda after Murchison Falls National Park. Since that time the protected area had been encroached due to intense pressure to allow the nomadic tribes to graze their cattle in the reserve. A development NGO even went as far as putting up a large health center within the reserve, reducing the limited space for threatened and endangered wildlife. When the senior warden told us that they had no conservation NGOs working in the park to help stop construction projects that were destroying the park, I felt sad. I started to imagine how we could expand our community-based One Health approach to conservation to Pian Upe, having seen an improvement in conservation attitudes and practices of communities in the pastoralist community at Queen Elizabeth National Park.

We applied for funding from the French Government and proceeded with caution as we approached the Karamojong, a Nilotic ethnic group of agro-pastoral herders who relied on their chief to make decisions. Our meeting with the local elder and chief went surprisingly well. He even declared that in Genesis, the first chapter of the Bible, God commanded that we look after the animals in the garden of Eden. When we recruited ten people to become community conservation animal health workers, their leader, Joshua Onyango, also declared that like my tribe—the Baganda, they had totems, including zebras and birds, that prevented them from killing their totems, which I saw as a golden opportunity to use culture to protect wildlife.

The animals in the reserve, including the eland and buffalo, were very shy. Having been heavily poached, they were wary of people and vehicles. Getting close enough to them to dart in order to conduct disease surveys was impossible. We decided to focus on training the rangers to monitor the health of wildlife through checking for clinical signs using binoculars and collecting samples from animals found dead in the park.

Sport hunting was allowed in Uganda as a way of gaining revenue to sustain conservation particularly in areas where there was hardly any tourism. One tour operator told me that Pian Upe had been one of the largest hunting grounds in the 1960s and 1970s; there was so much wildlife that vehicles would find it difficult to move. Now sadly there was very little wildlife, and what little there was ran away when a vehicle got close. I was a cynic of sport hunting when there was so little wildlife to hunt, but my experience in Pian Upe Wildlife Reserve changed my thinking. I started to see the value when the Community Conservation Warden, Tony Olinga, explained to me that the money from sport hunting was shared with the local communities and it was helping to reduce poaching for food. He also told me that the sport hunters helped to habituate the wild animals, so that they could hit their target, and they were only allowed to focus on old animals that were likely to die or become prey for lions. Ironically, once you got the animals used to vehicles and conducted regular patrols around the reserve, then it was easier to protect them.

Driving around the park, we came across Pokot tribesmen who had brought in their cattle from across the border in Kenya. Alarmed to realize that the park was not only threatened by pastoralists in Uganda, but also from Kenya, I still admired the stunning clothing of the Kenyan Karamojong. The women wore elaborate necklaces and earrings and the men wore feathers in their head gear. I was so touched when one of our community volunteer's wives made a beautiful traditional skirt for me. The Karamojong's determination to preserve their culture was another opportunity for them to earn a living through carefully organized cultural tourism.

We also visited the area homesteads to conduct surveys about the villagers' health and hygiene habits and conservation attitudes and practices. Their homestead fences were made using beautiful designs with twisted vines. My son Tendo, who had just turned five, took particular interest in helping us get samples from the goats of the Karamojong, though he hated the flies. Those flies were more than a nuisance; they were a red flag attracted by inadequate hygiene where cattle and people lived in the same quarters. While conducting surveys, Tendo became hysterical one day because of the flies that overwhelmed him. One concerned Karamojong woman asked if she could give him milk and the District Veterinary Officer, Dr. Arionga, was quick to say that Tendo didn't drink milk. Here, the milk was never boiled, it was only soured, putting the community at great risk from contracting brucellosis and other deadly preventable diseases. Boiling milk was one of the behaviors that CTPH was trying to encourage. Though we were not able to change this habit passed down the generations, we were able to get them to improve on sanitation and hygiene and they started to build and use pit latrines, which resulted in fewer flies. I was elated when the French Ambassador, Madame Sophie Makame, came to visit our project with her staff and remarked on this seemingly impossible change in behavior. It was her first visit to Pian Upe Wildlife Reserve. On top of admiring the amazing views of the vast and peaceful savanna plains, she expressed concern about the very low literacy levels where the majority of people had never been to elementary school.

A few months later, I received an interesting call from the Karimojong Overland Safaris sport hunting guides asking me for advice on how to feed two skinny orphan cheetahs that were found in local communities. Their mother was killed when she went after goats, and the rangers confiscated them. Their only chance of survival was Esbilac, a special milk for cats that could only be gotten in South Africa. If the seven-week-old cheetahs stayed in Pian Upe, they were unlikely to survive. One option was to place the cubs in captivity, where they could be taken care of. We chose to bring the cheetahs to Uganda Wildlife Education Centre so they could become ambassadors for their species—one that few Ugandans ever get to see— attracting more resources to protect them in the wild.

My sons came with me when we picked up the cheetahs from UWA offices to drive them to UWEC in Entebbe. The baby cheetahs preferred to sit on our shoulders, and the boys were particularly fascinated by their speed and non-retracting claws. I insisted that UWEC name them Pian and Upe so that people will always remember where they came from and Members of Parliament who visit the zoo would feel a sense of pride and be inspired to protect their wildlife reserve.

Pian and Upe became round playful balls of fur after just two weeks at UWEC and are now big and still quite friendly, having been brought up by humans from an early age. They've become a huge attraction at the Zoo. Tour operators now bring tourists to Pian Upe, providing another reason to keep the wildlife reserve intact. This has led to translocations by the UWA Veterinary Unit of giraffes and other species to boost the animal populations there, helping to restore its wildlife populations.

★ ★ ★

While serving on the UWA Board, a burning issue came up about Uganda's stance on international trade in elephants. The Tanzanian government was lobbying Uganda to allow trade and the Kenyan government was lobbying Uganda to ban the trade and the board was asked for advice. This important decision was to be made at the CITES (Convention of International Trade in Endangered Species of Wild Fauna and Flora) conference, which is one of the largest conservation forums in the world, occurring every three years to review this agreement between governments.

Captain Otekat felt that it was important for the board to take a stance on this, and we both strongly felt that allowing trade would cause the decimation of elephants in Uganda and poorer countries in Africa that didn't have enough manpower to protect the species. We decided to join the Uganda government delegation at the CITES conference held in Bangkok, Thailand.

There, we were able to influence the way Uganda voted—to ban the trade in elephant ivory. During that conference many countries held special events to lobby for different issues, so I suggested that at the next CITES conference, Uganda hold an event to share how improved livelihoods by engaging communities in conservation have reduced the illegal trade in wildlife. Three years later, this wish came true.

Luckily the illegal trade in mountain gorillas had almost stopped with support from the United Nations Environmental Programme (UNEP) Great Apes Survival Partnership (GRASP) of which CTPH had become a member with other conservation NGOs.

I was greatly honored to become a trustee of The Gorilla Organization based in UK, my first international board to serve on, where I had volunteered as a veterinary student stuffing envelopes of fundraising appeals to donors and was their first board member from Africa.

In 2015, I received the shocking news that Professor Eric Edroma, my mentor who gave me my dream job out of university had passed away. I was so devastated that I left an IUCN (International Union for the Conservation of Nature) regional meeting in Kenya to attend his funeral. When I was asked to step in his shoes as the Board Chairperson of Wildlife Clubs of Uganda, I was truly honored to continue Dr. Edroma's legacy in this leadership role to serve in an organization that nurtured my passion for wildlife conservation.

I was also truly humbled when the Prime Minister of Buganda, Owekitibwa Charles Peter Mayiga asked me to be the first Board Chairperson of the Buganda Heritage and Tourism Board, continuing the legacy of my maternal grandfather, who served as the kingdom's Prime Minister for twelve years.

I was particularly humbled to serve on the Board of Bwindi and Mgahinga Conservation Trust in 2019 when CTPH was nominated to represent the local NGOs.

Through my engagement on the Uganda Poverty and Conservation Learning Group, I was able to use my position as a Board member of UWA to double the revenue share to the local communities of Bwindi from each gorilla trekking permit from $5 to $10, where my walk with gorillas and career in wildlife conservation had begun.

PART IV

Sustaining Conservation

Chapter 24

Is Tourism a Necessary Evil?

A long my conservation journey, I often get asked if tourism is hurting or helping the mountain gorillas. When Dr. Dian Fossey studied the mountain gorillas in the Virungas in the 1970s, she came to believe that tourism would make the gorillas lose their fear of humans and therefore become more vulnerable to poaching, eventually leading to their extinction.

It is easy to understand her fears. In 1991, Bwindi Impenetrable Forest was turned into a National Park in the bid to protect the mountain gorillas and other wildlife, which was in sharp decline from habitat loss and unregulated hunting. However, this had a devastating impact on local communities, especially those who lived and depended on the forest for their livelihoods. Suddenly, they could not enter the park for timber or firewood; they could not collect honey, medicinal plants and reeds for weaving their baskets. Not surprisingly, this did nothing to deter poachers; some might say that new poachers were created overnight as a result.

However, by the time I visited Bwindi in 1994 as a veterinary student, there was a contagious air of hope as a result of the growing tourist industry in the area. It meant that for the first time in their lives, people could earn an honest, decent wage acting as park staff. Former poachers were hired as rangers. In fact, one of the first trackers who took me to see the gorillas told me that he was hired because the authorities got tired of arresting him for poaching in the national park.

In many ways, my conservation journey has mirrored the growth of great ape tourism in Uganda. When I started work as their first wildlife vet in 1996, there were two habituated gorilla groups. Now there are over twenty. Furthermore, the number of tourists able to visit a group of gorillas at any one time has grown from six to eight. So while in 1996 a maximum of twelve tourists could be trekking gorillas at once, now 160 tourists may be in the park at the same time.

In the 1990s conservation was shifting globally to engage communities as part of the solution. Uganda has been at the forefront of this sea change and created the Department of Community Conservation in Uganda Wildlife Authority to tackle any issues. In the early days, tensions were high. At one point, the local community set fire to the park out of resentment for not being allowed to enter. The chief wardens calmed the situation by improving the work culture of the staff and giving the local community jobs, as related by one of them in *Episodes and Tribulations of the African Ranger*.[17] As they started to earn a better living protecting rather than hunting wildlife, they became more supportive of the park.

When Dr. Eric Edroma lobbied Uganda's President Museveni to upgrade the status of Bwindi Impenetrable Forest from a forest reserve to a national park where no hunting or mining was allowed, one of the biggest draws was its potential to earn sustainable revenue from gorilla trekking tourists. This argument was even more convincing because in neighboring Rwanda, the park authorities were already reaping the benefits of having tourists visit the mountain gorillas in Volcanoes National Park.

I have seen this dream become a reality, seen Uganda returning as one of the top tourist destinations in Africa because of the mountain gorilla. On a personal level, developing my country in this way enables me to continue following my father's dream.

In 1993, with support from US Peace Corps Volunteers, Uganda National Parks built cottages in the local Bwindi community where tourists could stay. The community was so successful in managing the cottages that twenty years later they saved enough money to build a high-end lodge to earn more revenue from tourism. Some people developed crafts to sell to the tourists, and lodges and local restaurants cropped up, as well as village walking tours displaying the local cultures. Local community members hired as porters found they were earning more by carrying a tourist's bag to visit the gorillas than digging in their garden. I hired a young woman as a porter who carried my bags when checking on the gorillas during her high school holidays, which she used to pay her school fees.

As a veterinary student, I conducted research that showed that gorillas visited by tourists in Buhoma had a higher parasite burden that could be due to increased stress levels than gorillas only visited by a few researchers in Ruhija. In spite of that evidence, pressure rose for more visitors so much that the only gorilla group habituated for research purposes at Ruhija ended up becoming a gorilla group that was also visited by tourists. At Volcanoes National Park in Rwanda there was similar pressure, and tourists were taken to research groups at Karisoke.

As the number of habituated gorilla groups grew, the benefits to the local communities increased and revenue for both private local and international tour operators grew. On top of opportunities for employment and entrepreneurship, income to the local communities increased through a guaranteed revenue shared with the national parks. Through an act of parliament in Uganda, 20 percent of the park entry fees that tourists pay to Uganda Wildlife Authority is shared with the local community. Additionally some money from each gorilla permit was added to the community share due to the limited number of tourists who can visit. This "Gorilla Levy" fund unique to Bwindi and Mgahinga National Parks increased from $5 to $10 from every gorilla permit during the time that I served on the board of the Uganda Wildlife Authority, which meant that even more money was earmarked for local communities.

Within ten years, revenue from gorilla tourism was contributing 50 percent of the total operational budget for UWA, and some of the funds were used to support the operational costs of other protected areas with endangered and threatened wildlife that do not receive enough tourism revenue, such as Pian Upe Wildlife Reserve, where our two orphaned cheetah cubs were born. The other two districts, Kisoro and Kabale, around Bwindi also wanted gorilla groups to be habituated for tourism so that they could receive the benefits that the Kanungu district had garnered.

As the push grew to habituate more and more gorilla groups, con- servation organizations led by the International Gorilla Conservation Programme (IGCP), which helped Uganda to develop gorilla eco- tourism in 1993, warned against having too much tourism, which could essentially kill the treasured goose laying a constant supply of golden eggs.

Nevertheless, to spread the benefits to the southern sector of Bwindi, one gorilla group was habituated. After the first gorilla group's habituation, the demand grew for tourism in the southern sector, and one exceptional local entrepreneur, Fidelis Kanyamunyu, successfully lobbied for more groups to be habituated.

Since then, the number of lodges around Bwindi has grown from five to over sixty-four in the past twenty-eight years. This includes our own CTPH Gorilla Conservation Camp that we established in 2008 as a rustic camp hosting staff, volunteers, students, and visitors as well as gorilla trekking tourists.

However, with all the benefits come risks. When you habituate gorillas, they lose their fear of people and cannot tell the difference between someone who wants to protect or harm them. This makes them more vulnerable to poaching. To ensure their safety, whether or not there are tourists, they have to be visited every day by park rangers to make sure that they are healthy and safe from poachers and record their night nests and their GPS location. At Bwindi, we have seen that once gorillas lose their fear of people, groups of gorillas

close to the park edge often start to venture outside their forest habitat to forage on community land where they prefer the stems of the
banana plants to the fruit. They also like eating the bark of eucalyptus
trees that people have planted to reduce their need to cut hardwood
trees in the forest for firewood.

Once they leave the safety of the forest, they are vulnerable not
just to diseases but to angry community members.

However, if a local community has benefited from tourism, their
attitudes change. In 1995, just two years after gorilla tourism began,
four adult gorillas, including a mother and other group members
habituated for research, were killed by poachers when trying to protect an infant that was being taken for sale to a private collector.

Seven years later, in 2002, some community members were hired
to capture an infant mountain gorilla to be sold. This time however,
the local community tipped off UWA in time, and the poachers were
arrested as they were walking to the Nkuringo gorilla group. The
reason the community intervened was because they were starting to
see gorilla tourism as their livelihood, their future.

Of course, not everyone could see the benefits. In 2011, a playful
blackback, Mizano, was killed by a poacher when he got into a fight
with his hunting dog. Several years later during a period when tourism was suspended due to the COVID-19 pandemic, the Nkuringo
gorilla group tragically lost their silverback leader to a hungry poacher.

Without a doubt, we need to ensure that some of the gorillas are
not habituated in case of a fatal disease outbreak or massive poaching
incident.

Disease transmission from tourist to gorilla is all too real. The rule
of distance between tourists and mountain gorillas is seven meters,
but it's often broken due to either the curious nature of the tourist
or the gorilla or both that closes that gap. In 2011 two gorillas died
of human metapneumovirus in the Virungas.[18] This human pathogen,
known to be fatal to gorillas, was likely brought by a tourist who was
carrying the virus at the time.

But distance provides safety. I've become a passionate advocate of
enforcing gorilla tracking rules. I found it particularly difficult when
the number of tourists visiting a gorilla family was raised from six to

eight in 2010 due to the pressure to issue more gorilla permits, but we eventually agreed that this was preferable to habituating more gorilla groups to meet the increasing demand. But distance is hard to enforce. Observations showed that shockingly, 98 percent of the time tourists were viewing gorillas at three meters or less, much closer than the rules allowed. Tourists broke the rules 60 percent of the time, while the gorillas got this close to their human visitors 40 percent of the time.[19]

In 2011 I investigated the possibility of tourists' willingness to wear masks when tracking the gorillas as an additional preventative measure from airborne diseases. Our study was conducted with a master's student, Allison Hanes, from Oxford Brookes University in the UK, who returned ten years later to make a film encouraging tourists to wear masks. Our 2011 study showed that tourists simply lacked awareness about how great a threat a human virus could pose to a mountain gorilla. It's expensive to trek the gorillas, an investment that encourages most people not to cancel if they have a mild virus. As long as they can hike, they're likely to go. However, the research also revealed that 51 percent of tourists were willing to wear masks.[20] Three years later, another survey showed that 73 percent of tourists were willing to mask up.

Masks became an obvious necessity considering how difficult it was to enforce the rules of distance. But could we require masks as a rule? A global pandemic would answer that question for us, but that was yet to come.

On top of the threat of disease, tourism also has an effect on the behavior of mountain gorillas; even though visiting times are limited to an hour, the impact is significant. The gorillas eat less and the youngsters play more, showing off to their human visitors. Often you can tell when the hour is up when the silverback grunts and starts to move his group away.

So, this brings me back to my original question: Is tourism a necessary evil? I've come to the conclusion that it is because in spite of habituated gorillas being more vulnerable to poaching and disease, interestingly the only gorilla subspecies whose population is growing is the mountain gorilla, where a thriving tourism industry and revenue from gorilla trekking tourists is shared with the local communities. Gorilla tourism is a major contributor to tourism in Uganda, which is 8 percent of the gross domestic product, and it contributes as much as 60 percent of the revenue for the Uganda Wildlife Authority, proving that tourism income is enough of an incentive for local communities to protect and coexist with endangered mountain gorillas while providing revenue that sustains conservation. Because of gorilla tourism, what started out as trading centers selling local brew with the only employment available from the tea factory have now become flourishing urban centers with high-end lodges, comfortable basic accommodation mainly owned by local community members, craft shops, community walks, and schools, clinics, and roads.

The mountain gorilla has become a source of national pride in Uganda. The largest currency in Uganda, the 50,000 shs banknote, features this majestic endangered great ape.

In 2019, I invited some of the most experienced conservationists in the world to a primate ecotourism roundtable discussion to explore how we need to strike a balance between tourism and the threat of disease. Uganda had a lot to share about ecotourism that could guide other countries that were interested in it. The roundtable had diverse voices including the UWA, the Uganda Tourism Board, the Institute of Tropical Forest Conservation, the International Gorilla Conservation Programme, and the Arcus Foundation, the biggest donor in the world for great ape funding, and two of the most prominent tour operators—Praveen Moman from Volcanoes Safaris with a chain of lodges at protected gorilla areas in Uganda and Rwanda and Amos Wekesa from Great Lakes Safaris with a chain of lodges at protected chimpanzee areas in Uganda. It was a truly dynamic discussion where we talked about the "good, bad, and the ugly" aspects of great ape tourism. This included the need to find other options for tourists to reduce the pressure on the mountain gorillas, by developing tourism to other primates, other wildlife, and the local communities. Praveen stated it perfectly: "Without tourism it is difficult to protect great apes, but if tourism is not conducted in a responsible manner, great apes can become extinct." The roundtable concluded that while tourism has helped to take mountain gorillas off the critically endangered list, it has to be conducted responsibly to ensure that they remain healthy and their populations continue to grow.

Even then I thought to myself, *Is this the only way to sustain conservation or are there other possibilities we need to explore?* Gorilla tourism was turning out to be enough to ensure the protection of mountain gorillas at Bwindi, as long as it was conducted in a way that minimized human disease transmission to gorillas and ensured tangible benefits to the local communities. However, this conviction was challenged in the months to come.

Chapter 25

Saving Gorillas One Sip at a Time

CTPH had built a reputation for innovation, and it is this type of thinking that led us to explore another way to sustain conservation—developing a global coffee brand that could save gorillas. I often passed coffee farms when trekking the steep hills to reach my gorilla patients, and the ranger guides stopped to show the farms to tourists, many of whom were coffee drinkers but had never seen a coffee tree. But I didn't realize that these farmers were not getting a steady market or fair price until we started engaging with them.

In 2007, Lawrence became interested in developing a coffee brand that supported gorilla conservation. He had come across a project where this was already a reality. Source Café was working with smallholder arabica coffee farmers at Mount Elgon, where a donation from every bag of Kifara Kawa sold went to the Rhino Fund Uganda.

He approached their American director, Adam Langford, to develop a Gorilla Kawa brand with a donation to CTPH from every bag they sold. Adam was excited to partner with us. Source Café agreed to produce and package the coffee for us, with our label, and give us 2 percent of sales. We were also able to buy the coffee from them at wholesale price and sell it at retail through the CTPH Telecentre and UWA Visitor Information Centre at the Queen Elizabeth National Park crater drive gate.

We even sold the coffee in the United States when I was invited as a guest speaker at the Wildlife Conservation Network Expo in San Francisco.

Tragically, Adam Langford and the Ugandan manager and church leader, Moses Kimeze, died in an accident when their vehicle crashed in the valley over the steep hills of Mount Elgon at Kapchorwa.

Source Café regrouped and pressed on, continuing to produce our Gorilla Kawa brand. Lawrence convinced the Entebbe International Airport duty-free shop to begin selling Gorilla Kawa. Source Café then also sold their two other brands, Kifara Kawa and Kiira Kawa, named after the source of the river Nile at Jinja. Gorilla Kawa was the most popular coffee, which the Shop sold at the highest price of $12 for a 500-gram bag simply because of the gorilla on the package.

While we got very little revenue because the overall number of bags sold was very small, it raised awareness about our work, and it showed us that people were willing to buy coffee supporting gorilla conservation. But we got criticism from conservationists that the Gorilla Kawa wasn't supporting farmers around Bwindi where the gorillas were found. They were right. We desperately wanted to support these smallholder farmers, but did not know where to begin.

After some false starts getting funding to engage the local coffee growers, I realized we needed to rethink the coffee project as a for-profit business, something I knew nothing about.

With support from World Wildlife Fund for Nature Switzerland (WWF CH), I traveled to Zurich and received training in setting up a for-profit social enterprise that could also attract financing from investors in the form of equity. I learned that there are investors who are not only interested in a financial return on their investment but also wanted to see that people received a fair price for their product and that the environment was protected or, at the very least, not destroyed. I also learned that the kind of customers who would be willing to pay more for coffee with a cause were known as lifestyle of health and sustainability consumers, introducing me to a whole new world of business for good.

But as Conservation Through Public Health was an NGO, no one could invest in it. This meant that we had to create a new entity, a for-profit company limited by shareholding, which we called "Gorilla Conservation Coffee." But the name sounded similar to "Gorilla Coffee" owned by a New York–based company in the Bronx selling coffee from Ethiopia and other countries where gorillas did not exist. In Uganda, there were other companies, Big Gorilla which sourced coffee from smallholder farmers at Mount Elgon where there are no gorillas, and Gorilla Summit and Gorilla Highlands that sourced coffee from farmers in Uganda, some of whom were from the Kigezi region where gorillas are found, but not necessarily from the frontline communities impacting the mountain gorillas. We also felt that it was necessary to obtain trademarks in the United States, the European Union, and Switzerland, the three countries that imported the most coffee, and ensure that we sell the coffee commercially within five years so as not to lose the trademark.

I had no idea about operating a coffee company, especially one that sold roasted branded coffee internationally, and turned to Andrew Rugasira, who had studied at the University of London at the same time as me and who had developed the first international Ugandan coffee brand, Good African Coffee, which was sold in Waitrose and other supermarkets in the UK and South Africa. Over lunch in one of his cafés in Kampala, he very generously talked to us about what we needed to set up such a company and encouraged us to sell the coffee as a finished product. Most Ugandan coffees were sold as raw green coffee, and he was pleased to know that we were following in his footsteps to build a global coffee brand that owned the whole value chain. He introduced us to his Kenyan manager, Samuel Maina, who gave very useful feedback on the financial plan I was developing. Reading Andrew's book *A Good African Story* on my plane ride from

Uganda to Switzerland gave me additional insights and valuable lessons on the challenges of raising financing.

After pitching, World Wildlife Fund for Nature Switzerland gave us our first loan of 100,000 euros to develop a high-impact coffee brand that would contribute to saving gorillas. It was wonderful to meet the impact investor who provided half of this loan, Juerg Hunziker, and his lovely wife and daughter in Zurich.

Now it was time to take the challenge home. I turned to one of the community members, Safari Joseph, who we had engaged when setting up the telecentre and asked him if he knew of any arabica coffee farmers. He revealed to me that not only was he a coffee farmer, but he was also growing arabica coffee. I asked him to reach out to others, and found out that the former parish chief—local council III chairperson Sam Karibwende, was also an arabica coffee farmer. In December 2015 we had a meeting at Sam's farm in Kyumbugushu village, adjacent to Bwindi Impenetrable National Park, with about thirty farmers they had mobilized. The farmers were not receiving a steady market or fair price. One question that I struggled to answer was "Is this about promoting organic coffee or promoting gorillas?" I told them that Gorilla Conservation Coffee was founded to protect gorillas through supporting coffee farmers. Safari then pulled me aside and said "It is very good that you are engaging these farmers because some of them are still hunting animals in the park. If we keep them busy growing good coffee, they will not have time to enter the park to poach and collect firewood." This was exactly the information I needed to create a conservation enterprise by developing a global coffee brand that would save gorillas one sip at a time.

I was surprised to find that there was no coffee cooperative in the area, and first encouraged the farmers to create one. This way, we could train them in the same way to produce good coffee that we would market. They decided to call it the Bwindi Coffee Growers Cooperative, restricted to farmers in subcounties bordering Bwindi who were most likely to affect the gorillas' habitat in the three surrounding districts.

I was then introduced to a German company that wanted to buy the coffee from the Bwindi farmers. However, before they could make an offer, they asked to test the coffee for quality. It was my first time at a cupping session, and I found it very exciting. The coffee was cupped from the top coffee-producing areas in Uganda, including Mount Elgon and Mount Rwenzori, that also have national parks conserving important biodiversity. Though I believed that the Bwindi coffee was good because of the high altitude of between 1,600 and 2,600 meters, we were all surprised when the coffee from one of our farmers' crops scored the highest points!

They wanted to make an offer, but needed to be sure that we could provide them with thousands of kilograms of the same quality coffee. I was not sure that all farmers in the first seventy-five we engaged had the same coffee quality as Sam, and realized that we were not yet ready to take up such offers. This was further confirmed when I took one kilogram of coffee to Switzerland to a Swiss roaster and trader, Carlo Delfs from Sense of Coffee, who was also amazed at the quality. However, on a second trip I took him more coffee and he was disgusted about how bad the quality was. This is when I realized that we had to train the Bwindi farmers to consistently produce good coffee; it was the only way we could ensure them a steady market and good price.

I found the answer to this problem when I connected with Joseph Nkandu, an Ashoka Fellow and founder of the National Union of Coffee Agribusinesses and Farmer Enterprises (NUCAFE). He was passionate about getting coffee farmers a fair price for their coffee and excited to partner with Gorilla Conservation Coffee to train the farmers. I learned a lot from his team and that of Africa Coffee Academy—founded by my cousin Robert Nsibirwa, at the first training session, as did the farmers. Coffee seedlings should be planted at a particular spacing and pruned and weeded all throughout their growth. To produce high-quality washed arabica coffee, the red cherries must be harvested, pulped (to remove the outer coat), and fermented on the same day. Then the coffee is dried in the shade to produce what's called parchment. Rural farmers sold their coffee as red cherries or parchment.

I also learned that the coffee traders—the middlemen—had the upper hand when it came to buying coffee. The price would fluctuate from $2 to 80 cents per kilogram of parchment particularly when farmers were desperately needing money for fixed costs, such as school fees to send their children back to school. Another disappointing discovery was that after being bought by the traders the raw coffee from Bwindi farmers was combined with coffee from known coffee-growing regions like Mount Rwenzori and could never be traced again to Bwindi.

We wanted fair practices and credit where credit was due. After WWF CH sent funds, we bought a central pulper that could remove the coat of the coffee cherries, and placed it at Safari's home. We then asked Safari to buy all coffee from the farmers at a premium price of 1,300 shillings per kilogram of red cherries, which was equivalent to $2 per kilogram of parchment and $3 per kilogram of green coffee (the stage after parchment). When Peter Ebinu joined us as the operations manager, he realized that we were losing money as we were paying an above-market price for good coffee cherries as well as the bad unripe or over-ripened cherries that we could not use, meaning that there was a lot of waste. This led me to make a difficult but strategic decision to only buy good coffee cherries from the farmers.

It made a huge difference to the financial sustainability of the social enterprise. The farmers soon learned that if they wanted a good price for coffee, they had to pick the coffee at the right time when it was ripe like a fresh red cherry and not when it was overripe or eaten by insects or still green and raw. We assured them that if they selectively harvested the coffee they would get a better price, which would ultimately make them better farmers who would earn a larger income. We trained them to keep consistent records and grow and process good coffee, spaced adequately with trenches to drain the water, and pruning, which gave them a higher yield for each tree.

We also taught them to grow shade trees or fruit trees with the coffee to help maintain a constant temperature around the coffee tree by preventing excessive heat and wind. When the shade trees' leaves fall and decompose, the soil's nutrient content and texture is improved, enabling it to retain more water for the coffee trees.

I found out that if the pulping of the cherries doesn't happen on the same day that they are picked, the coffee loses quality, and most farmers did not have hand pulpers. Therefore, at the beginning to be sure that we could have consistently good coffee, we bought fresh red cherries from the farmers on the day that they were harvested so that we could pulp and ferment the cherries on the same day. After fermentation, the coffee was washed and placed on racks to dry in the shade to become parchment coffee that could be taken to Kampala to be hulled to produce green coffee.

Now that we had mastered our manufacturing, our next step was to sell the coffee. Betty Aliba, a highly enterprising young woman, came to my office to tell me she was starting a Uganda Cultural Fair that could promote culture, conservation, and tourism together. Richard Bagyenyi, our program assistant, developed a rapport with Betty, who convinced him that we should sell Gorilla Conservation Coffee at her new fair.

The fair would have just the sort of people we were targeting to buy the coffee: local conservationists and expatriates in Uganda who have a passion for conservation and Ugandan culture. We worked with a local graphic designer to produce the first brand, which I decided should be named after my favorite gorilla, Kanyonyi. We used his photo for the package and developed a few words similar to the ones we had used for Gorilla Kawa. We even sourced bags from the UK, of two different types, shiny silver foil and matte brown recyclable kraft paper, because we thought that it would help us determine which bag people preferred. We developed brochures and waited excitedly for people's reaction to the coffee.

The day arrived. Some people came to our stall because they knew me and had heard about CTPH, while others came because they wanted to buy coffee, which we were serving. It turned out to be the most valuable time to test the market because it showed that people were keen to buy a product linked to a cause.

We also received valuable feedback on how to improve the packaging and create a brand look. We decided to go with the kraft bag made out of recycled paper with a stylized version of a photograph of Kanyonyi creatively designed by Add Value in Kampala.

The Entebbe International Airport duty-free shop became our first retail outlet for the coffee in December 2016. They also became our largest customer, placing weekly orders.

I realized that Gorilla Conservation Coffee was not a mass-market product because it could only be sourced from farmers where the gorillas were found. Most supermarkets competed on price and were unlikely to pay more than what we paid the farmers, so I also reached out to my other contacts, one of them being Suni Magyar, the owner of the Banana Boat retail shops. They had previously sold Gorilla Kawa and were selling other high-quality products with a cause, including crafts made by disabled groups. Recognizing that it was a niche market product, she was immediately interested in having Gorilla Conservation Coffee in her shop.

To launch our first brand of Gorilla Conservation Coffee globally, we developed a six-week crowdfunding campaign to reach out to many people in a short space of time and raise funds to buy coffee from the farmers, as well as pay for the costs to unveil the brand. We also needed a website, which was developed by a British blogger based in Uganda, Charlotte Beauvoisin. We would not have been able to pull off this crowdfunding campaign without the support of Werner Krendi, my financial adviser on Gorilla Conservation Coffee assigned by WWF CH, who compiled relevant information, and Amy Roll, a Global Health Corps fellow with CTPH, who developed the content.

And it proved successful, as I began to make some important and influential connections outside Uganda, including Melanie Hawkin, founder of Lionesses of Africa, who promotes African women-led businesses developing high-impact brands. This led to conferences in South Africa and London, where I was able to spread the story and brand of Gorilla Conservation Coffee. In 2017, Gorilla Conservation Coffee won its first award, the Switch Africa Green SEED award for ecoinclusive enterprises, from the European Union and United Nations. It came with funding and expertise to develop a business plan to attract investment. Gorilla Conservation Coffee subsequently joined the Conservation International Sustainable Coffee Challenge.

AidChild Café and Gallery located at the Equator, a favorite stop for many tourists traveling to Bwindi, was serving coffee that was not from Uganda; it came from Kenya. The manager, Sylvia Nanyunja, was keen on changing to Gorilla Conservation Coffee because most of the visitors who stopped by were going to trek gorillas and would be excited to buy locally grown coffee. AidChild became another major outlet.

We entered another global coffee competition and sent our product as roasted branded coffee to the United States. Again, we were all pleasantly surprised when Gorilla Conservation Coffee scored 92 points out of 100, as a specialty coffee, and even more elated when the Kanyonyi Coffee brand was among the top thirty coffees they cupped in 2018, and came in as number twenty-nine along with the best coffees in the world from South America, and countries closer to home in Rwanda and Burundi. This gave us the confidence to increase the price and brand value as a specialty coffee protecting endangered mountain gorillas, which increased our revenue to cover the costs of producing and marketing it.

We partnered with a conservation enterprise called Pangols that markets products made by local people who share a habitat with wildlife, to reduce their need to poach and destroy their habitat—a perfect fit for Gorilla Conservation Coffee. Through their founder, we started selling coffee outside Uganda as a co-branded product and continued to build our brand in the United States.

CTPH board member Dr. Lynn Murrell convinced Catherine Rasco from Arabica's Coffee House to sell Gorilla Conservation Coffee in her high-end cafés in Portland, Maine. We were elated when Cathy was willing to buy the coffee at a higher price of $7 per kilogram of green coffee ($2 higher than previous offers), which led to her becoming our first brick-and-mortar retail outlet in the United States. Lawrence and I were elated, even more so when a gorilla trekking tourist recognized the packaging from a shop in Maine.

Natural Habitat Safaris, which was affiliated with WWF US, convinced us to start coffee safaris and became our first customer. They visited the coffee farm of Sam Karibwende, who practiced organic farming and taught other farmers to adopt his methods.

Uganda Coffee Development Authority (UCDA) was excited about our brand that was enabling Ugandan coffee to be known internationally. When I met their executive director, Dr. Emmanuel Iyamulemye, while participating in a panel discussion on coffee tourism, he offered us space at the UCDA stall at the Specialty Coffee Expo in Boston. Lawrence and I were also invited to the Sustainable Tourism and Trade Association (STTA) conference in Mombasa, Kenya, to talk about the coffee safaris we had developed for gorilla trekking tourists to meet Bwindi coffee farmers and learn how coffee is saving gorillas.

As word of Gorilla Conservation Coffee's success spread, we were invited to join the Growth Africa accelerator program to help us realize our potential. Through this program, I learned a lot, especially that we could not be all things to all people, so we needed to understand who our customer was and be more strategic about our marketing.

I was encouraged that the coffee was also being sold extensively in lodges at Bwindi, and their guests preferred it because sometimes they met the farmers as they trekked the mountain gorillas and that was more meaningful than buying cheaper brands in supermarkets. I discovered that our main customers were tourists visiting Bwindi and other parts of Uganda and East Africa, expatriates, and the growing number of coffee-drinking Ugandans. Though Uganda is the largest coffee-exporting country in Africa, less than 6 percent of the coffee is consumed locally. I felt this was a big lost opportunity and wondered what we could do about it.

The next natural evolution was to establish a chain of coffee shops. Our first café was a rented room in a bar and restaurant. We now needed to hire baristas. We debated whether to hire people who were passionate about wildlife and teach them about making a good cup of coffee or people who were passionate about coffee and teach them about gorillas and wildlife conservation. Realizing that we needed to sell a good cup of coffee to get people to keep coming back, we opted for the latter.

Just as we were about to launch the Gorilla Conservation Café in December 2017, I received the shocking news that Kanyonyi, the gorilla after whom our coffee had been named, had died. He had been one of my favorite gorillas, and I'd known him since he was a baby. Kanyonyi had taken over the leadership of the Mubare gorilla group from his father Ruhondeza five years earlier. I'd last checked on him with my CTPH team two weeks before his death. Not long before, Kanyonyi had fallen off a tree and developed an infection in his hip. He was treated with antibiotics, but he'd fought with a habituated lone silverback, Maraya, and never fully recovered. The day we visited, he was weak and moving very slowly and built a day nest in front of us, which was highly unusual among gorillas. They usually prefer to build their nests in the evening when they are retiring for the night. But Kanyonyi was weak and needed to rest comfortably. One of his mates, Karungyi, was guarding him with her infant.

I felt that I had lost a dear friend. Kanyonyi had grown up around tourists. Even as a silverback and leader of his gorilla group, he would deliberately set out to frighten tourists to see their reaction—his idea of humor, which was definitely lost on the unsuspecting tourists.

People reached out with condolences and asked whether we intended to keep the same name for our coffee. I felt strongly that we should continue Kanyonyi's legacy through this brand and the new Gorilla Conservation Café. His individual story would help tell the larger story about how helping communities who share a habitat with critically endangered gorillas can prevent them from becoming extinct. I hoped that Kanyonyi's legacy could also continue naturally through his only surviving offspring, Masanyu, an infant who joined the Rushegura gorilla group with his mother Nyampazi. Masanyu had managed not to be killed by the lead silverback, Kabukojo, which is a miracle, because gorillas typically kill offspring that are not their own. Instead Masanyu was protected by the other females in the group. Nevertheless, I became concerned when his mother, Nyampazi, left him with the stepfather less than two years later and moved to Mubare gorilla group, which is also unusual. Sadly, Masanyu did not survive this separation from his mother.

Our first bulk order of coffee was five hundred bags of 250 grams each to be gifts for donors to Population Connection, an organization that supported us. We sent the bags co-branded with information about both organizations. More opportunities arose with the Great Apes Survival Programme (GRASP) at the International Primatological Society (IPS) conference in Nairobi. We provided co-branded coffee as gifts for the delegates, because they wanted to have a fully sustainable conference, where aluminum water bottles and local crafts were also given away. The next year, CTPH hosted the second African Primatological Society Conference affiliated to IPS, in Uganda. We served coffee that people could buy at the venue, and two hundred 125-gram co-branded bags of Gorilla Conservation Coffee were provided to the delegates in their gift bags.

Soon after, Tusk Trust generously offered for Gorilla Conservation Coffee to be served during the award ceremony where I was honored to be a finalist for the Tusk Award for Conservation in Africa.

The challenge of attracting investors remained. I had come to realize that sourcing coffee from seventy-five farmers wasn't enough of a draw to investors, but had no idea how to increase the numbers of coffee farmers within the Bwindi Coffee Growers Cooperative. Our funding from WWF CH had run out, so our working capital was limited to the revenue from the coffee we could sell. With the help of Solidaridad, an organization that supports small-scale farmers in their efforts to establish supply chains, we expanded to five hundred farmers through the model farmer system, where each of the twenty-five "model farmers" mentored other farmers. Now Gorilla Conservation Coffee was more attractive to investors. That year, we participated in an Italian Startup Africa Roadtrip accelerator program that made our pitch more appealing to investors. Gorilla Conservation Coffee won second prize, which meant that we could travel to Italy to meet potential investors.

We were introduced to Simon Leveldt, a two-hundred-year-old family-owned coffee business in the Netherlands. After we sent them a coffee sample, they were keen to buy six thousand kilograms. I was very excited, but concerned that we did not have this much coffee. We had to find a way to engage more coffee farmers around Bwindi so that when such a buyer came around, we had enough supply. This would also enable us to achieve our goal of reducing the number of farmers poaching in the gorillas' habitat. The newly enrolled five hundred farmers gave me hope. However, Simon Leveldt only sold organic coffee, and our farmers were not yet certified though most of them grew coffee organically primarily because they couldn't afford the commonly sold nonorganic fertilizer.

Even without the official organic label, by the end of 2019, the demand for Gorilla Conservation Coffee was far exceeding the supply.

And the situation was about to change, making Gorilla Conservation Coffee realize its potential to save gorillas when tourism ground to a halt.

Chapter 26

The COVID-19 Pandemic

In December 2019, the first whispers of a new coronavirus spreading very quickly across China reached me. Scientists rushed to find the center of this outbreak and initially concluded the most likely source was the sale of bats at the Huanan wet market in Wuhan, where the first human cases were reported.

The bats were caged in cramped conditions with other wild and domestic animals that did not ordinarily come into contact with each other. The close quarters and levels of stress experienced by the caged wild animals provided the perfect breeding ground for the virus to mutate and jump from one species to the next. As carriers of the virus, the bats would not have been affected, but this was not the case for other species.

Soon, reports came in pointing to a possibility of the pangolin as the intermediate host, meaning that they had contracted the virus from the bats. Consequently, those who ate pangolins also became infected. In China, eating pangolins for medicinal purposes is common practice and has fueled the commercial trade in pangolin meat, leading to a severe reduction in their numbers, even in Uganda, making them the next mammal after elephants and rhinos most impacted by the illegal wildlife trade. However, it was never proven and the search for another intermediate host continued.

This new strain of the coronavirus, COVID-19, was a definite cause for concern as the numbers of cases in China grew. The onset of the pandemic took me back to my early days and the reason I was hired as the first vet for the government wildlife agency: to protect the gorillas from contracting a fatal virus from humans. Yet, like the rest of the world, as much as I knew the mountain gorillas were at risk from this new strain of coronavirus, I didn't realize how contagious it was going to be and how much it was going to affect so many people in almost every country in the world, including Uganda. On January 30, 2020, the World Health Organization announced a public health emergency of international concern.

My years of dealing with zoonotic disease outbreaks such as Ebola and anthrax as a member of the Uganda Ministry of Health National Disease Task Force and sarcoptic mange (scabies) from my early days setting up the veterinary unit of Uganda Wildlife Authority, had somewhat prepared me for what lay ahead. Yet, unlike the Ebola outbreak, COVID-19 was far more contagious, and I knew we had to act fast.

COVID-19 wasn't the first respiratory disease to have the potential to spread from people to great apes. In 2011, human metapneumovirus infected Rwandan mountain gorillas, and two died. It was eventually traced back to South Africa, with the most likely host a tourist. In 2013 fifty-six chimpanzees became infected with a respiratory disease at Kibale National Park in Uganda, and five died. That event coincided with respiratory outbreaks in the local human communities and was associated with human rhinovirus C, another common cold virus in humans.[21] In 2016, wild chimpanzees at the research site within the Tai Forest in Ivory Coast contracted a human coronavirus, HCOV—OC43.[22] With all the available evidence, I persuaded UWA to require the wearing of masks by tourists, park staff, and any other visitors to protect the endangered mountain gorillas from contracting this new strain of coronavirus.

As airports started to shut down all over the world, we worked hard and fast to prepare the park staff of Bwindi Impenetrable National Park to enforce the health and safety rules for the mountain gorilla treks. We knew that we could not risk a single tourist getting close enough to a gorilla to potentially infect them with a virus that was already causing mounting numbers of deaths around the world. I convinced International Gorilla Conservation Programme (IGCP) to fund the training workshop and the Max Planck Institute donated hard-to-come-by surgical masks. The country had run out of surgical masks, and even our donated allotment was not sufficient. We knew we needed to find another source to obtain enough masks to protect the mountain gorillas and park rangers. That's when an inspiring local social enterprise called Ride for a Woman stepped up. This organization promoted women's financial independence and empowerment. They made tablecloths from local Kitenge material for tourists, but with travel affected, their market had dried up, and the enterprise was in trouble. Consequently, the founder jumped at the opportunity to produce cloth masks instead, saving her from having to lay off the women from the local Bwindi community.

Masks weren't our only stumbling block. Hand sanitizers and infrared thermometers were also in short supply. I eventually sourced one thermometer in Kampala from Doctor's Clinic at double the price—$120 instead of the usual $60—and hand sanitizer from Freicca Pharmacy in Kampala.

The first COVID-19 case in Uganda was reported on March 21, 2020, leading to panic, anxiety, and the beginning of social gathering restrictions. Schools had closed a few days earlier on March 18, and Lawrence collected our boys, Ndhego, fifteen, and Tendo, eleven, from their boarding school. They came home with their luggage and one month's homework. It was a relief to have my boys home safe and also an opportunity to widen their educational experience by taking them with me as I began the COVID training course. Though they had attended protocol training courses before, I knew that this one was somehow different. Now the stakes were not only the fate of the gorillas, but the fate of humanity as well. I believed the action we took now would shape the future of the mountain gorilla tourist treks and it would be something my sons would remember for the rest of their lives.

The first training workshop was held at the UWA Visitor Information Center at Buhoma, Bwindi's main tourist site, a spacious building that could allow social distancing of one meter between participants. The center proved to be a perfect setting, with the backdrop of the forest offering a calm environment for this critical training in a time of fear and anxiety. This landmark workshop was the beginning of a series of training days held in five tourist trekking locations in Bwindi. In just four days, we trained 130 staff to embrace the new gorilla viewing guidelines. We upgraded the usual protocols and procedures for all visitors with emphasis on preventing anyone with signs of a cough, flu, or fever from going on the treks and required the wearing of masks for all people visiting the gorillas. Particular attention was paid on maintaining the seven-meter distance between humans and gorillas. Although the gorillas might break the distance rules, it was even more essential that people did not. These updated regulations became the new policy not only for the gorillas in Uganda, but also for the chimpanzees.

We were also able to offer practical training to tourists using volunteers to trek to the gorilla groups. The age restriction had been part of the gorilla viewing guidelines for some time to minimize the risk of the gorillas picking up childhood diseases such as measles from young children. But Ndhego was now fifteen, old enough to visit the gorillas. His first trek as a volunteer was probably as memorable for me as it was for him. As parents we always hope to pass on our legacy to the next generation, and to be able to share the importance of protecting the mountain gorillas with my son was such a gift.

During the trek, our ranger, Goreth Nyibiza, received a message on her phone that the Uganda Wildlife Authority had suspended primate tourism from March 26 until the end of April 2020 to protect the gorillas and chimpanzees during the COVID-19 pandemic. I was greatly relieved, as well as concerned. Even though the gorillas would be safe from contracting COVID-19 from tourists, they would be even more vulnerable to potential poachers and their snares. With the growth of gorilla tourism, more and more communities had given up farming and become dependent on the revenue that tourism brought. With the suspension of tourism and a loss of revenue, local communities would feel they had no choice but to venture back into the forest for bushmeat to feed their families and earn a living. Not only would the gorillas be vulnerable to snares, but the potential for conflict between the gorillas and the community could also develop. More exposure to community meant more exposure to COVID-19. And even in normal times gorillas sometimes left the park boundary to forage for banana plants and eucalyptus trees on community land. Now they risked picking up a lethal virus. The vital role of the trackers and rangers was more urgent than ever, and I emphasized the importance of continuing to check on the gorillas every day to ensure their safety and continued health.

The fundamental principle behind setting up Conservation Through Public Health (CTPH) was precisely to avoid the transmission of diseases between human and gorilla communities, as well as resolving the conflict between them so that they could coexist in harmony and peace. Consequently, we already had in place a program for local communities who either trained to become gorilla guardians as members of the human and gorilla conflict resolution teams (HUGOs) or were part of the village health and conservation teams (VHCTs).

Over the past thirteen years, CTPH had facilitated the formation of 270 VHCTs in six frontline parishes with high human and gorilla conflict around Bwindi. However, with the onset of COVID-19, I knew we would need to newly train these two sets of community volunteers regarding the risks of this highly contagious disease. With this in mind, we'd sent a proposal to the Arcus Foundation to help us train them, and their donation was our first emergency grant during the pandemic. Perhaps we would be ahead of the game and deal with potential problems before they arose.

We were anxious to conduct this training especially when the tourism warden, Peter Mbwebwe, told me that the Habinyanja gorilla group had come outside the park, and the affected community member was asking for a lot of money for the loss of his eucalyptus trees that had been debarked by this gorilla family. In the southern sector another gorilla group, Nkuringo, who were notorious for coming out of the park, had also ranged into community land. It was a sign of things to come, and little did we know that this gorilla group was going to face the greatest tragedy of all.

With primate tourism suspended, the local communities had suffered a significant loss of income. We started to receive donations from generous individuals who had visited Bwindi, who wanted to support the local porters and other members of the community. However, despite the generosity of donations, I began to receive disturbing but not unexpected reports that some members of the Bwindi community had returned to the forest to poach. With a rise in poaching, it was only a matter of time before disaster struck.

At the beginning of June 2020, just two months after primate tourism was suspended, I received a report that the lead silverback of Nkuringo gorilla group, Rafiki, had died. I had last visited that gorilla group that February, when we left him mating with an adult female, Kizza. He kept to himself most of the time, leaving the younger blackbacks, Tabu and Muhoozi, to entertain us. I was confident that he was ably leading his group and received the utmost respect from his family members, as the only silverback. Enos Nahabwe, our wildlife health technician, was particularly shocked at the news of Rafiki's death because when he had checked on him the previous week, he looked healthy and was behaving normally. However, after the postmortem, we found out that it wasn't sickness that had killed Rafiki, but something more sinister. Rafiki's death was the result of a sharp object penetrating the left upper part of his abdomen up to the internal organs. A sharp object, most likely a spear, that could only have been deliberately inserted. Our worst fears had come to pass; he was killed by hungry and desperate poachers.

Three days after Rafiki's killing, bushmeat and several hunting devices including a spear, rope snares, wire snares, and a dog hunting bell were recovered from a house. The poacher had been driven into the forest to feed his family and to earn a living from selling the bushmeat at the local market. He claimed that when he entered

Bwindi Impenetrable National Park in the early hours of the morning, to check on the snares he had set for duiker and bush pigs, he was attacked by Rafiki, and killed him with a spear in self-defense. The poacher was arrested by UWA along with three others with whom he claimed to have shared the bushmeat.

My first reaction was disbelief. After having worked in the Bwindi community for over fifteen years through CTPH field programs, I could not imagine how someone could kill Rafiki, particularly when gorilla tourism had transformed and lifted many of the local community members at Bwindi out of poverty. Murole village, where the poachers came from, is in one of the target parishes, Nteko, with high human and gorilla conflict that CTPH has been working in for ten years.

I realized just how hungry people were and how the absence of tourism income had contributed to this tragedy. Tourism had become a lucrative business; the amount of money that someone earns from a day of carrying tourists' luggage to track gorillas is the same as most members of the community earn in one month. Those relying on selling crafts, food, and accommodation to tourists were equally suffering. The Nteko parish community suffered even more than most because their land is barren, forcing them to acquire more fertile land across the border in DR Congo where they planted their crops. With lockdowns and the closing of the borders between Uganda and DR Congo, they had not been able to harvest their crops.

Two communities had been devastated by this tragedy; the poacher facing eleven years' imprisonment and no longer able to support his family, and the gorillas who had lost their leader.

I first met Rafiki as a six-year-old juvenile gorilla in 2001 when I was conducting my tuberculosis research. Rafiki grew up seeing people in the forest, because the Nkuringo gorilla group had been habituated in 1997, and by the time he became the lead silverback in 2008 after his father died he trusted all human beings. This made it easier for the poacher to get close enough to him and, out of fear, instead of avoiding Rafiki, the poacher speared him. Sadly, this tragic incident left the Nkuringo gorilla group without a leader. Within just two weeks, they shrank from seventeen gorillas to ten. Three gorillas left the group to join a silverback we named Christmas. His group grew from five to eight gorillas, including two females without babies and one blackback called Muhoozi. Three other gorillas also left the Nkuringo gorilla group and started wandering on their own, eventually joining the Bishaho gorilla group that was also ranging nearby. The females with infants did not leave Nkuringo gorilla group because their infants could be killed by a new silverback. Though the Nkuringo gorilla group did not yet have a clear leader, I suspected one of the two older remaining blackbacks, Rwamutwe or Tabu, would take over the group. I prayed the Nkuringo group would eventually stabilize and recover from the trauma of Rafiki's death. Thankfully, a month after leaving, Muhoozi returned from the Christmas group and Rwamutwe, who had stayed, at the age of sixteen and about to start silvering, stepped into the shoes of Rafiki to lead a gorilla family of eleven.

This poaching incident showed us the urgent need to intensify our conservation education and community health programs to reach every single resident, including these four poachers and their families. I also realized that although providing emergency food relief to local communities is not what we do at CTPH, we needed to address hunger at Bwindi brought about by the COVID-19 pandemic. We devised a plan to support the local communities by providing seedlings of fast-growing food crops to meet their nutritional needs during this time. It was also an opportunity to teach the Bwindi communities to embrace sustainable farming as a longer-term measure to reduce their dependence on tourism revenue to feed their families.

While distributing fast-growing seedlings and seeds consisting of ten "ready to grow" crops—pumpkins, maize, ground nuts, beans, onions, tomatoes, amaranthus, spinach, kale, and cabbages—to the first one thousand most vulnerable households around Bwindi, we visited the family of the poacher together with Jane Flanagan from the London *Times*, who was doing a story on COVID-19 and conservation for an appeal for Tusk Trust. The community lined up to receive their seedlings with an air of hope in this desperate situation. Among them was the poacher's wife, who had been identified by our VHCT. At her home made of mud and wattle, I discovered that she was only twenty-two and had three children under the age of three. She was among the poorest people in her village, renting land from her husband's grandfather, who relied on her husband to provide for him. Coincidentally, the grandfather's brother had been a ranger when we dealt with the gorilla that settled in community land twenty-four years ago. Her grandfather's brother warmed up to us and told us that when the poacher speared the bush pig it screamed, and Rafiki, who wanted to protect his family, charged. The poacher in self-defense speared the gorilla several times until he died. Though it did not bring Rafiki back, I was more at peace knowing the full story. Hunger had driven community members to poach during the pandemic, and we were actively trying to do something about that.

Meanwhile, the park rangers also needed more support. Tusk Trust funded our ability to buy rangers food rations to take into the forest while monitoring the gorillas and patrolling their habitat to look for snares, and other signs of illegal activity. We also obtained funds from the British High Commission and IUCN to purchase camera traps and GPS units to support their antipoaching efforts.

Coffee farmers around Bwindi also needed support during the pandemic. Our main coffee market prior to the pandemic was the gorilla trekking tourists. However, now that they had stopped traveling to Uganda, we had to look for buyers outside Uganda. Fortunately, we were able to get our first distributor from the UK, Moneyrowbeans, just in time.

The impact of the COVID-19 pandemic on the local communities really hit home. It was clear to me that this overdependence on tourism simply was not sustainable, and I recognized that engaging the Bwindi community in longer-term alternative livelihoods such as Gorilla Conservation Coffee was even more essential.

Soon, though, the pandemic was brought home in a very personal way when we received news of the death of my husband's aunt, Erina Zikusoka, in London. She was a great supporter of our work, and it came as a shock to us all when we received the news. Only a week later, we received yet more news from London of the death of my closest friend's mother, Margaret Ssali, who was also a great supporter of the work at CTPH. Later in the year we lost a renown environmentalist and wetland defender, Paul Mafabi, and three more close relatives and family friends in Uganda, Betty Mdoe, Ambassador Stephen Nabeta and Dr. Edward Kigonya, a prominent physician.

As the devastation of COVID-19 stretched across the world, we received news about asymptomatic zookeepers unwittingly spreading the virus to tigers and lions at the Bronx Zoo in New York. Cats and dogs also contracted the virus from their owners. Then the shocking report of farmed mink contracting COVID-19 from asymptomatic handlers, developing respiratory symptoms, and then transmitting it back to other handlers. The Netherlands and Danish governments decided to cull millions of farmed mink because they feared that they would become a new reservoir of more virulent strains of COVID-19.

Several studies soon showed that old-world primates were susceptible to the virus. In fact, great apes have the same angiotensin converting enzyme (ACE2) protein receptors as humans; the SARS-COV-2 virus attaches to them easily.[23, 24] We already had an early warning system for disease outbreaks through noninvasive collection of gorilla fecal samples from their night nest and trails, and we immediately began testing samples for COVID-19.

In June 2020 Uganda partially eased lockdowns. I was elated that three decades of advocacy was paying off when President Museveni stated that tourism to gorillas and chimpanzees would not open yet because he did not want our "cousins" to get sick. He echoed a concern we had raised in a joint publication with great ape experts at the beginning of the pandemic in March 2020.[25] I lobbied for prioritizing the testing of park staff, conservation staff, porters, gorilla guardians, VHCTs, indigenous Batwa (hunter-gatherers who were evicted from the forest when it became a national park), reformed poachers associations, and villagers whose homes were visited by wandering gorillas. The National Disease Task Force granted our request. We made arrangements with the local health centers around Bwindi to collect their nasal and oral swabs.

These plans were timely because great ape tourism reopened at the end of September 2020.[26] Just two months later, Uganda was in the grips of its first severe wave of COVID-19. We got wind of this when conducting a second formal training of the park rangers in stricter management of tourists and more intensive gorilla health monitoring. In the middle of the training, one of the CTPH staff developed a sore throat and mild cough; it was a shock to us all when he tested positive and we had to immediately cancel the next workshop for the next set of rangers. Those of us who were with him immediately went into quarantine. This created a lot of anxiety and tension for the partner organizations of CTPH who participated in the training. It was an even greater shock when staff at our office in Entebbe also tested positive and so did staff of several institutions in Entebbe and Uganda's capital, Kampala. COVID-19 had arrived in Uganda in a big way. On top of minimizing further spread within my team, I found myself having to counsel my staff who tested positive, and encouraged them to take the medications recommended by the government of Uganda: azithromycin, vitamin C, and zinc oxide. Luckily, during this outbreak everyone developed mild symptoms and quickly recovered. (We were not always to be this lucky.) I realized we needed to develop stricter preventive measures through more frequent testing of the staff who now had to upgrade from cloth masks to putting on fresh surgical masks or N95 masks when they were within ten meters of the gorillas.

However, in spite of all these imminent threats to the great apes, including humans, I saw COVID-19's silver lining. Now, we'd be more likely to see a change in people's behavior and government policies to prevent future pandemics. Since the COVID-19 pandemic, I have been encouraged to see tourists demanding that adequate social distancing and other protection measures are put in place to protect the great apes.

The COVID-19 crisis drew attention to many of the key safety measures and approaches and health issues that CTPH has been highlighting for years, addressing the One Health interface between humans and wildlife. Within a few weeks, our established CTPH programs were able to mitigate the impact of the virus on endangered mountain gorillas and on the local communities with whom they share their fragile habitat. This in turn helped communities to cope better during the COVID-19 pandemic.

The pandemic illustrated how diseases can easily spread between wild animals and people and demonstrated the need for greater protection of wildlife habitats. Sixty percent of emerging zoonotic diseases in humans come from animals including wild animals where deforestation and other forms of habitat destruction bring people in closer contact with wildlife. It also showed the need to ban animals that are likely to harbor such contagious diseases from wet markets and improve the welfare of animals that find themselves in these situations.

The COVID-19 pandemic brought the world's economies to their knees, and a realization that life will never be the same again where we all have to learn to live in a new "normal." This includes learning to respect and value nature and wildlife to prevent the next pandemic.

Chapter 27

The COVID-19 Nightmare Continues into 2021

2021 began with the shocking news that all gorillas living in the same troop in San Diego Zoo Safari Park in the United States contracted COVID-19 from an asymptomatic keeper. It was diagnosed through testing their fecal samples. Eight captive western lowland gorillas developed mild to moderate symptoms; however, one of them, Winston, a forty-eight-year-old silverback, developed severe symptoms that only improved after he was treated with monoclonal antibodies, a very expensive treatment that had only just started to be used on humans.

This prompted the San Diego Zoo to vaccinate another troop of gorillas that had not contracted COVID-19, as well as chimpanzees and other susceptible species, with an experimental animal vaccine produced by Zoetis. They were willing to take the risk though it was not yet approved for commercial use in animals. But vaccinating a wild ape population would be much more difficult, if not impossible.

A month later, gorillas in Prague Zoo in Czechoslovakia also got COVID-19 from asymptomatic keepers.

Again, a silver lining. After the captive gorillas got COVID-19, CTPH was able to successfully advocate at a Ministry of Health COVID-19 task force meeting in January for park staff and conservation personnel working with great apes to be among the priority groups of people to be vaccinated along with health workers and teachers.

As in the rest of the world, COVID-19 cases were rising in Uganda and surrounding African countries. It was a fear we all lived with. In February while in Burundi training veterinarians, I became one of the growing number of COVID-19 patients.

Far from home and confined to a hotel room, it was a lonely and difficult time especially letting my son, Tendo, know that I would be missing his twelfth birthday celebration. It was particularly frustrating because we had all been in quarantine for a period of six days after arriving in Burundi. Having been declared free from COVID-19, we found that our trainees were not wearing masks, and we had to buy them masks and sanitizers to protect each other.

I woke up the following morning with a heavy feeling of sadness that I was not going to be around for Tendo's birthday and apprehension about the next few days. After being given medicine to treat the COVID-19, which consisted of three sets of tablets—azithromycin antibiotics, zinc oxide, and hydroxychloroquine—it hit me that the bungalow I had transferred to from the hotel was to be my home of solitary confinement for the next week or until I tested negative, which could even last as long as one month.

I broke the news to my sister Veronica, who was looking after my mother, who at the age of ninety-one had recently become weaker and less mobile. We made a decision not to tell my mother I had fallen ill. I also did not want to make Tendo more anxious and did not tell him why I added an extra twelve days to my stay. My sister called me every day, and whenever I sounded anxious, would insist that I measure my oxygen levels on the pulse oximeter I carried with me from Uganda, while she was on the call, and advised me to call a doctor if the reading went below 90. My husband tried to cheer me up with photos of Tendo's birthday celebration.

However, after taking the hydroxychloroquine, I developed an intense headache that prevented me from looking at a computer screen for two days, which added to my anxiety. After finding out that this drug had been banned for treatment of COVID-19 by the Food and Drug Administration (FDA) in the United States, I stopped taking it and my headaches went away. Though I was beginning to lose concentration, I forced myself to fulfill previous obligations, which kept me sane.

This included media training with National Geographic Society, having become a National Geographic Explorer in 2018, and a presentation at the Global Banking for Values conference, having become a finalist for the Tallberg Eliasson Leadership Prize in 2020. I also found the energy to facilitate a virtual meeting where we shared findings from surveys of over one thousand travelers to determine their willingness to adopt stricter COVID-19 protocols when visiting great apes.[27] These virtual interactions helped to take my mind off my isolation. I was also cheered up daily by several black birds that perched on the ground near my bedroom window.

On day two, I lost my sense of taste and smell. I lost my appetite completely. As a veterinarian I knew the consequences of not eating for several days could be dehydration and even coma. It was a struggle to drink a cup of tea or glass of water. I was only able to eat a bit of melon and mango and consoled myself that our great ape cousins, gorillas and chimpanzees, thrive on a diet of fruit, leaves, shoots, and stems. When the skin on my feet started to shrivel up, I began to doubt my sparse fruit-only diet. By day four, I started to develop a cough, which progressively got worse, especially at night. At my lowest moments, I sought God's reassurance that I would not succumb to the very disease that I sought to protect gorillas and people they shared their habitat with from contracting.

Ten days later, my two colleagues and I were taken to be tested again. It was the first time out of solitary confinement, and I felt like a bird that had been let out of its cage. Thankfully, we were given the all clear, which meant that we could go home. As I took my seat on the airplane, I felt joy about going home, but was having trouble catching my breath after climbing the stairs to board the plane. I could not eat the plane food, and during the journey I had difficulty breathing. My condition worsened while I was in transit in Ethiopia, but I tried to keep a brave face. Upon landing in Entebbe, I was greeted by Lawrence and Tendo with a big bunch of flowers. I joyfully greeted them back with a request to take me to the closest hospital.

I was immediately admitted to Victoria Medical Centre, and put on a vitamin drip, which was followed by a dextrose drip and one dose of intravenous dexamethasone. I woke up the following day feeling much better and relieved to be on the road to recovery. The following evening, when Lawrence brought me dinner from home, I enjoyed eating for the first time since getting sick. It was our traditional meal of matoke (savory banana) and groundnut sauce. I was so glad that my taste and smell were coming back!

My staff from CTPH came to visit and were shocked especially because I had not told them that I was sick with COVID-19, because we did not want this news to spread in Uganda and all over the world while we were still in Burundi for fear that the Burundian government may delay our return to Uganda even further. Now that I was safe at home, I felt comfortable telling people and also felt an ethical obligation to share the news with my team and others so that they would take the disease more seriously and follow the COVID-19 protection measures even more strictly. I also got the courage to tell my mother, who took the news surprisingly well and was concerned that I had left the hospital after only two nights. Just before I left the Victoria Medical Centre, I insisted on taking another COVID-19 test, because I needed to make sure that I had completely cleared the virus from my body.

When we got home that night, after many celebratory cheers I climbed up the stairs to my bedroom and became breathless. The first thought that came into my head was, "How am I going to get to the gorillas in Bwindi?" I flopped onto my bed to get my breath back, and it was only after ten minutes that I was able to start breathing normally again. I watched Tendo's favorite movie with him, but my mind was racing.

The following day Lawrence got a phone call from the hospital, which told him the devastating news that I was positive on both nasal and oral swab PCR tests. Now my whole family needed to quarantine. All the adults at home were put on prophylactic medication and immediately started wearing masks all the time. Though Tendo now knew that I had COVID-19 it was difficult to stop him from hugging me.

However, I still had a burning task. National Geographic Society wanted me to record a three-minute video talking about our work with the gorillas and how we were protecting them from COVID-19. I had told them that I could not record the video in Burundi, acknowledging that it was not safe for anybody to come to my bungalow and film me. So, I asked Tendo to record the video, and we walked, with me somehow slowly dragging myself, to a small forest three hundred meters from our home. At the edge of the forest, we found a nearby bush looking like the secondary growth at Bwindi Impenetrable Forest that the gorillas like to feed in, and Tendo did the recording. It came out surprisingly well though it wasn't until later on when I watched the finished version edited by the National Geographic Society, that I could hear how short of breath I sounded. When Tendo and I started to walk back to the house through the forest, I suddenly ran out of energy. Tendo raced ahead on his bicycle to get help. I had to be carried home and stayed in bed for the rest of the day. I realized that my symptoms were gradually getting worse.

The light at the end of the tunnel came unexpectedly from Mulago Hospital, the place of my birth. They were running clinical trials of a new herbal drug for treating COVID-19. When Mr. Kyaligonza, the health coordinator, saw my name on the database for people testing positive, he reached out to me. It did not take long for him to convince me to join the clinical trial. Doctors in Uganda and around the world were still grappling with how to treat COVID-19 patients. My symptoms had worsened, and I realized that I needed different medication. Now that I had COVID-19, I also felt obligated as a scientist to participate in this clinical trial and help find an effective treatment for the disease.

When my husband took me to the hospital, we were greeted by staff dressed in hazmat suits who came to take me into the COVID-19 ward, and he was banned from physically visiting me until I recovered. As I entered the general ward, I froze when I saw other patients with oxygen tubes. The next day, I was given a room on the sixth floor overlooking the parking lot where I could wave to Lawrence, Tendo, and the CTPH team when they came to "visit" me. This form of communication became our new norm.

Like the birds in Burundi, the marabou storks perched outside helped connect me with nature and improve my mental state.

I had never felt so helpless in my life; my morale was at an all-time low. When after a CT scan, I was told that I had 80 percent lung damage, as well as multiple blood clots in the pulmonary arteries in my lungs, the shock of it really hit me. So, I was receptive when a psychologist came to my room and counseled me about seeking spiritual support, adding that "though doctors treat, healing comes from God." When other doctors recommended that I should go to the intensive care unit (ICU) because of the clots, I rejected their advice. I felt strongly that my mental health would be affected by being in a room with people succumbing to the same disease and would slow my healing. In addition to receiving the UBV-01N herbal drug or placebo in a blind clinical trial, I was given intravenous dexamethasone and twice-daily injections of an anticoagulant. Thankfully I steadily improved.

Realizing the importance of having a positive outlook, I promised myself to start reading again, books written by famous conservationists I had met. Sir David Attenborough's book *A Life on Our Planet* increased my determination to keep going, and Dr. Jane Goodall's book *Reason for Hope*, about her spiritual journey, really helped me to get closer to God and reaffirm my calling while in the hospital.

At the hospital I received the news that President Magufuli of neighboring Tanzania had succumbed to COVID-19. He had publicly dismissed the importance of the virus, preventing his nation from taking any measures to protect themselves, which sadly led to many deaths that could have been prevented.

Yet again, a silver lining. In between my treatments in the hospital, it was an amazing opportunity to have conversations with the doctors and nurses about COVID-19, One Health, and conservation of gorillas. It meant that I was able to gain a greater understanding of COVID-19 from a medical perspective, which would help me in managing the disease should it reach the gorillas. Coincidentally, my mother had sponsored Dr. Bruce Kirenga—one of the senior doctors who attended to me—early in his career.

When I was given permission to see my family again, seeing them in my room after two weeks of only being able to wave to them from the isolation ward brought tears to my eyes. I felt so grateful to God for healing me and became more determined to recover fully by pacing myself and delegating more.

While I was in the hospital, the vaccines arrived in Uganda. It became much more important for me to encourage my staff and others in Uganda to vaccinate against COVID-19. I followed up with Dr. Ssebudde, the district health officer of Kanungu working in the Bwindi area to see if he could help to get the national park staff and conservation personnel of CTPH and other conservation NGOs to be in the first group of people to get vaccinated. After managing to convince my team that severe COVID-19 was far worse for them, their families, and the gorillas than any side effects from the vaccination, Dr. Ssebudde arranged for the CTPH staff to get vaccinated at Bwindi Community Hospital in March. Lawrence and most members of the CTPH team got vaccinated, but many people in Uganda remained reluctant, including the rangers. This was a huge disappointment after we had successfully advocated for park staff to be in the priority groups to be vaccinated. I decided that convincing people living next to wildlife to get vaccinated was the next priority for CTPH to mitigate the impact of the pandemic. In a subsequent training workshop, we helped the rangers overcome their hesitancy and they all got vaccinated.

Meanwhile, I continued to work from my hospital confinement. Dr. Fabian Leendertz, a renowned veterinarian and epidemiologist from the Robert Koch Institute, had invited me to become a coauthor on a short correspondence to the *Nature Journal* about vaccinating people in biodiversity hot spots to protect people and wildlife from each other.[28] Fabian was one of a team of ten scientists who was tasked to find the source of COVID-19, and some of them had traveled to Wuhan in China to make this key discovery. I immediately accepted to be a coauthor, and the paper came out in mid-March while I was in hospital.

Upon my release, I hit the ground running, though running more slowly than before. A few days after leaving the hospital, I participated in a World Health Organization virtual panel on community-led approaches to preventing disease outbreaks in light of the COVID-19 pandemic. Two weeks later, I attended an in-person meeting of the Global Health Security Agenda that was focused on zoonosis. They were impressed by CTPH community engagement and advised us to link up with the District One Health committees that had begun just before the pandemic. While there, I convinced the Ministry of Health, which was working with the USAID Social Behavior Change Activity program, to add the additional message about protecting wildlife and stimulating the return of tourism to the vaccination campaign. People needed incentives to balance their own reward/risk assessment of the vaccine.

Two months after I was discharged from the hospital, Uganda went into a severe second COVID-19 wave, with ten times as many cases and deaths as in the first wave, which was further complicated by the more contagious Delta variant. This steep rise in cases got me so anxious that I received my first AstraZeneca vaccine only two months after testing negative for COVID-19. I also immediately jumped into action to prevent COVID-19 from spreading to the gorillas. Tragically, Dr. Stephen Ssebudde, my dear mentor, succumbed to COVID-19. That same week, my cofounder of CTPH, Stephen Rubanga lost his mother-in-law to the virus after only three days in the hospital, a double tragedy for the CTPH family.

As a result of this sharp rise in cases, the president of Uganda imposed a full lockdown. The general public panicked and lined up to get vaccinated as the strategy at the Ministry of Health changed from focusing on vaccination education campaigns to preventing mild COVID-19 cases from becoming severe because there were not enough hospital beds and oxygen in intensive care units for the rapidly growing number of critical patients. Keeping people out of the hospital would be done through strengthening home-based care by training village health teams and initiating village COVID-19 task force committees. Desperate for support, the MOH turned to the NGOs. CTPH development director Mary Leakey quickly raised funds from individual donors and the Wildlife Conservation Network, and within two weeks, we were able to initiate village COVID-19 task force committees in eight frontline parishes with high human and gorilla conflict around Bwindi Impenetrable National Park. The fifty-nine committees from fifty-nine villages consisted of 472 people including village health and conservation teams (VHCTs) as the home-based care coordinators, Local Council 1 (Village Chiefs), UWA, the porters' association (who carry tourists' luggage to the gorillas), teachers, religious leaders, and women's groups. I attended the first village task force committee meeting to guide the process. Hearing stories from the community, we realized that on top of the stigma of having COVID-19, people were so desperate to earn a living, they might try and hide their symptoms. Village COVID-19 task force committee members were given pulse oximeters and noncontact infrared thermometers, masks, gloves, and hand sanitizers. They received home-based care training, learned how to do contact tracing, and how to be the link between patients and health centers or hospitals. Though the policy in Uganda offered free testing of patients showing symptoms, retesting after treatment was not free. People were unable to pay for that second test, which put the gorillas at risk.

September 2021 brought more shocking news that eighteen out of twenty captive western lowland gorillas at Zoo Atlanta in the United States had contracted the Delta variant of COVID-19 from a vaccinated keeper. Zoo Atlanta immediately embarked on vaccinating the rest of the great apes that had not gotten sick, including the orangutans, and susceptible felid species including lions, tigers and leopards with the Zoetis vaccine, which was still in the experimental phase for use in animals. Subsequently I arranged for Zoetis to donate this vaccine for susceptible wild animals in Uganda including captive chimpanzees at the Chimpanzee Trust and captive chimpanzees and felids at the Uganda Wildlife Education Centre. This news strengthened the argument for vaccinated tourists to get tested again when they arrive in Uganda. I also realized that the gorillas were still at great risk of picking up a severe variant when they ventured out of the park into community land no matter how carefully the tourists adhered to the rules. The only way to reduce this health risk to the endangered mountain gorillas was to strengthen the prevention measures we had put in place since the pandemic began in 2020. This included continuing to test people who interact with gorillas even when they are vaccinated and making sure that those who tested positive were treated and retested before they could resume their duties. This included all staff of CTPH and other conservation partners and the communities we work with.

Within two years, we had not seen health complications in the gorillas due to COVID-19, and we continue to intensively monitor them by testing fecal samples from all the 260 habituated gorillas and observing them for clinical signs.

Getting severe COVID-19 myself, and losing relatives, friends, and colleagues to the disease within a short space of time underscored the fragility of life, and with it the importance of strengthening my legacy by getting my team to take up more of my responsibilities. For the first time I put a senior staff member, Kaamu Bukenya, in charge of the day-to-day running of the organization, which freed me up to strengthen our collaborations, advocate, and keep inspiring the next generation.

I was humbled to be selected among twenty-seven independent experts from around the world to serve on the WHO Special Advisory Group for the Origin of Novel Pathogens to advise on further studies to determine the source of the COVID-19 pandemic and a framework to prevent emerging and reemerging diseases, such as monkeypox.

In mitigating COVID-19, CTPH's collaboration with health partners strengthened and our efforts were published in an issue of *Frontiers in Public Health* with a focus on Planetary Health.[29]

Chapter 28

One World, One Health: Preventing Anthrax and Ebola and Planning a Sustainable Future

How do you convince people to support your work when they don't understand it? When we started out in 2003, the idea of addressing human, animal, and environmental health together was just emerging. Very few understood that people and animals can make each other sick and that, in turn, this can have enormous impacts on conservation, public health, and sustainable development. At CTPH we developed a multidisciplinary approach to address these issues, but because it didn't fit into a neat category it was difficult for donors and policy makers to understand the potential benefits.

Today, there is a global effort known as One Health that aims to help people better understand and respond to the intricate connections between the health of humans, animals, and the environment. By the time the US Centers for Disease Control and Prevention (CDC) established its One Health office, Conservation Through Public Health had been implementing the approach for six years. The One Health approach really came into maturity during the COVID-19 pandemic. The government of Uganda has now embraced the approach by developing a National One Health Platform involving government sectors from human health, animal health, wildlife, and the environment to work together to prevent, detect, and respond to existing zoonotic diseases as well as emerging pandemic threats. Something as simple as children's viruses that they pick up from school being passed on to their parents who are asymptomatic, have unknowingly been passed on to endangered chimpanzees in Kibale National Park and Budongo Forest Reserve, causing sickness and death.[30] CTPH is collaborating with the Kibale Ecohealth project to prevent this happening in gorillas.

COVID-19 brought the CTPH concept to a broader acceptance, but wildlife veterinarians have been grappling with the reality of zoonotic disease outbreaks between people and wildlife for as long as there have been wildlife veterinarians. In 2001, chimpanzees in the Tai Forest in Ivory Coast started dying. The veterinarian investigating the deaths, Dr. Fabian Leendertz, initially suspected Ebola because of the symptoms of bleeding from the body orifices. But the culprit was anthrax. In 2004 hippos started dying in Queen Elizabeth National Park under mysterious circumstances. But this was happening only in the place where chimpanzees are naturally found, the Kyambura Gorge, which is a green oasis of forest in this vast savanna. I immediately suspected anthrax, having learned from veterinarians in South Africa that it commonly attacks hoofed animals in savanna habitats. I recalled that several years earlier, before I started working at UWA, there were unusual die-offs of hippos in the hippo pool in the southern sector of QENP that had not been investigated. The South African veterinarians discovered that the best way to prevent the spread of the disease was by putting acacia thorny bushes on carcasses, which prevented vultures from opening the bodies and releasing resistant anthrax spores that stay in the environment for several decades. Once vultures carry the spores to other parts of the national park, the disease spreads rapidly.

CTPH was only one year old when this anthrax outbreak occurred in 2004, and we were just getting things off the ground. I was also pregnant with our first child, Ndhego, and did not want to go anywhere near the investigations in case we got infected with this potentially fatal disease. Over three hundred hippos died along with several buffalos and livestock, which all grazed together. Thankfully the chimpanzees in Kyambura Gorge did not contract anthrax from the hippos. To prevent further spread, the UWA veterinary team initially resorted to burning the carcasses; however, twenty liters of diesel were needed for each hippo. It was not only expensive, but also horribly polluted the environment. They then resorted to burying the hippos in deep mass graves.

Two years later, while hosting a meeting of the Public Health and Conservation Technical Support Unit, we invited the conservation and health sectors to speak to each other, and see how best to prevent sicknesses and fatalities in future outbreaks. What came out of the meeting was extremely valuable. Whereas UWA had not come across any people eating hippo meat during the outbreak, the District Health Officer, Dr. Stephen Ssebudde, reported that over two hundred people became ill—six fatally so—after eating infected hippo meat in the market. Fortunately, unlike COVID-19 and other viral diseases, anthrax has a cure if cases are treated early enough with penicillin and other antibiotics, and those who reported to him on time recovered. This outbreak was alarming for the tour operators, who had also feared that tourists would cancel their bookings for fear of contracting the disease.

Though anthrax outbreaks typically occur every ten years, just six years later, in 2010, hippos started dying again, and this time around we were much readier to get involved in reducing the impact of the outbreak on animals and people.

CTPH swung into action. Our systems were in place. We trained the community conservation animal health workers (CCAHWs) to educate people not to eat meat from unknown sources, and they reached over five thousand people. We also joined the UWA team in quickly burying hippos, this time with lime, which kills the resistant spores. Thankfully, a vaccine had been developed, which the team from ministry of agriculture, animal industry, and fisheries (MAAIF) used to immunize the cattle grazing with hippos, thereby protecting people.

Lawrence came up with the idea of supporting the ministry of health with a communication platform and a dedicated website for disease outbreaks. With the help of Computer Frontiers, CTPH set up the website and a toll-free hotline that people could call for information on anthrax. Over ten thousand people called the hotline. As a result, we were runners-up for the 2010 Health Category of the Annual Uganda Communications Commission (UCC) Awards for our innovation. The 2010 and 2011 anthrax outbreak lasted for a shorter time with significantly fewer deaths than the 2004 outbreak. One hundred hippos and fifteen buffalo died. The death toll in hippos was 30 percent of the previous outbreak, and no humans or livestock died. Though the tour operators were anxious that tourists would not want to visit Uganda, their fears were short-lived. This multidisciplinary task force made all the difference in reducing the impact of the anthrax outbreak on wildlife, people's health, their livelihoods, and tourism. It revealed to me how the power of a One Health approach built on the foundation of a multidisciplinary team effort can save lives.

When deadlier Ebola and Marburg outbreaks occurred, the same national disease task force worked together to address it. Ebola and Marburg are highly contagious hemorrhagic fevers, caused by filoviruses. Though this task force was headed by the ministry of health (MOH) because the spread of infection was mainly through human-to-human contact, the disease likely came from contact with infected bat droppings or eating an infected monkey, and the same principles applied. African fruit bats living within caves in Mount Elgon had given Marburg to the local communities as well as to people working in mines. In the caves of Maramagambo Forest in Queen Elizabeth National Park, a tourist caught the fatal disease from bat droppings. This caused UWA to stop taking tourists in the caves and the CDC set up a viewing platform where the bats could safely be observed without the risk of contracting a zoonotic disease.

For this outbreak, we joined the ecological monitoring group headed by the MOH veterinary public health officer, Dr. Winyi Kaboyo. The website we had developed for anthrax was able to be used for Ebola, Marburg, and other disease outbreaks until the MOH designed a permanent one. It was exciting to develop a One Health communication platform that the MOH built upon to better manage fatal disease outbreaks in the country, including COVID-19.

In 2016, I was honored to be asked to serve on the task force to create the first Uganda National Institute of Public Health, which would be taking into account the concerns of wildlife. This proved important experience in designing action to reduce the impact of COVID-19 a few years later.

In 2014, I became a victim not of disease itself, but of the panic created by hemorrhagic fevers when I traveled to Washington, DC, to give presentations at the Wilson Centre, then on to the Explorers Club and WINGS World Quest retreat in New York City, and finally at Mississippi State University. Before leaving DC, I had lunch at a health food market where I made an adventurous decision to eat raw beef with salad.

I arrived in New York City by train and stayed at the home of my friend and colleague, primatology professor Jessica Rothman. On my first night I became severely ill. She was afraid to take me to an urgent care clinic because, having traveled from Uganda, they would suspect Ebola and put me in quarantine. We both assumed it had been food poisoning and would quickly pass. The next day, upon arrival at the Explorers Club, the President, Alan Nichols and his wife, Becky, who had been looking forward to seeing me because we all had visited the gorillas together in Uganda, immediately noticed that I was looking ill. They had put out a lovely display of sandwiches that I could not even look at, let alone eat. I had to throw up again before the meeting, and Will Roseman, director of the Explorers Club, took me to Lexington Hospital in Manhattan. When he told them that I had traveled from Uganda, I was put in an isolation room and could only be seen by one brave African American doctor dressed up in a full PPE hazmat suit.

Poor Will had to also be put in quarantine for carrying my bag and coat. He probably made matters worse by telling them that I was a gorilla veterinarian and needed to get immediate medical attention so that I could give a talk about my work. This only served to make the hospital panic even more about me carrying a deadly virus from the gorillas in Uganda to New York City! They probably were aware of the thousands of people in Gabon and other countries in Central Africa who had contracted Ebola after eating gorillas and chimpanzees that had died of the disease. The next question they asked me was "Do the gorillas you are treating have Ebola?" and I truthfully said that they did not. Their final question was if I had been in contact with anyone who had Marburg. Because I was getting regular updates from the task force that it had thankfully been contained, I was able to confidently tell them that there was no risk. I finally told the doctor that I likely had food poisoning and desperately needed IV hydration. They first took what seemed like gallons of blood from me before they put me on a drip. When Jessica came to see me, she told me that the hospital was very concerned about the media finding out I was in hospital with a suspected case of Ebola. Finally she was able to convince them to let me go back to her home. I was too sick to eat for a few days, but managed to attend the WINGS retreat and give a talk in Mississippi, as well as meet with my niece Nabaada and my nephews, Martin and Willie Kalema, who were equally amused at my close call.

But we knew our mirth hid our deeper frustrations. When an Ebola outbreak occurred in neighboring Democratic Republic of Congo (DRC) years later, three American University students we were hosting at CTPH rushed out of the country before we could convince them to stay. Having gone through the COVID-19 pandemic that affected all countries in the world, I feel that if such an incident was to happen again in Uganda, Americans may not rush back home. Uganda had another Ebola outbreak in September 2022. Thankfully an Ebola vaccine has been developed, which has protected health workers in DRC during recent outbreaks. However, the Ebola Zaire vaccine that reduced the spread of this outbreak was not protective against the Ebola Sudan virus in Uganda, and sadly some health workers succumbed to the disease. Unlike COVID-19, though, 90 percent of people who get Ebola die; you have to have physical contact with someone who has the disease and the symptoms are more obvious, making it easier to bring it under control than a highly contagious respiratory disease where infectious people can be asymptomatic. Nevertheless, because of the new technology of monoclonal antibodies that had been developed for use in COVID patients, the survival rate of Ebola Sudan patients increased from 10 percent to 60 percent. By the time Makerere University and Uganda Ministry of Health, with support from WHO, started clinical trials for a vaccine against Ebola Sudan, fifty-five people had died including seven health workers.

Our work on the national disease task forces attracted the attention of another department of the Ministry of Health (MOH), when they learned that we are promoting community-based family planning around Bwindi Impenetrable National Park. They now saw CTPH as a strategic partner in improving the health of mothers and their children and enabling families to better balance their family budget.

Uganda has among the highest population growth rates in the world, increasing at a rate of 3.3 percent, with one million people being added to the population every year. Population growth is a major contributing factor to the country's dwindling natural resources. The districts surrounding Bwindi Impenetrable National Park, where I started my life's work, have a population density as high as three hundred people per square kilometer. There is a hard edge between the community and the park almost all around the forest, apart from the southern sector, where there is a buffer zone of tea farms. This was established by UWA, with support from the International Gorilla Conservation Programme, and has helped to reduce the conflict between people and gorillas.

The minister of tourism, wildlife and antiquities, the Honorable Ephraim Kamuntu, had started to talk about how high human population growth rates were affecting the future of protected areas in Uganda. When I joined the UWA board, he tasked us to address the conservation issues at Mount Elgon. According to the Uganda Bureau of Statistics, this region has the country's highest population density of one thousand people per square kilometer, with a population growth rate of 3.4 percent per annum. Though there were no gorillas at Mount Elgon, I saw how our integrated approach to addressing population, health, and environment (PHE) could address the health needs of people, improve their attitudes to conservation, and reduce conflict with wildlife. In my experience, promoting community-based family planning in areas rich with wildlife and high human densities makes conservation relevant to other sectors including human health, population planning, and economic development.[31]

In 2014, I gave a presentation about the work of CTPH at the first national family planning conference in Uganda. The excitement in the room was electrifying when His Excellency the President of Uganda endorsed voluntary family planning to enable better education and economic opportunities for the young and rapidly growing population of Uganda. Several media houses hurriedly reported on it that very day to the extent that Alan Weisman, author of the book *Countdown*, excitedly contacted me. In his chapter on Uganda, Alan had written about our work at Bwindi and the Ugandan president's stance on having larger families in support of economic growth and development. After his earlier bestselling book, *The World Without Us*, we had hosted Alan at Bwindi so he could learn all about our integrated family planning and conservation model, which he wanted to feature in *Countdown*.[32] Alan, himself, is responsible for my choice to only have two children. When he saw me with our boys he asked, "Are you planning to have more?" He added, "If you stop at two, they are replacing you and your husband, and not contributing to the population growth rate of Uganda." Ndhego was five years old and Tendo less than one year old. I realized it was important to practice what we preach and be a role model to other couples facing the same questions in their lives. As a result of this conversation, we did not have any more children. It helped me to think about how stopping at two could enable us to provide the best opportunities that life had to offer for our two children. This would minimize consumption and use of natural resources, protecting the environment and helping nature thrive.

We are now introducing our PHE model to other protected gorilla areas in Africa.[33] Importantly, we understand that while the

PHE model is effective, there is no one-size-fits-all approach, and the unique needs of each community must be incorporated into the PHE response. In the Virungas (mostly in the Congo), for example, the local community is predominantly Catholic, and this religion has traditionally frowned upon contraceptive use. However, because of the high rates of extreme poverty in DRC, people responded positively to our message emphasizing balancing the family budget through limiting the number of children in order to afford to give them adequate healthcare and education.

The Wilson Center in Washington, DC, a neutral policy forum for addressing global issues through independent research and open discussion, supported us to advocate for our PHE approach in the United States. Our approach to family planning was also supported and celebrated by Population Connection, a grassroots nonprofit that advocates to the US Congress to increase funding for international family planning assistance to the United Nations Population Fund and supports other efforts to stabilize the world population at a level that can be sustained by Earth's resources. I was invited to speak at a Wilson Center panel with Ken Weiss, an environmental journalist who had visited us in Bwindi and written about our work. Speaking at such an important event really opened the door for us to connect with organizations who were also passionate about the impact of population growth, and supporting organizations, such as ours, who were addressing these issues.[34] Population Connection eventually became an important donor to and supporter of CTPH. Its president, John Seager, gave me valuable advice about fundraising and invited a senior member of my team to the United States to learn about their model, which strengthened our advocacy efforts. I was a bit hesitant to get into advocacy because my passion lies in program implementation, where I am happiest being in the wild with the animals and helping the local communities sharing a habitat with gorillas and other endangered wildlife. However, I also realized that our approach was difficult for most people to understand, making it problematic to raise support and garner much-needed funds to improve things at the local level. I needed to be out there convincing people about the benefits of our holistic approach. It became strategic to join forces with other organizations to be able to influence decision and policy makers within the donor community, governments, and NGOs that could potentially take our model to scale. Earning global recognition, particularly during the COVID-19 pandemic, helped to raise additional support for One Health approaches to achieve a planet in balance. This included the Edinburgh Medal for Science and Humanity in 2022. My parents had studied at Edinburgh University, which made the award even more special.

It has been truly humbling to have received so much media attention for our work. And it's been necessary. The media has been a great strategic partner in our advocacy efforts at the local, national, and international levels.

Putting CTPH on the map has enabled me to spread the message of One Health in the hopes that our future can become brighter as we discover new ways of living in balance and harmony with our environment, the animals, and each other.

Chapter 29

Women in Conservation

Trailblazing Women

African conservation has been traditionally dominated by men from the Western world. I actually heard a male colleague from the UK whom I had invited to Uganda to assist me say in all seriousness that conservation got spoiled when women got involved. The truth is that being a woman has both hindered and enabled me and other women to make a significant impact in conservation. The world has been conditioned to think that a woman cannot do something before a man, yet this is exactly what happened when I began my career in 1996. Even in my native country, I didn't realize how many barriers I broke when I became the first wildlife veterinarian in Uganda. Later I would hear myself referred to internationally as the first female wildlife veterinarian in Uganda, yet I was the first wildlife veterinarian in my country, period! There was no man who came before me. I just happened to be female.

Ironically, my mother's concern for me working at the age of twenty-four with the mountain gorillas in the wild was, in fact, a barrier I had to overcome, but she herself is one of the most empowered and well-respected female leaders in Uganda.

For better or worse, she raised me to be a determined independent woman, like herself. And I proceeded with my plan despite her initial maternal objections. But I couldn't have done it without the pathfinders before me: Dr. Jane Goodall, Dr. Dian Fossey, and Dr. Biurite Galdikas. These three women, referred to as the Trimates, were selected by the trailblazing archaeologist and paleontologist Louis Leakey to study the three nonhuman great apes—chimpanzees, gorillas and orangutans—and help us understand ourselves better. I was delighted when Mary Leakey, his granddaughter, joined our team at CTPH.

Dr. Jane Goodall. who conducted the first study of chimpanzees in the wild at the tender age of twenty-six, with no university education, made a groundbreaking scientific discovery that chimpanzees make tools out of blades of grass to fish termites out of holes in trees so that they can eat them. This made Professor Louis Leakey state that "Now we must redefine tool, redefine Man, or accept chimpanzees as human." In spite of this discovery, when Jane got her PhD, she still had to work twice as hard as the male scientists for the scientific community to take her findings seriously.

Dr. Dian Fossey conducted the first long-term study in the world on a different great ape, the mountain gorilla, and made people realize how tolerant and accommodating gorillas are to human presence. The Hollywood film about her memoir, *Gorillas in the Mist*, opened up the world's attention to the plight of the mountain gorillas and changed the perception of gorillas from "King Kong" to "gentle giants," making them among the greatest wild animal tourist attractions in the world. Dian became concerned about the gorilla injuries from snares, and her advocacy led to one of the first field veterinary programs dedicated to a single animal in the wild, the Mountain Gorilla Veterinary Project. I am privileged to continue her legacy in my walk with gorillas both as a wildlife veterinarian and a conservationist.

Dr. Biurite Galdikas conducted the first study of orangutans, "the orange ape," in the wild. When she signed her book that I bought after attending her talk in London as a vet student, she wrote "Follow your dreams and the rest will follow." I took the words to heart.

A fourth woman also inspired me: Dr. Liz Macfie, the Uganda country director of the International Gorilla Conservation Programme, both as a role model and mentor, when she gave me my first opportunity to study mountain gorillas at Bwindi as a twenty-four-year-old vet student. I was encouraged that she managed to have a rewarding career in wildlife conservation, starting out as a mountain gorilla veterinarian in Rwanda, while also having a family.

As much as I had these four amazing role models to inspire me, I had another hurdle to overcome—being a Black woman in conservation. I was glad that people did not doubt my abilities at home in Uganda. In fact, many people celebrated me because I challenged their thinking that wildlife is only for foreigners. However, whenever I traveled abroad, I had to work twice as hard to be taken seriously as a veterinarian and a conservationist who is Black and female.

When Tusk Trust asked me to be on a panel of building conservation leaders, where I was the only woman on the panel of five, I realized that I had unique challenges when compared to my fellow African panelists.

People often asked me if I am taken seriously as a woman in my career, primarily because it is in a male-dominated field. In my first job as the first full-time wildlife veterinarian for Uganda, I did not dwell on the fact that I was a woman; I was more concerned about making a difference through my work. Since I brought a unique expertise to the organization, I was taken seriously as a professional, even though I was among the youngest members of the team and a woman. UWA being a paramilitary organization meant that rangers, who at the time were only men, respected the strict hierarchy and saluted me, which I took in stride, though my family found it amusing.

When I started out at UWA, I was essentially one of the only women out in the field working directly with the wild animals, treating and moving them, and it raised a few eyebrows and doubt in my abilities among my male colleagues. Thankfully they did not outwardly show this. I only found out about this twenty years later from a female colleague in conservation who was elated that I had proved them wrong.

I recall when tracking the gorillas, the rangers (all men) would let me walk in front as the team leader, but also so I could set the pace, as I was slower than them. The rangers also pulled me uphill and helped me along whenever necessary, and they respected that though I joined them in the field as a senior staff member, I shared their hardships in the field, the physical exertion, extreme weather conditions, not enough water and food, as well as the threat of attacks from elephants and other dangerous wild animals in the forest.

When I graduated as a veterinarian from the Royal Veterinary College, University of London, 60 percent of us were women. In contrast, when I gave a talk three years later at Makerere University—with the only veterinary school in Uganda—women made up only 5 percent of the class. When I returned home to set up the veterinary department at UWA, only 5 percent of people in the organization were women. They were mainly doing office and administrative work as support staff at the headquarters, and only a few were in management and engaging communities in the field. However, they were strong women, and I remember a time when one of them told me she'd heard a new senior administrator refer to me, saying "that cheeky naughty girl is too close to donors." She was so outraged that she had to tell me. I was so upset that it made me cry, after all that I had done to get the UWA veterinary department up and running! But it made me even more determined to succeed.

Even back in 1999, when I was recognized as a Model of Excellence by the Forum for African Women Educationalists in Uganda, there were impressive women at the forefront of Ugandan politics. The vice president of Uganda who presided over the ceremony was a woman: Hon. Specioza Kazibwe. My own mother was one as well, Hon. Rhoda Kalema,[35] pioneer of the women's movement in Uganda and one of the first women members of parliament, paving the way for other women to join politics. We have had a female speaker of parliament, Hon. Rebecca Kadaga, who was mentored by my mother. My mother, now ninety-three years old, has dedicated her life to uplifting women in Uganda and began this journey in the 1950s when she joined the Uganda Council of Women subcommittee on the status of women that successfully lobbied for women to vote after the country gained independence in 1962. She had been blessed to have a forward-thinking father, who made sure that both his daughters and sons went to school, and eventually even took his daughters to a coeducational school, Kings College Budo, an unusual practice in Uganda in the 1930s. She became a member of Parliament in the 1980s. After Idi Amin abolished women's movements in the 1970s, she became the link between the old and new women's movement in the Museveni era and advocated for an additional seat in parliament for women in every district. This has resulted in Uganda having among the highest proportion of women in parliament, increasing female participation in the governance of the country. I am proud of her for pushing for these important steps in women's emancipation not only in Uganda, but the rest of the world. It was during her time in parliament that the first Uganda Wildlife Act was passed that led to the creation of the Uganda Wildlife Authority in August 1996 by merging the Uganda National Parks and the Game Department.

However, as founder and CEO of CTPH, I saw that the field of conservation, in particular, had very few women, not only in UWA, but also in Uganda, and shockingly few women were heading conservation organizations around the world. This meant that women's voices are rarely heard. Thus over the years, I have learned that it is often necessary to raise my voice in a room that mainly has men.

My thirty-year journey in conservation has shown me that when you don't engage and empower women, conservation is unlikely to work in the long term. I first began to understand this when I led a team of men to conduct health education workshops to reduce the risk of human and gorilla disease transmission, and caught the whispers of women attending the workshop telling each other that they must educate their girl children. If I could become a leader, what might their daughters achieve?

When we decided to add family planning to our community programs, the local leaders selected trusted volunteers, half of whom were women, which was important for our approach of couple peer education. Subsequently these women became leaders in their communities working on an equal footing with fellow male volunteers who also got more involved in family planning and healthcare promotion.

One of the biggest threats to wildlife conservation is poaching. When we started to engage reformed poachers it was their wives who joined the meetings and admitted that when their children are sick or they don't have food on the table, they put their husbands under pressure to go into the gorillas' forest habitat and collect bushmeat, which is also believed to have medicinal properties. When this confession was made, I (the only other woman at the meeting) realized how often we miss the other half of the puzzle by only speaking to the men.

Men and women need to be engaged equally for long-term gains to be achieved in conservation and sustainable development. Where necessary, women may need an extra push to compete on the same level as men. I was convinced that it was important for me to be able to provide this platform in my team and in the communities where we are working. Having focused discussions with groups of women has enabled them to open up about their fears of engaging in conservation.

I am pleased to say that twenty-five years after I joined the UWA, the number of female rangers has grown from 0 to 20 percent. However, some roles are still all male like the human and gorilla conflict resolution (HUGOs) teams of volunteers from the Bwindi community—gorilla guardians who herd gorillas from community land to the park. Some of these men have stated that women can't manage this job because they will faint when they see a gorilla! I wonder how they think I've survived all these years.

We went through a phase at the beginning of CTPH where I felt obligated to have affirmative action for hiring women, but I found that so early in the startup of the NGO we needed skill and talent regardless of gender. So it was that I have ended up having an organization that currently has only 30 percent women, yet I am a female founder, president, and CEO. Some of my Ugandan male staff told me that they joined CTPH because I inspired them. Interestingly, some of the male volunteers from other countries have found it much harder taking instructions from an African woman because of the stereotypes out there in the wider world.

On International Women's Day in 2017, I received a Golden Jubilee Award from the president of Uganda for distinguished service to the nation as a veterinarian and conservationist, the same award my mother received a few years before me for her leadership role in engaging women in politics.

In spite of the great progress made in breaking societal norms over the past two decades, an expatriate referred to me as the *secretary* of the minister of tourism, wildlife and antiquities at a conservation event. At that, the minister, Hon. Ephraim Kamuntu, corrected him, saying, "This doctor is my boss."

While getting my MBA in Global Business and Sustainability on the social entrepreneurship track at Tangaza University College in Kenya, I met a dynamic Kenyan woman who had founded a coffee company in Kenya. One of her main challenges was not being taken seriously as a woman in a man's world of coffee trading. I often get asked how we are engaging women in Gorilla Conservation Coffee and my initial answer was that women don't own land, so we are engaging farmers as a family unit where women play a key role on the coffee farm. Few of our farmers allowed their wives to have their own coffee farms. One who did is Sam Karibwende, the chairperson of the Bwindi Coffee Growers Cooperative that we helped to create, where his wife has one of the best coffee farms among our farmers. Now women make up 120 out of five hundred farmers, of which six out of twenty-five are female "model farmers."

I traveled to India and connected with conservationists to give a keynote presentation about our work at the Student Conference on Conservation Science (SCCS) in Bangalore. I was impressed to find that 50 percent of the audience were women. Until my presentation, they had only met male keynote speakers from UK, Europe, or the United States talking about wildlife in Africa.

Through BBC World Service radio, I connected with a Sri Lankan vet and Ashoka Fellow, Dr. Nalinika Obyesekera, who founded an animal rescue center for dogs and cats in Colombo. *The Conversation*, a program connecting two people in the same profession, but doing different things, gave us a platform to share our lives as veterinarians, where we discovered that the gender stereotypes of women in both our societies were similar and a big barrier to women who wanted to work in remote locations. Female Asian students who have volunteered with CTPH have faced similar challenges.

My first international recognition as a woman in conservation was by WINGS World Quest, a foundation that supports women in conservation. I received the 2011 Women of Discovery and Exploration Humanity Award from WINGS in the presence of my mother, parents-in-law, and niece Baada and nephew Ntale (who live in New York). My mother is petrified of snakes, but was won over by Kate Jackson who received the Courage Award for protecting snakes in the central African jungle.

It was refreshing to find an organization that focused on women, who need to be taken seriously on a professional front and have to balance work and family on a personal front. I was inspired by the WINGS fellows who shared their stories through their books, including Anne Bancroft, who went to Antarctica on her own.

WINGS fellow Leela Hazzah, an inspiring Egyptian woman and cofounder of Lion Guardians, convinced me to join the Women for the Environment—Africa Leadership council that she initiated. I joined WE—Africa, to empower female managers to achieve their leadership potential in conservation through training and mentoring. I was so excited when Lilly Ajarova broke a glass ceiling by becoming the first female CEO of the Uganda Tourism Board in 2019, exactly what WE—Africa is advocating for.

The global celebration of women in conservation has been inspiring. But while I've been on the receiving end of awards and recognition, I know how many women working for the cause there are behind each and every celebrated female leader. We could not achieve what we do without the women who have come before us and the women whose continued daily work make it all possible.

Balancing parenting and the call of the wild

As a wildlife veterinarian, I found it challenging to balance parenting with the call of the wild, and support from my family and colleagues was essential. We have often left our children with my mother and Lawrence's grandparents when we travel abroad to raise awareness and funds for CTPH. Dr. Margaret Driciru, a wildlife veterinarian and Warden for Ecological Monitoring and Research, also had children the same age as mine and they often played together at her home in Queen Elizabeth National Park while their mothers went to test buffalo and other dangerous animals for zoonotic diseases. Our staff and volunteers often helped with the children when they accompanied me.

It is so important where possible to have the support of your spouse in your life's calling. When I met Lawrence, he liked the fact that I was happy to be dirty in the bush. He thought I was the only person who was crazy about gorillas until we visited Jane Dewar at Gorilla Haven in Atlanta, Georgia, who was somehow even crazier about gorillas. She invited me to be on her board and has been a great supporter of our work ever since. Setting up an organization with my husband gave depth to our marriage beyond having children, and has come with its own set of interesting opportunities and challenges. Having embarked on journeys together with CTPH and later the Gorilla Conservation Camp and Gorilla Conservation Coffee, Lawrence has always understood that my priority is wildlife when I have to be away for many days in the bush or traveling abroad to raise awareness and funds for our work.

This has made parenting and balancing with the call of the wild easier. He has also understood why I have taken our sons to Bwindi from the tender age of two months where Ndhego recognized his first elephant in the national park, and not in a storybook. It has been a joy teaching my children to appreciate and love animals and nature and to have empathy for poorer people we meet in rural areas like Bwindi. The Batwa traditional hunter-gatherers who lived in Bwindi Impenetrable Forest before it became a national park have become their good friends and have taught them many life skills such as making fire in the traditional way.

I have applied what I have learned from the gorillas to my family, where we spaced our two boys using the same interbirth interval of gorillas of four and half years. This spacing is perfect because the older child is emotionally independent by the time the next baby is born and can even help to babysit and teach the younger child many important life skills. Our older son Ndhego has taught his brother how to play soccer and how to handle animals, and I have always felt safe leaving Tendo under Ndhego's watch. Like a four-year-old gorilla, who can build its own nest and will be able to play in a healthy manner with its younger sibling while helping mother to babysit.

★ ★ ★

My career has also been defined by my faith in God, where I found my calling working with gorillas. Whenever I am with the gorillas I feel peaceful and at one with nature. I have experienced spiritual growth on the conservation journey while getting to know and protect gorillas and other species, which has given me a reason to keep going in spite of hardships, knowing that this is my calling and it is for a greater purpose.

I have always seen my career as a way to continue my father's legacy to develop Uganda. I was destined to meet Margaret and David Ritchie, and eventually did in 2011. Margaret had been my father's personal secretary when he was the commerce and industry minister in the government of Obote immediately after Uganda had attained independence from the British. Through the Whitley Fund for Nature, our families reconnected when I was invited to give a talk at World Wildlife Fund for Nature UK, where Margaret and David's daughter Liz worked. I was flabbergasted when I received an email from Margaret Ritchie, who must have heard about me from her daughter. My mother reconnected with Margaret after forty years. It was like opening an old wound as my heart started bleeding again for my father who I had never gotten to know. When together with my husband Lawrence, we met Margaret and David, they told us stories about my father, which I was hungry to hear. One that stood out for me was that my father changed the English name he had been given to William Wilberforce after learning about his huge contribution to the abolition of the slave trade. The Ritchies were in the last photo taken of my father when he took them out on a boat called

The African Queen to welcome Margaret's family who had come to Uganda to attend her and David's wedding at All Saints Cathedral in Kampala.

Sadly, my parents never made it to Margaret's wedding because my father was abducted a few weeks before it. I felt closer to my father when Margaret told me that he was very proud when I was born and had made a decision to spend more time with me, having recently resigned from the busy schedule of politics when he returned to Uganda from exile in Tanzania following Amin's grasp for power.

When I was a child, after my mother joined politics to continue my father's dream, I was often invited by her to attend community meetings. Though at the time I sometimes grew bored, I later realized my mother was showing me how to be a leading woman in politics and advocacy for rural education and community development.

After I became a wildlife vet and beyond, my mother, despite her fears for me, supported me always. She visited me in Budongo Forest to follow chimpanzees and later allowed me to take her to the gorillas in Bwindi Impenetrable Forest. I have never seen my mother wearing trousers and she was probably the first person to trek the mountain gorillas in a skirt! The people digging in the gardens excitedly shouted out to her "Mukeikuru—old woman, why are you going to see the gorillas?" My brother and sister had also tracked the gorillas at separate times and jokingly complained that I brought the gorillas closer for our mother who had a shorter hike of forty-five minutes to get to the gorillas, while it took them four hours. The park rangers and tourists were also thrilled to meet her and walked extra slowly to make sure she kept up with them. She was amazed and reassured to see that the gorillas were gentle vegetarian giants.

Like many parents, the pandemic brought challenges and gifts. As a result, Ndhego and Tendo have participated in the trainings I've conducted with the park rangers and village health and conservation teams and have become experts on COVID-19, particularly Tendo, who actively contributed to the discussions during the trainings with the rangers. For World Gorilla Day, he wrote an article about COVID-19 and gorillas in the *New Vision* national newspaper children's *Toto* magazine. Tendo also started a backyard chicken farm at the age of eleven during COVID-19. When he was fifteen, Ndhego wrote his book[36] about being a junior zookeeper at the Uganda Wildlife Education Centre; I saw in him the spark that was nurtured in myself at his age. I am delighted that my children are doing interesting and important things in their lives and hope that I've inspired them in the same way that my parents inspired me to pursue my dreams regardless of the challenges I faced. They inspired me to do my part through my work with gorillas and other wildlife to change the world for the better.

Author's Note

As this memoir reflects, to protect the world's remaining endangered mountain gorillas, my walk with gorillas has evolved into also helping people who they share their fragile habitats with.

Two organizations I founded, Conservation Through Public Health in 2003 and Gorilla Conservation Coffee in 2015, are focused on reducing threats to biodiversity by enabling people to coexist with gorillas and other wildlife. We strive to achieve this through improving the health of people and animals (gorillas, other wildlife and livestock) in and around Africa's protected areas and other wildlife-rich habitats, and improving the livelihoods of coffee farmers living around gorilla habitats, reducing their need to go into the Bwindi Impenetrable National Park in search of food and fuelwood.

Together we can make a difference in reducing the threats of dis¬ease, habitat loss, and poaching to ensure a secure future for gorillas and other wildlife in Africa. I hope that you will visit ctph.org and gccoffee.org to learn more about these two organizations, and see how you can get involved in our work and support conservation efforts on the ground.

Epilogue:
Shaping the Future

I believe that the future of conservation is bright, but precarious. If we don't act fast to build upon what we have learned, more species will become extinct. If we don't engage the next generation in conservation, we will lose natural habitats and precious wildlife forever. Organizations like Wildlife Clubs of Uganda that nurtured my childhood passion for conservation and Roots and Shoots initiative of the Jane Goodall Institute must be supported.

One of the ways I am encouraging our future generations is to participate in initiatives where children are the main audience. I was featured in an episode of the *N*Gen Science* TV show that encourages African children, especially girls, to have a career in science. Two teenagers from the Bwindi community were selected to appear on the show, Deus, fifteen, and Briona, seventeen. Ndhego, who was sixteen, and Tendo, who was twelve, also joined in. I took the three teenagers to check on the Rushegura gorilla group. They were excited to see the gorillas, and asked many questions about the brown baby, Butime, whose mother, Kibande, was very old. The baby had lost his hair due to genetic abnormalities and poor nutrition, but was still holding on to life. Tendo was too young to visit the gorillas, so his main role in the film was as a narrator. He took center stage at the CTPH Gorilla Health and Community Conservation Centre laboratory, as well as working with the Bwindi ecological monitoring and research warden, Joseph Arinaitwe, in setting up wildlife cameras that captured the many animals that share a home with the gorillas, including chimpanzees, elephants, duikers, bush pigs, and pangolins. Unexpectedly, we all got involved in the release of a pangolin back to the forest, that had been captured in the local community, reminding me of how endangered and widely trafficked they are around the world. I hope that the memories of these highly engaging experiences will stay in the children's minds and influence their career choices or decisions that they make about wildlife within their communities of Bwindi, Uganda, and the world.

What kind of future do we want for our children, and how many species will remain for the future generations to see? Extinction stared me in the face after visiting the last two northern white rhinos in the world, at Ol Pajeta ranch in northern Kenya. Northern white rhinos had been poached to extinction in Uganda in the early 1980s and the last herd of northern white rhinos was decimated most likely by soldiers in Garamba National Park in DRC in 2007. This was particularly painful having been a founder member of Rhino Fund Uganda in the late 1990s, where plans that had been made to translocate northern white rhinos from Garamba to Uganda or Kenya were not followed through for various reasons. I am now serving on the Board of Ziwa Rhino Sanctuary, where over thirty southern white rhinos are being kept by a private Ugandan landowner, Captain Joe Roy, in partnership with Uganda Wildlife Authority.

We must make conservation relevant to the general public. How can we ensure that the One Health approach is on the forefront of international environmental conservation? We must combat poverty, disease, and high human population growth simultaneously with addressing climate change and wildlife conservation. It is worth exploring the potential of multidisciplinary approaches to making the world a better place.

In 2018, mountain gorillas were reclassified from critically endangered to endangered, after their numbers surpassed the threshold of one thousand and showed a positive growth trend to a minimum of 1,063 individuals with the latest census of gorillas at Bwindi. In fact, they are the only gorilla subspecies to be taken off the IUCN critically endangered list. Sadly, all the other gorilla subspecies are rapidly declining in number. Habitat loss, poaching, bushmeat trade, disease, conflict with humans, and climate change continue to threaten all gorilla subspecies, including mountain gorillas, eastern lowland gorillas, western lowland gorillas, and Cross River gorillas, which are all worsened by poverty and high human population growth rates.

When I am asked what the most important threats are to mountain gorillas, I have found that the order of priority of threats to gorillas changes according to the local situation. Before tourism, the threats to mountain gorillas were the same as all other gorilla subspecies in Africa currently are today. When Bwindi Impenetrable Forest was upgraded from a forest reserve where you could enter and cut trees in a controlled manner to a national park where timber cutting could no longer be permitted, the mountain gorillas were not habituated and the local communities were resentful that they could no longer get timber and other products from the forest. Dr. Adonia Bintoora and Joseph Serugo, who were the first chief wardens of Mgahinga and Bwindi Impenetrable National Parks, told me how the community threatened to burn the forest park. When Bwindi gorillas were habituated for tourism, and local communities started to earn a meaningful living from gorilla ecotourism, their attitude to conservation started to change, and now they cannot live without the gorillas, which have become their future. With habituation, human disease has become one of the most important threats to mountain gorillas who come into close contact with humans in the form of tourists, researchers, and local communities when gorillas venture outside the park to forage in people's gardens. Gorillas are also threatened by retaliatory killings when they destroy people's crops. At Bwindi, these issues are being addressed through regular monitoring of wildlife, improved veterinary care, targeted conservation education, health-care, and livelihoods improvement in the local communities, as well as effective law enforcement.

What's next for me and CTPH? We are looking forward to the exciting challenge of scaling the Bwindi model to other gorilla sub-species in Africa, as well as to other biodiversity hot spots through partnerships with local stakeholders. When CTPH won the 2020 Saint Andrews Prize for the Environment, this dream became a reality where we are replicating our model to protect eastern low-land gorillas in DRC. The main threats to eastern lowland goril-las, western lowland gorillas, and Cross River gorillas are the same as when Bwindi Impenetrable Forest first became a national park. These include habitat destruction where some gorilla populations in Africa are not found in protected areas and are considered a delicacy. Additionally, there's often retaliatory killing when gorillas destroy community property, particularly in areas where they are ranging far from protected areas. Having tested our model in different habitats, we have been able to better understand and plan how next to scale up our Conservation Through Public Health model.

During the COVID-19 pandemic, elements of CTPH model started being scaled up through the Africa CSO Biodiversity Alliance. I coauthored a policy brief with IGCP on responsible tourism to great apes, targeting African governments, donors, tour companies (and tourists) who all have a role to play in minimizing disease trans-mission and maximizing benefits to communities.[37] It was launched at the first IUCN Africa Protected Areas congress targeting thirteen of twenty-one countries in Africa with gorilla and chimpanzee tour-ism at thirty-three sites.

Bottom-up approaches have promise for a sustainable approach that empowers landowners to become dignified partners in managing wildlife together with authorities.

Ironically, our success has brought new challenges. Now that the number of mountain gorillas has almost doubled in the past twenty-five years, the gorillas are running out of space in Bwindi Impenetrable National Park and will soon have nowhere to expand. Rainforest Trust provided funding for a feasibility study to expand the protected habitat of gorillas, including how we can fulfill the needs of the local communities who are selling (or putting aside) their land to create a larger home for mountain gorillas.

The rate of human population growth needs to continue to be addressed. Awareness of overpopulation has contributed to an average drop in birthrates in Uganda's rural areas from 7 to 5.5. We are pleased to have contributed to further reducing the rate in Kanungu District from 7 to 4.1. We need to see the same momentum in the two other districts neighboring Bwindi Impenetrable National Park, the Kisoro and Rubanda districts.

However, for natural habitats to be protected, remain intact, or expand, we need to build the leadership of people from where the wildlife is found. In 2016, I helped launch the African Primatological Society (APS), to build African leadership in primate research and conservation through enabling aspiring primatologists from these countries to attend conferences, present papers, and network with other scientists to support each other's projects. In my travels to conferences, I was alarmed to find that fewer than 10 percent of delegates representing primate organizations were from countries where these primates are found. The first APS conference was held in 2017 in Ivory Coast with 150 delegates, 80 percent of whom were native Africans. Dr. Inza Kone became the president of APS, and I became the vice president.

In 2019, I headed the organizing committee to host the second APS conference in Entebbe, Uganda. With aggressive fundraising we were able to raise over $100,000 from the Arcus Foundation, Margot Marsh Foundation, Houston Zoo and other donors to sponsor native Africans from all over the continent to attend the conference. Ernest Kleinwort Charitable Trust gave $10,000 toward simultaneous translation to enable the delegates from French-speaking countries, where half the primates are found, to participate fully in the conference. Knowing that political support is essential for building a homegrown African movement of primatologists, we were thrilled when the minister of tourism, wildlife and antiquities, Hon. Ephraim Kamuntu, opened the conference. Hosting a high-profile guest of honor attracted media coverage that helped to amplify the message that the future of wildlife lies in the hands of those who live where it occurs naturally, and they should be empowered to protect the wild-life for future generations.

We exceeded our goal with over three hundred delegates from twenty-four countries attending of whom 85 percent were local Africans who gave scientific presentations and presented posters.

The APS conference was a family affair for me. My husband was on the organizing committee, my sister and mother—the oldest del-egate—attended the conference, and my two sons helped with serv-ing coffee. Students from Uganda Canadian International School, my sons' former school, came with their headmistress, Miriam Odermatt, and asked very thoughtful questions. Elizabeth Veilleux, who was most vocal, told me a few years later that I inspired her to follow a career with wildlife, which was amazing. In his keynote speech, Professor Vernon Reynolds (my old mentor) shared a photograph of me when I first conducted research on primates in the wild at the age of twenty-two in Budongo Forest, which excited the delegates, and I was delighted that it inspired others to take up primatology as a career, including two young women from Uganda and Kenya. The Nigerian delegation was the largest delegation outside Uganda, and a place where primate meat is a delicacy and widely eaten. They brought the message back to their countries that gorilla tourism was a way to preserve the species and create livelihoods at the same time.

For several decades the Japanese have supported primatology in Africa, so I was thrilled to have the Japanese Ambassador, Kazuaki Kameda, attend the conference, particularly as Kyoto in Japan is one of the most prominent centers of primate research in the world.

We gave lifetime achievement awards to people who have nur-tured African leadership in primatology over several decades, includ-ing Dr. Jane Goodall, Prof. Vernon Reynolds, Prof. John Oates, and Dr. Russ Mittermeier from UK and the United States, Prof. Jonah Ratsimbazafy from Madagascar, and the Ugandan Professor Isabirye Basuta, a chimpanzee expert who has trained many Ugandan prima-tologists. I was honored to win the 2020 Aldo Leopold Award from the American Society of Mammologists for my work with goril-las and other wildlife as well as nurturing Ugandans in the field of conservation.

In the next five to ten years I would like our multidisciplinary One Health approach to conservation to have an impact beyond Uganda to the ten countries in Africa that are home to gorillas and to other countries in the world. Winning the United Nation's highest environmental honor in 2021, the Champions of the Earth Award in Science and Innovation, for our One Health approach to conservation, is helping to make this a reality. After I gave a talk at the Masai Mara University conference in Kenya, one of the professors told me that she was impressed with our approach that was meeting the needs of both wild animals and people. She was outraged that orphaned elephants in Nairobi were getting the most expensive milk formula when children living just next door couldn't afford milk and were starving and malnourished. For conservation to have a lasting impact, it is vital to build a homegrown movement of local conservationists who are in a better position to balance the concerns of wildlife with the human needs in their countries.

Over time, I have come to realize that conserving wildlife is complex and therefore needs many different actors. To help tell the story of my personal journey, I have sometimes had to tell other people's stories as well. I would like to close with words from a heroine I never had an opportunity to meet, Prof. Wangari Maathai, who was the first African to win the Sierra Club Earthcare Award, and in whose footsteps I was humbled to follow when I became the second African to win this prestigious award.

She said:

"I'm very conscious of the fact that you can't do it alone. It's team work. When you do it alone you run the risk that when you are no longer there nobody else will do it."

Acknowledgments

I would like to deeply thank my family, friends, and colleagues who have supported me on this incredible journey, as well as our donors and partners who have generously kept our work going. It is not possible to individually thank everyone, but I thank them collectively and if they come across their names in this memoir, they know that their part in shaping my journey is deeply appreciated.

Yet, I would like to mention a number of other organizations and individuals—some of whom departed from this world—who have been instrumental at various stages of my life and career, as well as in publishing this memoir.

People who helped me to write

I'll start off by acknowledging those who have enabled this book to be in your hands. The following authors gave encouragement, insightful advice and support in writing and publishing this memoir: bestselling author Sabriye Tenberken and her husband, Paul

Kronenberg—founders of Braille Without Borders-Kanthari; Cathy
Kreutter also mentored my teenage son to write *Zookeeper for a Week*
that won the Moonbeam Gold Award; Kings College Budo class-
mate and lawyer David Mpanga took a keen interest in my work
with gorillas; lawyer Peter Mulira also pushed me to write a book
about my career with wildlife and offered financial support; bestselling author Alan Weisman featured our work with gorillas and
Bwindi local communities in his book *Countdown*; Dr. Rob Brown
also arranged a book signing; Robert Kibuuka, Martin Lwanga,
and Elizabeth Kanyogonya also supported my mother in writing
her autobiography, and Helen Lang through Wildlife Conservation
Network is a major donor to our work with the gorillas and local
communities.

I am extremely grateful to Jane Marie Franklyn, who put me
on the international stage in 1997 at the beginning of my career
through a documentary on my work at Uganda Wildlife Authority
on BBC1, and subsequently gave advice on the writing of this memoir; and John Davey, her cameraman, who told my mother that he
was going to make me famous. The legendary CNN producer Zain
Verjee sparked my interest to start writing again while interview-
ing me for CNN African Voices at our field office at Bwindi. Sarah
Marshall took a keen interest in this book after featuring me in several articles including in the *Telegraph UK*, and Dr. Anthony Collins
from the Jane Goodall Institute momentously supported our work
and the promotion of this book. Thank you all for this critical support
in my journey.

I would like to greatly thank my veterinary colleagues and
friends who encouraged me to document my experiences and write
a book: Dr. Sam Okech, Professor at Makerere University College of
Veterinary Medicine, Animal Resources and Bio-Security; Dr. Robert
Aruho, Uganda Wildlife Authority Senior Veterinary Officer, and Dr.
Peter Apell, senior manager at the Jane Goodall Institute Uganda.

I am grateful to the Women for the Environment, Africa leadership council, who encouraged me to take some time off to write,
especially Dr. Leela Hazzah who reviewed the chapter on women
and conservation as well as other members of the WINGS family

of Women in Discovery and Exploration, in particular Milbry Polk, Anne Bancroft, Yael Jaekogin Beth Nixon, and the conservation legends and National Geographic Explorers, Dr. Jane Goodall[38], Dr. Sylvia Earle[39], and Dr. Meg Lowman[40] "Canopy Meg," whose books have inspired and guided me.

A special thank you to Suzanne York from Transition Earth who helped develop chapter outlines; A.Tianna Scozzaro from the Sierra Club headquarters who engaged publishers; John Seager from Population Connection who gave funding toward writing the book; and Naz Ahsun my literary agent who has dedicated countless hours to help me write and edit my memoir. Allison Hanes not only helped me to find Skyhorse Publishing but also created a wonderful documentary to accompany the book through her company One Health Productions, together with Alex Campbell and Arden Kelley from her team. Tony Lyons took a great interest in the book and Lilly Golden diligently edited it from a very wordy draft to a concise and compelling memoir; the Wilson Center extensively supported our work, including making the first offer to host a book launch; Joy Chesborough in San Francisco and Christine Gibbons in the UK for offering to hold a book signings. I am grateful to African Writers Trust and Uganda Christian Writers Forum for their advice and support.

I would like to greatly thank CTPH Patron HRH Queen Sylvia Nagginda of Buganda for her unlimited support and encouragement of our work. I am grateful to the Board of Conservation Through Public Health: Pauline Nantongo, Beatrice Adimola, Dr. Lynn Murrell, Phillip Kiboneka, and Luke Nkuubi, for believing in me and granting me time to write; and the CTPH staff, in particular Stephen Rubanga, who has been with me for a large part of this journey; and Kityo Emmanuel and Kakande William, who have been with me since CTPH began. Kaamu Bukenya and Mary Leakey Sudra, who encouraged me to write and document our unique approach to conservation in this book; and Elizabeth Kaniwabo and Richard Bagyenyi, who helped to compile photos and other important material for the book.

I could not have written this book without the help of family, who supported and encouraged me: my nephew Willie Kalema, who reviewed drafts; my mother; my brother Dr. William Kalema;

my sister, Dr. Veronica Naki Kalema, who gave advice; my husband, Lawrence, who triggered my memory; my sons, Ndhego and Tendo, who inspired me with their curiosity and boundless energy; Auntie Rita Kiwana and her daughter Babirye D'Arbela; my parents-in-law, Retired Lieutenant Colonel Kenneth Dako and Mrs. Sarah Zikusoka Dako; and Uncle Aggrey and Auntie Betsy Zikusoka.

Women

While my mother, Rhoda Kalema, tops the list, there have been many women who inspired me on my journey:

- Patron of CTPH, HRH Queen Sylvia of Buganda who founded the Nnabagereka Development Foundation that leverages culture to support children, youth, and women
- Professor Wangari Maathai—Nobel prize winner who founded the Green Belt Movement
- Dr. Shirley McGrael, founder of the International Primate Protection League
- Dr. Laurie Marker, who founded Cheetah Conservation Fund in Namibia
- Anita Roddick, founder of the Body Shop, who early on created products not tested on animals and later sourced goods from women in Africa and other developing countries
- Dr. Meg Lowman, one of the first "Arbonauts" in the world studying wildlife on top of trees and founder of the Tree Foundation
- Dr. Christine Dranzoa, for her pioneering role in promoting wildlife health within wildlife management at Makerere University College of Veterinary Medicine and supporting girls to achieve higher education
- Beatrice Adimola, former director at National Environment Management Authority

I was recognized together with four Ugandan women by the African Wildlife Foundation for our impact in wildlife conservation:

- Pauline Nantongo, our current CTPH Board Chair, and executive director of Ecotrust
- Lilly Ajarova, CEO of Uganda Tourism Board and former executive director of the Chimpanzee Trust
- Helen Lubowa, executive director of Uganda Community Tourism Association
- Diana Nalwanga, Director of Programmes at Nature Uganda and formerly a board member of UWA

To those with whom we have fought together to amplify the role of women in conservation and sustainable development—thank you so much—Dr. Winnie Kiiru, Dr. Colleen Begg, Fiesta Warinwa, Rosette Rugamba, Anne Kahihia, and Dr. Nyawira Muthiga from the WE-Africa Leadership Council; and other forces of change: Hind Alowais, Vice President of the Dubai Expo 2020; Hon. Jesca Eriyo, former Uganda Minister of State for the Environment; Doreen Katusiime, Permanent Secretary in the Ministry of Tourism, Wildlife and Antiquities; Bessie Kikoyo, Apohia Muhumbira, Eunice Duli, Lilian Nsubuga, Agnes Nakidde and Robina Gangiriba from UWA; Rebecca Harrington, Marian Starkey, and Lee Polansky from Population Connection; Brenda Berry and Karl Morrison from Planet Women; Helena Cotton, Angela Yang, Amanda Vincent, Jo-Anne McArthur, Sharon Ryan, Dr. Elaine Millam, Crystal Dimiceli, Alexander Blair, Dr. Laly Lichtenfield, Dr. Paula Kahumba, Helena Nambogwe, Jacqueline Shimanya Edith Kabesiime, Winnie Lawoko, Cathy Watson, Rehema Kasule, Maria Kasule, Margaret Othieno, Angela Nduhukire, Lydia Obbo, Doreen Kabasindi Wandera, Alice Ruhweeza, Pat Awori, Dominique Goncalves, Rosamira Guillen, Shivani Bhalla, Iroro Tanshi, Prof. Kathleen Ragsdale, Dr. Barbara Barungi, Bea Karanja, Sarah Watson, Ivy Wairimu, Maaike Manten, Judy Brey, Betty Aliba, Sarah Margiotta, Gertrude Kenyangi Jacqueline Asiimwe, Patricia Bageine, Yogi Birigwa, Sonya Willet, Catherine Ruhweza (Mama Tendo), Dorothy Kirumira, Kebirungi Pheonah, Fiona Saunderman, magistrate Gladys Kamasanyu; Lisa Randolph, author of *Wildlife Divas*, Stephanie Williams and actress Catherine Wolf who are also donors.

I was greatly honored to be featured with my mother in Goretti Bamwanga's book *Footmarks* about Uganda's women pioneers and humbled when Avance Media listed me in the 100 Most Influential Women in Africa along with environmentalist Dr. Musonda Mumba and Ellen Johnson Sirleaf, the former president of Sierra Leone whose foundation nominated me as a COVID-19 heroine, and Winnie Byanyima, Executive Director of UNAIDS.

I thank women veterinarians who have mentored me and followed in my footsteps: Dr. Mary Brancker, Dr. Liz Macfie, Dr. Elizabeth Wambwa, Dr. Sharon Redrobe, Dr. Anita Michel, Dr. Anneke Moresco, Dr. Barb Wolfe, Dr. Linda Munson, Dr. Linda Lowenstein, Dr. Josephine Afema, Dr. Sylvia Baluka, Dr. Bena Nakanwagi, Dr. Margaret Driciru, Dr. Carol Asiimwe, Dr. Rachel Mbabazi, and Dr. Jessica Kurere.

I thank women primatologists with whom we have lifted each other up: Jillian Miller, Janie Reynolds, Dr. Jessica Rothman, Dr. Emily Otali, Julia Lloyd, Debbie Cox, Cherry Montgomery, Racquel Costa, Jane Dewar, Helga Rainer, Alice Mbayahi, Anna Behm Masozera, Dr. Martha Robbins, Dr. Tara Stoinski, Dr. Winnie Eckert, Dr. Katie Faucett, Dr. Jennifer Verdolin, Dr. Tatyana Humle, Dr. Kim Hockings, Dr. Liz Williamson, Dr. Janette Wallis, Dr. Riashna Sithaldeen, Dr. Jo Thompson, Dr. Jill Preutz, Dr. Rachel Ikemeh, Prof. Catherine Hill, Dr. Magdalena Svensson, Dr. Cat Hobaiter, Dr. Joe Setchell, Maryke Gray, Chloe Chesney, Amy Clannin, Amy Roll, Cristina Gomes, and Dr. Susan Cork.

Establishment of CTPH

I am grateful to Mrs. Joyce Mpanga who connected us to Kulika Charitable Trust, who sponsored my veterinary degree in the UK; Alex Muhweezi, who gave CTPH our first office space as the Uganda Country Director of International Union for the Conservation of Nature; Charles Goodsill and Professor Ellen Kraly from upstate New York enabled the setting up of a CTPH US office for three years at Colgate University campus. American Jewish World Service Volunteers Carol and Geoffrey Howard, Masha Katz, Daniela Amodei, and Susan Rothstein gave critical support in organizational development and marketing in the first few years; and Sam Bisase, Allan Matovu, CTPH staff Richard Tibita and Rose Mugide , and volunteer David Opio, helped to build administrative systems; Connie Alezuyo, Sylvia Nandago, and Joseph Byonanebye helped to build our public health programs; Richard Kibalama, Paul Ntungwa and Emmanuel Nsaba provided critical IT and marketing support.

I thank Ambassador Steve Browning and his wife Sue Browning and Ambassador Natalie Brown from USA, Ambassador Sophie Makame from France, and the British High Commissioner Kate Airey who visited or hosted us and promoted our work at CTPH.

I thank Severine Dieudonne, Sarah Parfitt, Lisa Peters, Angela Robson and my sister Veronica who graciously arranged the memorable ten-year celebration of CTPH in the UK.

A big thanks to former CTPH board members Dr. Allison Alberts, Hon. Johnson Nkuuhe, Dr. Ian Clark and his wife Robbie, Alexandra Karekaho, Dr. Noelina Nantima, Katia Allard, Charmaine Donnelly and Dr. Gerry Noble.

I am indebted to Laura Arndt from Global Green STEM for support toward the Gorilla Guardians, including getting Hunter to design a beautiful logo for their t-shirts, which she provided, and critical support in establishing a STEAM program among the Bwindi youth funded by National Geographic.

Donors

CTPH is grateful to many donors for ongoing support to these programs since inception in 2003, including Wildlife Conservation Network, Population Connection, Tusk Trust, Darwin Initiative, Whitley Fund for Nature, Critical Ecosystem Partnership Fund, Global Development Network, Mulago Foundation, Disney Conservation Fund, National Geographic Society, USAID, United States Fish and Wildlife Service, John D. and Catherine T. MacArthur Foundation, Wildlife Conservation Society, African Wildlife Foundation, Family Health International FHI360, Population Reference Bureau, Ashoka, North Carolina Zoological Park, San Diego Zoo Global, Cotswold Wildlife Park, Forix Foundation, The Gorilla Organization, Zoos Victoria, Primate Conservation Inc., Rain Forest Trust, Milkywire,

Rare Species Fund, Empowers Africa, World Wildlife Fund for Nature, Growth Africa, Solidaridad, Babel Foundation, Planet Women, GAIA, Maliasili, Arcus Foundation, British High Commission to Uganda, International Union for the Conservation of Nature (IUCN), The International Development Research Centre, Dietrich American Foundation, European Commission through Nestlar, and several individual and other institutional donors who have enabled us to reach this far.

Telecentre

I thank Hon. Dr. Johnson Nkuuhe, Prof. Aramanzan Madanda from Makerere University Department of Women and Gender Studies Technology Program, Bill Farmer from Uganda Carbon Bureau, Daniel Stern from U-Connect, Sean Nicolson from Microsoft and Renee Francis from Ericsson for supporting our telecentres together with our key partners from Uganda Communications Commission: Eng. Patrick Mwesigwa and Eng. Patrick Musambu, among others in the ICT for Development community.

Gorilla Conservation Coffee

For helping Gorilla Conservation Coffee realize its potential: Rahel Gerber, Sybille Bonner, Nicolaus Hutter and Werner Krendi from WWF Switzerland Impact Investment for Conservation Program; Jan-Willem Loggers; Robert Nsibirwa from Africa Coffee Academy; Frederick Kawuma, Colin Hakiza, Annemarie Weeden, Marianne Boye from Add Value Creators Ltd; Joseph Nkandu from Nucafe; Dr. Nathaniel Dunigan from Aidchild; Dr. Emmanuel Iyamulemye and Laura Mulenga Walusimbi from Uganda Coffee Development Authority, Peter Seligman, Bambi Semroc, and Valerie Beard from Conservation International Sustainable Coffee Challenge; Romal from Safari Lounge in Kenya; John Probert, Vicky Weddell, Andrew Warren, Mwambu Wanandeya, Melanie Perry, and Dr. Nina Wanandeya Milne from Carico Café; Susan Muhweezi, Meg Hilbert from Jakana Foods; Fabio Cappellin from Vanilla Dreams; Andrea Cesoni, Francesco Rubino and Filippo Sala from Startup Africa Roadtrip; Nancy

Rapando, Julius Semyalo, Joan Kantu Else, Glen Jampol, and Judy Kephers working together to promote coffee tourism. I thank the operations and farmer extension teams: Peter Ebinu, Safari Joseph, Godfrey Ssekabira, Rita Kyomuhingire, Joel Muwonge, Nicholas Ainebyona, Edward Sekandi, the dedicated staff at the Gorilla Conservation Café; the Bwindi Coffee Growers Cooperative and the inspiring coffee farmers living in subcounties around Bwindi Impenetrable National Park.

Leadership Journey

I also thank several inspiring partners along my leadership journey—the African Primatological Society, Mulago Foundation, Maliasili, and partner organizations, Alan Stoga, Tom Cummings Maarten Koets, Zahara Abdul and other members of the Tallberg Foundation family, Francesco Raeli and other members of the Rolex Award family, Brian Stranko, AfriVet founder and The Explorers Club where I serve as the Chairperson of the Africa Chapter.

I am indebted to Ashoka who nurtured my entrepreneurial spirit and the many inspiring Ashoka fellows and staff who supported my entrepreneurial journey: Debbie Kaddu Serwadda, Abu Musuuza, Nassir Katuramu, Mwalimu Musheshe, Bill Carter, Bev Schwartz, Maria Baryamujura, Rita Sembuya, Lilian Keene Mugerwa, Irene Mutumba, Claire Wavamuno, Haron Wachira, Alexandra Ertler, and Vincent Odhiambo; and University of Milan and Tangaza University College, for their support in obtaining an MBA in Global Business and Sustainability—Social Entrepreneurship Track. The folks from United Nations Environmental Program (UNEP) have greatly amplified our work: Doug Cress, Dr. Johannes Refisch, Alejandra Perez, Florian Fussstetter, Kibuuka Mukisa, and Dr. Julian Blanc.

To my inspiring fellow National Geographic Explorers and the dedicated team of staff including Alexander Moen, Dr. Ian Miller, Debra Adam Simmons, Dr. Claire McNulty, Chloé Cipolletta, Shivan Parusnath, Cheryl Zooks, Stacey McClain, Rosemary Martin, Catherine Workman, Sarah Van Duyn, Sarah Davidson, Danielle Cales, Jenny Lim, Christine Zirneklis and Lisa Feit, who featured me in the National Geographic Women of Impact documentary.

The Government

Sam Mwandha, Dr. Andrew Seguya, Moses Mapesa, Dr. Arthur Mugisha, Dr. Yakobo Moyini, and Prof. Eric Edroma have greatly supported me in their role as UWA Executive Directors, which has been critical to my journey. I am also grateful to the hardworking and dedicated Wardens and Rangers who have bravely protected the precious wildlife against all odds. I also thank my fellow UWA board members: Ben Otto, Mani Khan, Captain Otekat, Boniface Byamukama, Hon. Janet Okorimoe, Grace Aulo, Michael Ariyo, and Zeridah Zigiti; and Dr. Akankwasah Barirega, National Environment Management Authority ED, and Tom Okello, National Forest Authority Executive Director. I am grateful to the Ministers of Tourism, Wildlife and Antiquities: Hon Ephraim Kamuntu, Hon Tom Butime, and Hon Maria Mutagamba; Assistant Director General of L'Institut Congolais pour la Conservation de la Nature (ICCN), Mr. Benoit Kisuki, and Dr. Georges Muamba former executive secretary of Great Virunga Transboundary Collaboration. I also thank the Uganda district local governments in particular Kanungu, Kisoro, and Rubanda who we have worked closely with to uplift the Bwindi communities.

Cannon Ben Rullonga, Josephine Kasya, and Dr. Stephen Ssebudde from Kanungu District Local Government were instrumental in getting CTPH established and launched when we hosted the Nnabagereka, Hon. Apollo Makubya and Hon. Apollonia Lugemwa from the Buganda Kingdom. I thank the Prime Minister Katikiro of Buganda Owekitibwa Charles Peter Mayiga, Treasurer Omuwanika of Buganda Owekitibwa Robert Waggwa Nsibirwa, and all the dedicated members of the Buganda Heritage and Tourism Board that I chaired.

Conservationists

A big thank you to conservationists who have offered support at critical stages of my journey: Wilhelm and Ursula Moeller, Peter and Elke Moeller, Dr. James Musinguzi, David Musingo, Frank Ruhinirwa, Prof. Vernon and Frankie Reynolds, Jake Reynolds, Dr. Andrew Plumptre, Dr. Alistair McNeilage, Kaddu Sebunya, Frederick Kumah,

Philip Muruthi, Daudi Sumba, Linda Greenberg, Stany Nyandwi, Pradeep Suthram, Andrea Santy, Nancy Gelman, Dirck Byler, Dr. Russ Mittermeir, Prof. Richard Wrangham, Prof. Bernie Tershy, Aggrey Rwetsiba, Dr. Adonia Bintoora, Captain Otekat, Walter Odwokorot, Joseph Serugo, James Byamukama, Charles Tumwesige, Samuel Besigye, Stephen Masaba, Bashir Hangi, Charles Etoru, Samson Werikhe, Bernard Twinomugisha, James Omoding, Michael Keigwin, Dickson Kaelo, Tom Lalaampa, Agostinho Jorge, Dr. Inza Kone, Dr. Ekwoge Abwe, Dr. Jonah Ratsimbazafy, Dr. Takeshi Furichi, Prof. Colin Chapman, Prof. Thomas Struhsaker, Dr. Jean Claude Kyungu, Dr. Vital Kakembo, Dr. Dominic Bikaba, Badru Mugerwa, Stan Miller, Dieter Beller and Stephen and Helga Tomkins, Penny Havnar from Elephants for Africa–Wildlife for Africa Trust in Zimbabwe and former USAID Environmental Officer, Dr. Jody Stallings, Prof. Derek Pomeroy, Dr. Panta Kasoma, Dr. Tony Sainsbury, George Owesigire, Tom Sengalama, Adalbert Aine-omcunguzi, Fidelis Kanyamunywa, Max Graham, Mark Mwine, Katia Allard, Kim and David Chase, Dr. Felix Ndagijimana, and Prosper Uwingeli.

I thank wildlife veterinarians Prof. John Cooper and his wife environmental lawyer Margaret Cooper, Prof. Mark Fox, Prof. Richard Kock, Dr. John Wambua, Dr. Jacob Mwanzia, Dr. Ludwig Siefert, Dr. Jonathan Sleeman, Dr. Tony Mudakikwa, Dr. John Bosco Nizeyi, Dr. Billy Karesh, Dr. Steve Osofsky, Dr. Ed Ramsay, Dr. Roy Bengis, Dr. Cobus Raath, Dr. Pete Morkel, Dr. Tony Goldberg, Dr. Fabian Leendertz, Dr. Thomas Gillespie, Dr. Dominic Travis, Dr. Joseph Okori, Dr. Innocent Rwego, Dr. Joseph Mavisi, Dr. Chris Whittier, Dr. Felicia Nutter, Dr. David Hyeroba, Dr. Noel Arinteireho, Dr. Richard Ssuuna, Dr. Patrick Atimnedi, Dr. Eric Enyell, Dr. Joshua Rukundo, Dr. Wayne Boardman, Dr. Steve Unwin, Prof. Alonso Aguirre, Dr. Ben Davidson, Dr. Olivier Nsengimana, and Dr. Arthur Kalonji, Dr. Richard Muvunyi, Dr. Mark Okot, and other veterinarians for their great support: Dr Sam Byagagaire, Dr. Dan Semambo, Dr. Innocent Djossou, Dr. Jesus Muro, Dr. Patrick Vudriko, Dr. Wilson Engena, Dr. Joseph Mubiru, Dr. David Kakwa among others.

I thank my fellow members of the IUCN Wildlife Health Specialist Group, IUCN ESARO (East and Southern Africa)

Regional Committee and the section on Great Apes (SGA) of the IUCN Species Survival Commission Primate Specialist Group; and the British Veterinary Zoological Society of which I am an honorary member; the British Veterinary Association; and the Uganda Veterinary Association for all the great support.

Public Health Community

Dr. Lynne Gaffikin introduced me to donors who support Population, Health and Environment (PHE) and was instrumental in making our public health programs achieve the intended goal of bringing benefits to conservation. I also thank other PHE champions who have greatly supported our work: Negash Teklu from Ethiopia PHE Consortium, Linda Bruce, Dr. Paul Blumenthal, Dr. Amy Voedisch, Jason Bremner, Kristen Patterson, and Rachel Yavinsky with Population Reference Bureau; Dr. Angela Akol, Patrica Wamala and Tricia Petruney from FHI360; Charles Kabiswa and Isaac Kabong from Ecological Christian Organization; Raymond Ruyoka and Roseline Achola strengthened our engagement with THETA and UNFPA; Roger-Mark De Souza, Meaghan Parker, and Lauren Risi from the Wilson Center; Carina Hirsch and David Johnson from Margaret Pyke Trust; Issa Makumbi, Atek Kagirita, and Hon. Dr. Monica Musenero from the MOH national disease taskforces and Dr. Sarah Paige from USAID made our One Health model realize its potential in reducing the impact of disease outbreaks and pandemics. Dr. Birungi Mutahunga and Edson Niyonzima from Bwindi Community Hospital (BCH) for their unlimited support. Nina Gobat, Dr. Sarah Olsen, Barbara Natifu, Dr. Julius Lutwama, John Kayiwa, Musa Sekamatte; my fellow advisory committee members from the International Livestock Research Institute (ILRI) One Health Research Education and Outreach Centre (OHRECA): Dr. Dieter Schillinger, fellow author Dr. Caradee Wright, Dr. Doreen Robinson, Dr. Bernard Bett and Dr. Hung Yen from ILRI with whom we serve on the World Health Organization Scientific Advisory Group for the Origin of Novel Pathogens (WHO SAGO); Cheryl Stroud from the One Health Commission; Dr. Doreen Othero; Margaret from NEKEKI; and Prof. EJ Milner Gulland, Dilys Roe and Francesca Booker who through research to policy engagement increased awareness of the health benefits of the CTPH model to conservation and sustainable development.

Tourism Community

A big thank you to Karl Whiffler, Praveen Moman, Amos Wekesa, Jane and Paul Goldring, Jonathan and Pamela Wright, Roni Madhvani, Corne Schwalkwyk, Brian Mugume, Tony Kirungi, Glorious Tumwesgiye, Herbert Byaruhanga, Johnnie Kamugisha, Evelyne and Dennisa Habassa, Barbara Adoso, Lydia Eva Mpanga, Phillip Brennan, Saul Ampeire, Lilian Kansiime, Rachel Kakungulu Kirama, Emmy Gongo, Tom Bakara, Katie Rees, Alexandra Avila, Scovia Kyasmira, among others.

University and Other Educational Partnerships

From the student and university community: Dr. Nancy Stevens and Dr. Geoff Dabelko from Ohio University, Dean Prof. Kabassa, Prof. Sam Majalija, Prof. Frank Mwine, Prof. Francis Ejobi, Prof. George Niseyemana, and Prof. Johnson Acon from Makerere University College of Veterinary Medicine, Animal Resources and Bio-security (MUK COVAB) in Uganda, the Open University, Dr. Jay Levine, Dr. Peter Cowen, and Dr. Andy Stringer from North Carolina State University, Prof. Gad Ruzaaza, Dr. Robert Bitariho, Prof. Dominic Byarugaba and Dr. Medard Twinamatsiko from MUST, who have supported work to conduct field research, Dr. Ryoma Otsuka and Dr. Mike Huffman from Kyoto University, Prof. Dwight Bowman from Cornell University, Prof. David Hayman from Massey University, Prof. Francisco Olea-Popelka from Colorado State University, Prof. Margaret Khaitsa, a Ugandan professor of Veterinary Medicine at Mississippi State University, Dr. Robert Kabuusu from St. George's University in Grenada, Dr. Neil Anderson from Edinburgh University, and Dr. Dominic Mundrugo-Lali from Uganda National Commission for UNESCO. During the COVID-19 pandemic, we started working with Dr. Tony Goldberg at the University of Wisconsin-Madison, who founded the Kibale Ecohealth project, to also protect the mountain gorillas from common flu viruses.

I was one of seven alumni featured for their distinctive careers at the University of London Royal Veterinary College Hobday Building wall of achievement opened by HRH Princess Anne and extremely grateful to Vicki Laing, other faculty and students for this very great honor.

A big thank you to students we hosted at CTPH who inspired us and continue to promote our work: Dr. Ben Ssenkera from Makerere University Faculty of Veterinary Medicine; Dr. Divya Krishnan from Christchurch University in Bangalore, India; Dr. Melissa Turner, Dr. Amy Trey and Dr. William Fugina from Cornell University; Kelly Sambucci from RVC; Vishaka Vasuki from St. George's University in Grenada; Dr. Jalika Joyner and Dr. Jenna Herrington from North Carolina State University; Dr. Robert Stenger from Mississippi State University; Ursula Brown from Allderdice High School; and Emily de Moor, a teacher from St. Matthew's Episcopal Day School in the US, and Isabella Mazariegos from Colorado State University arranged for me to speak to her One Health club there.

The Wider Community

Special thank you to the local communities of Bwindi and other protected areas who we have worked with to learn how to take care of the precious wildlife and secure a brighter future together.

I am indebted to even more friends, colleagues and organizations from the conservation, primatology, veterinary, public health, tourism, and development community many of whom have been mentioned in this memoir—thank you for believing in me. To those who joined my journey when we founded Gorilla Conservation Coffee social enterprise, a big thank you for having faith in developing a global coffee brand to save gorillas.

Family friends

British family friends who looked after me in my student days in Scotland and London were instrumental in encouraging me to pursue my dream of working with animals and changing the world. Mary Klopper convinced my mother that it was safe for me to study the mountain gorillas in Bwindi Impenetrable Forest, along with her husband, Prof. Arnold Klopper whose home became a base for me, my siblings and cousins; Sue and Peter Woodsford became my first individual donors early in my career when working at UWA and built upon this at CTPH; Prof. David and Ilske Carter provided encouragement even later in life as my conservation journey became shaped by One Health. Margaret and David Ritchie enabled me to understand my father more and encouraged me to continue his dream of developing Uganda through my passion for conservation.

Friends

I am grateful to Maureen Kiyingi, also a donor, Lisa Sihotang, Cathy Sebukima, Herbert Sebukima, Arigye Mpairwe, Susan Batwala, Dr. Flavia Mpanga Kaggwa, Dr. Susie Mpanga Kiggundu, Farida Kyamanywa, Regina Lule, Ethel Nsubuga, Deborah Rutiba, Alexa Sasha Lewin, Brad Rister, Kelly and Francisco Ojeda, Debbie and Phillip Betts, Trina Scott-Zuor, Christine Mwambi and International School of Uganda community, Oskar Semweya-Musoke, Paul Mwambi and Taibah International School community, Beat Odermatt and Miriam Odermatt and U-Can International School community, Jonathan and Christelle Ouellet, Dr. Martin Aliker and Mrs. Camille Aliker, Marcella Mukasa, Dr. Maggie Kigozi, Anne Awori, Angela Walakira, Angelina Kironde, Elizabeth and Badru Ntege, Captain Joe Roy and Salma Buwembo for their long-standing friendship and support to our work with wildlife.

Family

CTPH would not exist without the support of my family. I thank my grandmother Jaaja Veronica for her love and care. I am indebted to my cousin Eleanor Nsubuga, her husband Peter and daughter Joy for their generosity to host CTPH US office for most of the past two decades; my cousins Deborah and Eric Kironde provided a base for me in London as a veterinary student; Grandparents Engineer James Zikusoka and Anita Katiti Zikusoka greatly supported our work and looked after the boys when we travelled. I am extremely lucky to have extended family: cousins, aunties, uncles, nephews and nieces who have supported our work with wildlife and attended several events in Uganda and around the world, the Anindo, Buwembo, Byagagaire, Collyer, Dako, D'Arbela, Ejalu, Gowa, Hillier, Jingo, Juko, Kasirye, Kawuma, Kigonya, Kitheka, Kironde, Kiwana, Kiwanuka, Lubale, Lutalo, Mamus, Maraka, Mdoe, Mukasa, Musasizi, Nsibirwa, Nsubuga, Nyonyintono, Semambya, Strain, Suubi, Wambuzi, Wanandeya, Wandera, and Zikusoka families.

My mother, brother, sister, and niece Nabaada Rhoda Kalema and nephews Juko Kayondo, Martin Ntale Kalema, and Willie Kalema have greatly supported my work and became donors to CTPH over the years and so have my sisters-in-law Felling Chalele and Juliet Semambo Kalema. I thank my cousin Maria Kiwanuka who got me one of my first interviews in Uganda on her Radio One station early in my career while setting up the veterinary unit at UWA; and Deborah Kironde Mugerwa and Eric Kironde and Nakato Kiwana and John Scott who provided a home base in London; Janet and Keith Collyer who became donors and Esita and Jingo Buwembo who regularly promote our work and Nakato Nsibirwa who first marketed the Gorilla Conservation Camp internationally. I am grateful to family friends who have taken a keen interest in my wildlife career and supported my work with wildlife: Barbara Mulwana Kulubya also a donor, Joyce Semaganda, Mrs. Adelina Lubogo and Ivan Lubogo, Mrs. Catherine Kisumba and Ssali Kisumba, Prof. Mondo Kagonyera, Major General Apollo Gowa, Brigadier Andrew Lutaya, Dr. Lydia Mpanga, Adengo, Batwala, Kaijuka, Kanyerezi, Kavuma, Mulwana, Musoke, Rutega, Semaganda families.

School friends

I thank my childhood friends from Kitante Primary School, Greensteds School, and Kabale Preparatory School for their support and interest in my career with wildlife; and friends from Dollar Academy in Scotland who made me feel at home far away from home and continue to support and follow my career, as well as the Rector Ian Munro who invited me back thirty-eight years later to give a presentation at my old school and Jacqueline Smith who reconnected me with the school after filming our work at Bwindi for BBC2 Science

Department, which she headed, Bex Bohea who came out to Uganda, and my alumni Elizabeth Meagre, Ian Murray, Kate Carroll, and Phil Stewart. I greatly thank all my classmates from King's College Budo in Uganda who have become lifelong friends and supporters.

Friends from Kibuli Secondary School, Madina Nakibirige and Sarah Kolo who served as board members of CTPH, and my biology teacher, Mr. Justus Acungwire, who gave me the opportunity to revive the school's Wildlife Club. Herbert Sebukima and Patricia Bageine who went on to win the Miss Wildlife competition kept the legacy going. I also thank University of London RVC housemates and friends, Angela Kerton, Emma Pillow and Sarah Burgess.

Artists

A special thank you to Gasuza Lwanga, a highly talented Ugandan musician, who composed "Team Gorilla" to raise funds for CTPH; Brigitta Best and her team at Voice, Art and Social organization who made a concert in Luxembourg to support our work with the gorillas and to Taga Nuwagaba for donating his beautiful and vivid wildlife paintings to raise funds for our work with wildlife. The famous Japanese artist Abe Chisato donated beautiful paintings of gorillas and photographer Gavin Bowyer of The Sympathetic Lens donated postcards with beautiful photos of gorillas to support our work. Katie Losey took photos and redesigned CTPH website when she travelled to Uganda with Absolute Travel and Volcanoes Safaris.

Recognition

I have been both honored and humbled to receive numerous awards and recognition. John Lwere from Uganda Export Promotion Board and his team made me Uganda's face for the Dubai Expo 2020. I am truly grateful for this, and to the national and international media who have extensively covered my journey from the very beginning. Special thanks to the New Vision in Uganda and BBC media. I thank Victoria Wilson Darrah who filmed my veterinary work at UWA on her inspiring UBC television program *Eye on Uganda* and Marie Lais Emond who hosted me at her home after featuring my wildlife veterinary work in *Fair Lady* magazine. A big thanks to Deborah

Steller of Calabass films, who did the first film *Living on the Edge* about our work at CTPH, and Adele Cutler for promoting our work through several media houses, as well as Richard Vaughan, Helen Mukiibi, Robert Kabushenga, Conan Tumusiime, Shaban Senyange, Solomon Olweny, Abraham Mutalyebwa, Musinguzi Bamuturwaki, Gerald Tenywa, Julius Luwemba, Zadock Amanyisa, Curtis Abraham and bloggers Brian Atuheirwe, Arans Tibaruka, Charlotte Beauvoisin, Fred Mwebya, Sarah Kagingo and Baluku Geoffrey among others for continuously for covering our work.

Lastly, I would like to thank the almighty God for giving me the steadiness of purpose on several phases of my journey, strength when I felt like giving up, and inspiration to complete my memoir.

Endnotes

1. Wambuzi, Sam. 2014. *An Odyssey of a Judicial Career in Precarious Times*. Cross House Books. Edinburgh, Scotland.
2. https://eden.uktv.co.uk/eden-heroes/sir-david-attenborough/article /more-sir-david-attenborough-quotes/
3. Hanson, Thor. 2001. *The Impenetrable Forest: My Gorilla Years in Uganda*. 1500 books. USA.
4. Kalema-Zikusoka, G., J. M. Rothman, and M. T. Fox 2005. Intestinal parasites and bacteria of mountain gorillas (*Gorilla beringei beringei*) in Bwindi Impenetrable National Park, Uganda. *Primates* 46:59–63.
5. Kalema, G. 1994. Letter. "Veterinarians and Zoological Medicine" to the *Veterinary Record*, Raising My Concern for Trained Wildlife Veterinarians in Developing Countries Like Uganda. *Veterinary Record* 135 (1).
6. *New York Times*. 1974. https://www.nytimes.com/1974/05/18/archives /the-screen-men-of-karamoja-is-a-study-of-africa.html.
7. Gladys the African Vet. 1997. https://www2.bfi.org.uk/films-tv-people /4ce2b80bb12a3.
8. Kalema-Zikusoka, G., R. A. Kock, and E. J. Macfie. 2002. Scabies in free-ranging mountain gorillas (*Gorilla beringei beringei*) in Bwindi Impenetrable National Park, Uganda. *Veterinary Record* 150 (1):12–15.
9. Kalema-Zikusoka, G. and L. Lowenstine. 2001. Rectal prolapse in a free-ranging mountain gorilla (*Gorilla beringei beringei*): clinical presentation and surgical management. *Journal of Zoo and Wildlife Medicine* 32 (4): 509–513.
10. Galdikas, B. M., and J. W. Wood. 1990. Birth spacing patterns in humans and apes. Comparative Study. *American Journal of Physical Anthropology*. 1990 Oct.; 83 (2):185–91. doi: 10.1002/ajpa.1330830207, https://pubmed.ncbi.nlm.nih.gov/2248378/
11. Munn, J., and G. Kalema. 1999–2000. Death of a chimpanzee in a trap in Kasokwa Forest Reserve, Uganda. *African Primates* 4 (1&2): 58–62.
12. Kalema-Zikusoka, G., Stephen Rubanga, Birungi Mutahunga, and Ryan Sadler. 14 December 2018. Prevention of Cryptosporidium and Giardia

at the Human/Gorilla/Livestock Interface. *Frontiers in Public Health*. Brief Research Report. doi: 10.3389/fpubh.2018.00364.

13. https://www.balancingactafrica.com/news/telecoms_en/6993/ugandas -bwindi-telecentre-collects-data-on-gorillas-and-targets-tourists-and -locals.

14. Costa, Raquel, Masaki Tomonaga, Ryoma Otsuka, Michael A. Huffman, Fred B. Bercovitch, Gladys Kalema-Zikusoka, and Misato Hayashi. 1 March 2021. The dispersal dilemma among female mountain gorillas: Risk infanticide and gain protection. *African Journal of Ecology*.

15. Nolan, Matthew J., Melisa Unger, Yuen-Ting Yeap, Emma Rogers, Ilary Millet, Kimberley Harman, Mark Fox, Gladys Kalema-Zikusoka and Damer P. Blake. 2017. Molecular characterisation of protist parasites in human-habituated mountain gorillas (*Gorilla beringei beringei*), humans and livestock, from Bwindi Impenetrable National Park, Uganda. *Parasites & Vectors* 10: 340; doi: 10.1186/s13071-017-2283-5.

16. Aguilar, Xavier Fernandez, Mana Mahapatra, Mattia Begovoeva, Gladys Kalema-Zikusoka, Margaret Driciru, Chrisostom Ayebazibwe, David Solomon Adwok, Michael Kock, Jean-Paul Kabemba Lukusa, Jesus Muro, Ignasi Marco, Andreu Colom-Cadena, Johan Espunyes, Natascha Meunier, Oscar Cabezón, Alexandre Caron, Arnaud Bataille, Genevieve Libeau, Krupali Parekh, Satya Parida, and Richard Kock (2020). Peste des Petits Ruminants at the Wildlife–Livestock Interface in the Northern Albertine Rift and Nile Basin, East Africa. *Viruses* 12 (12): 293; doi:10.3390 /v12030293.

17. Serugo, Joseph. 2020. *Episodes and Tribulations of the African Ranger*. Kampala: FTK Luminary Publishers.

18. Palacios, Gustavo, Linda J. Lowenstine, Michael R. Cranfield, Kirsten V. K. Gilardi, Lucy Spelman, Magda Lukasik-Braum, Jean-Felix Kinani, Antoine Mudakikwa, Elisabeth Nyirakaragire, Ana Valeria Bussetti, Nazir Savji, Stephen Hutchison, Michael Egholm, and W. Ian Lipkin. April 2011. Human Metapneumovirus Infection in Wild Mountain Gorillas, Rwanda. *Emerg Infect Dis.* 17(4): 711–13. doi: 10.3201/eid1704.100883.

19. Weber, Annalisa, Gladys Kalema-Zikusoka, and Nancy J. Stevens. (13 February 2020). Lack of Rule-Adherence During Mountain Gorilla Tourism Encounters in Bwindi Impenetrable National Park, Uganda, Places Gorillas at Risk from Human Disease. *Frontiers in Public Health*. doi: 10.3389/fpubh.2020.0000.1.

20. Hanes, Allison C., Gladys Kalema-Zikusoka, Magdalena S. Svensson, and Catherine M. Hill. 2018. Assessment of Health Risks Posed by Tourists Visiting Mountain Gorillas in Bwindi Impenetrable National Park, Uganda. *Primate Conservation* (32): 10 pp.

21. Scully, Erik J., Sarmi Basnet, Richard W. Wrangham, Martin N. Muller, Emily Otali, David Hyeroba, Kristine A. Grindle, Tressa E. Pappas, Melissa Emery Thompson, Zarin Machanda, Kelly E. Watters, Ann C. Palmenberg, James E. Gern, and Tony L. Goldberg. February 2018. Lethal Respiratory Disease Associated with Human Rhinovirus C in Wild Chimpanzees, Uganda, 2013. *Emerging Infectious Diseases*. doi: 10.3201/eid2402.170778.

22. Patrono, Livia V., Liran Samuni, Victor M. Corman, Leila Nourifar, Caroline Röthemeier, Roman M. Wittig, Christian Drosten, Sébastien Calvignac-Spencer, and Fabian H. Leendertz. 2018. Human coronavirus OC43 outbreak in wild chimpanzees, Côte d'Ivoire. *Emerging Microbes & Infections* 7:118 doi: 10.1038/s41426-018-0121-2.

23. Melin, Amanda D., Mareike C. Janiak, Frank Marrone, Paramjit S. Arora, and James P. Higham. 2020. Comparative ACE2 variation and primate COVID-19 risk. *Communications Biology*. /doi.org/10.1038/s42003-020-01370-w.

24. Damas, Joana, Graham M. Hughes, Kathleen C. Keough, Corrie A. Painter, Nicole S. Persky, Marco Corbo, Michael Hiller, Klaus-Peter Koepfli, Andreas R. Pfenning, Huabin Zhao, Diane P. Genereux, Ross Swofford, Katherine S. Pollard, Oliver A. Ryder, Martin T. Nweeia, Kerstin Lindblad-Toh, Emma C. Teeling, Elinor K. Karlsson, and Harris A. Lewin. Broad Host Range of SARS-CoV-2 Predicted by Comparative and Structural Analysis of ACE2 in Vertebrates. https://www.ncbi.nlm.nih.gov/pmc/articles/PMC7486773/ Proc Natl Acad Sci U S A. 2020 Sep 8; 117(36): 22311–22322. Published online 2020 Aug 21. doi: https://doi.org/10.1073%2Fpnas.201014611710.1073/pnas.2010146117.

25. Gillespie, Thomas R., Fabian H. Leendertz, Steve Ahouka, Christelle-Patricia Lumbu Banza, Marc Ancrenaz, Richard Berg, Sebastien Calvignac-Spencer, Ariane Düx, Jan F. Gogarten, Livia Victoria Patrono, Emmanuel Couacy-Hymann, Tobias Deschner, Martha Robbins, Roman Wittig, Terence Fuh-Neba, Ilka Herbinger, Gladys Kalema-Zikusoka, Inza Kone, Elizabeth V. Lonsdorf, Patrice Makouloutou Nzassi, Jane Raphael, Deus Cyprian Mjungu, Johannes Refisch, Innocent B. Rwego, Dominic Travis, Martin Surbeck, and Serge Wich. 2020. COVID-19: Protect Great Apes During Human Pandemic, https://www.nature.com/articles/d41586-020-00859-y.

26. Uganda Wildlife Authority. (2020). Standard operating procedure for tourism services and research activities in UWA estates and the reopening of the protected areas to the general public during COVID-19 pandemic. Retrieved from https://www.ugandawildlife.org/covid-19-sops.

27. Nuno, Ana, Chloe Chesney, Maia Wellbelove, Elena Bersacola, Gladys Kalema-Zikusoka, Fabian Leendertz, Amanda D. Webber, Kimberley

J. Hockings. 2022. Protecting great apes from disease: Compliance with measures to reduce anthroponotic disease transmission. *People and Nature.* Research Article. doi: 10.1002/pan3.10396 www.protectgreatapesfromdisease.com.

28. Leendertz, Fabian H., and Gladys Kalema-Zikusoka. 2021. Vaccinate in biodiversity hotspots to protect people and wildlife from each other. *Nature* 591, (2021). p. 369. doi: https://doi.org/10.1038/d41586-021-00690-z.

29. Kalema-Zikusoka, Gladys. Stephen Rubanga, Alex Ngabirano, and Lawrence Zikusoka. 12 August 2021. Mitigating Impacts of the COVID-19 Pandemic on Gorilla Conservation: Lessons From Bwindi Impenetrable Forest, Uganda. *Frontiers in Public Health.* doi: 10.3389/fpubh.2021.655175.

30. Negrey, J., R. Reddy, E. Scully, S. Phillips-Garcia, L. Owens, K. Langergraber, J. Mitani, M. E. Thomson, R. Wrangham, M. Muller, E. Otali, Z. Machanda, D. Hyeroba, K. Grindle, T. Pappas, A. Palmenberg, J. Gern and T. Goldberg (2019). Simultaneous outbreaks of respiratory disease in wild chimpanzees caused by distinct viruses of human origin. *Emerging Microbes and Infections* 8: 139–149.

31. Kalema-Zikusoka, G., and J. Byonanebye. 2019. Scaling up a one-health model of conservation through public health: Experiences in Uganda and the Democratic Republic of the Congo. *The Lancet Global Health* 7: S34. doi: 10.1016/S2214-109X(19)30119-6.

32. Weisman, Alan. 2013. *Countdown: Our Last, Best Hope for a Future on Earth?* New York: Little, Brown.

33. Kalema-Zikusoka, Gladys. 2013. In Uganda, Integrating Population, Health, and Environment to Meet Development Goals. *New Security.* https://www.newsecuritybeat.org/2013/03/uganda-integrating-population-health-environment-meet-development-goals/

34. Kalema-Zikusoka, Gladys. February 2010. Comprehensive Conservation—Gorillas on the List. *The Reporter,* a publication of Population Connection. 42, no. 1.

35. Kalema, Rhoda. 2021. *My Life Is but a Weaving.* Moran Publishers. Nairobi, Kenya.

36. Zikusoka, Ndhego J. W. 2021. *Zoo Keeper for a Week.* https://ctph.org/zookeeperforaweek/

37. Mbayayi, A., and G. Kalema-Zikusoka. 2020. COVID-19 and Africa's Great Apes. Challenges and Threats Amidst the COVID-19 Pandemic for Sustaining Conservation through Responsible Great Ape Tourism. Africa Biodiversity Alliance, Civil Society Alliance.

38. Goodall, Jane. 1971. *In the Shadow of Man.* Houghton Mifflin. Boston.

39. Earle, Sylvia. 2021. *Ocean: A Global Odyssey.* National Geographic.

40. Lowman, Meg. 2021. *The Arbornaut: A Life Discovering the Eighth Continent in the Trees Above Us.* Farrar, Straus and Giroux. New York.

Index